Strategic Business Forecasting

Strategic Business Forecasting

Including Business Forecasting Tools and Applications

Dr Jae K Shim

Professor of Business Administration, California State University, Long Beach and
CEO, Delta Consulting Company

GLOBAL
professional
publishing

Global Professional Publishing

Random Acres
Slip Mill Lane
Hawkhurst
Cranbrook
Kent

Email: publishing@gppbooks.com

ISBN 978-1-906403-47-8

Printed by IBT

For full details of Global Professional Publishing titles in

Finance and Banking see our website at:

www.gppbooks.com

Contents

Contents

Contents

Preface

Business forecasting is of extreme importance to managers at practically all levels. It is required for top managers to make long-term strategic decisions. Middle management uses sales forecasts to develop their departmental budgets. Every other plan such as a production plan, purchasing plan, manpower plan, and financial plan follows from sales forecasting. The book is designed for business professionals such as director of forecasting and planning, forecast manager, director of strategic planning, director of marketing, sales manager, advertising manager, CFO, financial officer, controller, treasurer, financial analyst, production manager, brand/product manager, new product manager, supply chain manager, logistics manager, material management manager, purchasing agent, scheduling manager, and director of information systems.

The goal of this book is to provide a working knowledge of the fundamentals of business forecasting that can be applied in the real world regardless of firm size. We walk you through basic forecasting methodology, and then practical applications. All aspects of business forecasting are discussed making this book a comprehensive, valuable reference.

What is unique about this book is threefold. First, this book is practically oriented. It will try to avoid theoretical, rigorous, and mathematical discussions. It will directly get into how to use it, when to use, what it is used for, and what resources are required of it. It will include many practical examples, applications, illustrations, guidelines, measures, checklists, rules of thumb, "tips," graphs, diagrams, and tables to aid your comprehension of the subject.

Secondly, it incorporates the use of computer technology--especially PC. Actual computer printouts obtained via spreadsheet programs such as *Microsoft Excel*, *Lotus 1-2-3*, *Spreadsheet-based add-ins* (such as *Budget Maestro*), and, and popular software packages such as SPSS, Minitab, and SAS, are be displayed and explained.

Thirdly, the book goes much beyond just sales forecasting. It encompasses a wide range of topics of major importance to practical business managers, including economic forecasting, cash flow forecasting, cost prediction, earnings forecasts, bankruptcy prediction, foreign exchange forecasting, interest rate forecasting, and much more.

Jae K Shim

Los Alamitos, California

Part 1

Introduction

Chapter 1

Forecasting and Managerial Planning

Management in both private and public organizations and in both manufacturing and service organizations typically operate under conditions of uncertainty or risk. Probably the most important function of business is forecasting. A forecast is a starting point for planning. The objective of forecasting is to reduce risk in decision making. In business, forecasts are the basis for capacity planning, production and inventory planning, manpower planning, planning for sales and market share, financial planning and budgeting, planning for research and development and top management's strategic planning. Sales forecasts are especially crucial aspects of many financial management activities, including budgets, profit planning, capital expenditure analysis, and acquisition and merger analysis.

Figure 1.1 illustrates how sales forecasts relate to various managerial functions of business.

Who Uses Forecasts?

Forecasts are needed for marketing, production, purchasing, manpower, and financial planning. Further, top management needs forecasts for planning and implementing long-term strategic objectives and planning for capital expenditures.

Marketing managers use sales forecasts to determine (1) optimal sales force allocations, (2) set sales goals, and (3) plan promotions and advertising. Other things such as market share, prices, and trends in new product development are required.

Production planners need forecasts in order to:

◆ Schedule production activities

◆ Order materials

◆ Establish inventory levels

◆ Plan shipments

Figure 1.1: Sales forecasts and managerial functions

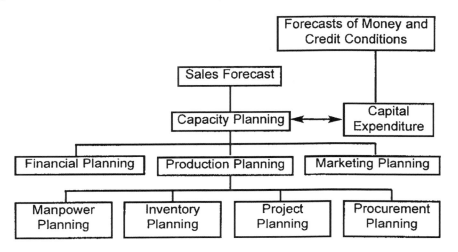

Production/operations managers need long-range forecasts to make strategic decisions about products, processes, and facilities. They also need short-range forecasts to assist them in making decisions about production issues that span only the next few weeks. Table 1.1 cites some examples of things that are commonly forecasted. Long-range forecasts usually span a year or longer and estimate demand for entire product lines such as lawn products. Medium-range forecasts usually span several months and group products into product families such as lawn mowers. Short-range forecasts usually span a few weeks and focus on specific products such as lawn mower model #101.

Some other areas that need forecasts include material requirements (purchasing and procurement), labor scheduling, equipment purchases, maintenance requirements, and plant capacity planning. Managers are also interested in forecasting costs, prices, and delivery times.

As shown in Figure 1.1, as soon as the company makes sure that it has enough capacity, the production plan is developed. If the company does not have enough capacity, it will require planning and budgeting decisions for capital spending for capacity expansion.

On this basis, the financial manager must estimate the future cash inflow and outflow. He must plan cash and borrowing needs for the company's future operations. Forecasts of cash flows and the rates of expenses and revenues are needed to maintain corporate liquidity and operating efficiency. In planning for capital investments, predictions about future economic activity are required so that returns or cash inflows accruing from the investment may be estimated.

Table 1.1: Forecast variables and time horizon

Forecast Horizon	Time Span	Examples of Things That Must Be Forecasted	Some Typical Units of Forecasts
Long-range	Years	New product lines	Dollars
		Old product lines	Dollars
		Factory capacities	Gallons, hours, pounds, units, or customers per time period
		Capital funds	Dollars
		Facility needs	Space, volume
Medium-range	Months	Product groups	Units
		Departmental capacities	Hours, strokes, pounds, gallons, units, or customers per time period
		Work force	Workers, hours
		Purchased materials	Units, pounds, gallons
		Inventories	Units, dollars
Short-range	Weeks	Specific products	Units
		Labor-skill classes	Workers, hours
		Machine capacities	Units, hours, gallons, strokes, pounds, or customers per time period
		Cash	Dollars
		Inventories	Units, dollars

Forecasts must also be made of money and credit conditions and interest rates so that the cash needs of the firm may be met at the lowest possible cost. The finance and accounting functions must also forecast interest rates to support the acquisition of new capital, the collection of accounts receivable to help in planning working capital needs, and capital equipment expenditure rates to help balance the flow of funds in the organization. Sound predictions of foreign exchange rates are increasingly important to financial managers of multinational companies (MNCs).

Long-term forecasts are needed for the planning of changes in the company's capital structure. Decisions as to whether to issue stock or debt in order to maintain the desired financial structure of the firm require forecasts of money and credit conditions.

The personnel department requires a number of forecasts in planning for human resources in the business. Workers must be hired and trained, and for these personnel there must be benefits provided that are competitive with those available in the firm's labor market. Also, trends that affect such variables as labor turnover, retirement age, absenteeism, and tardiness need to be forecast as input for planning and decision making in this function.

Managers of nonprofit institutions and public administrators must also make forecasts. Hospital administrators face the problem of forecasting the health care needs of the community. In order to do this efficiently, a projection has to be made of:

◆ The growth in absolute size of population

◆ The changes in the number of people in various age groupings

◆ The varying medical needs these different age groups will have.

Universities forecast student enrollments, cost of operations, and in many cases, what level of funds will be provided by tuition and by government appropriations.

Forecasting is also important to managers of service organizations. For example, managers in the travel and tourism industry need seasonal forecasts of demand. City planners need forecasts of population trends in order to plan highways and mass transit systems, and restaurants need forecasts in order to be able to plan for food purchases. The service sector which today account for 70 percent of the U.S. gross domestic product (GDP), including banks, insurance companies, and cruiseships, need various projections for their operational and long-term strategic planning. Take a bank, for example. The bank has to forecast:

◆ Demands of various loans and deposits

◆ Money and credit conditions so that it can determine the cost of money it lends

Types of Forecasts

The types of forecasts used by businesses and other organizations may be classified in several categories, depending on the objective and the situation for which a forecast is to be used. Four types are discussed below.

Sales Forecasts

As discussed in the previous section, the sales forecast gives the expected level of sales for the company's goods or services throughout some future period and is instrumental in the company's planning and budgeting functions. It is the key to other forecasts and plans.

Economic Forecasts

Economic forecasts, or statements of expected future business conditions, are published by governmental agencies and private economic forecasting firms. Business can use these forecasts and develop its own forecasts about external business outlook that will affect its product demand. Economic forecasts cover a variety of topics including GDP, levels of employment, interest rates, and foreign exchange rates.

Financial Forecasts

Although the sales forecast is the primary input to many financial decisions, some financial forecasts need to be made independently of sales forecasts. This includes forecasts of financial variables such as the amount of external financing needed, earnings, and cash flows and prediction of corporate bankruptcy.

Technological Forecasts

A technological forecast is an estimate of rates of technological progress. Certainly, software makers are interested in the rates of technological advancement in computer hardware and its peripheral equipment. Technological changes will provide many businesses with new products and materials to offer for sale, while other companies will encounter competition from other businesses. Technological forecasting is probably best performed by experts in the particular technology.

Forecasts for Supply Chain Management

Supply management involves the integration of the functions, information, and materials that flow across multiple firms in a supply chain-- i.e., buying materials, transforming materials, and shipping to customers. All participants in the supply chain need to know what the forecast is for all items. For example, if a retail store chain decides to offer a promotion on Hershey's chocolate bars in a certain week, this will tend to increase the demand for those bars as prices will be discounted. In order to assure customers of an adequate supply, the manufacturer needs to know when the promotion will take place and make adjustments to its manufacturing and production capacity to meet those needs. In addition, wholesalers must have adequate inventory on hand to meet the retailer's needs. All too often, retailers do not share their strategic plans with supply chain partners, which results in stock-outs. The collaboration with supply chain partners should not only be a one-time event; there should be a cross-functional team appointed that includes all supply chain partners: the manufacturer, the wholesale distributor and the retailer. This team should plan all of the supply chain activities such as production, inventory, transportation and warehousing in order to successfully meet planned objectives. This should be facilitated through a shared forecast.

Forecasting Methods

There is a wide range of forecasting techniques that the company may choose from. There are basically two approaches to forecasting: qualitative and quantitative. They are as follows:

1.   Qualitative approach - forecasts based on judgment and opinion.

    (1)   Executive opinions

    (2)   Delphi technique

    (3)   Sales force polling

    (4)   Consumer surveys

2.   Quantitative approach

    a)   Forecasts based on historical data

- Naive methods
- Moving averages
- Exponential smoothing
- Trend analysis
- Decomposition of time series

    b)   Associative (Causal) forecasts

- Simple regression
- Multiple regression
- Econometric modeling

    c)   Indirect methods

- Market surveys
- Input-output analysis
- Barometric forecasting
- Forecasts based on consumer behavior - Markov approach

Figure 1.2 summarizes the forecasting methods.

Figure 1.2: Forecasting methods

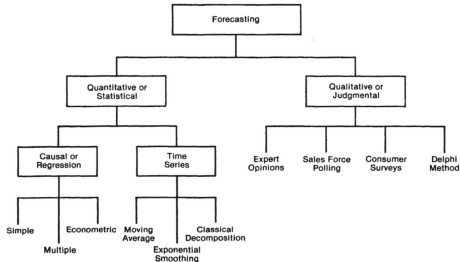

Quantitative models work superbly as long as little or no systematic change in the environment takes place. When patterns or relationships do change, by themselves, the objective models are of little use. It is here where the qualitative approach based on human judgment is indispensable. Because judgmental forecasting also bases forecasts on observation of existing trends, they too are subject to a number of shortcomings. The advantage, however, is that they can identify systematic change more quickly and interpret better the effect of such change on the future.

We will discuss the qualitative method here in this chapter, while various quantitative methods along with their illustrations will be taken up in subsequent chapters.

Selection of Forecasting Method

The choice of a forecasting technique is significantly influenced by the stage of the product life cycle, and sometimes by the firm or industry for which a decision is being made.

In the beginning of the product life cycle, relatively small expenditures are made for research and market investigation. During the first phase of product introduction, these expenditures start to increase. In the rapid growth stage, considerable amounts of money are involved in the decisions; therefore a high level of accuracy is desirable. After the product has entered the maturity stage, the decisions are more routine, involving marketing and manufacturing. These are important considerations when determining the appropriate sales forecast technique.

9

After evaluating the particular stages of the product, and firm and industry life cycles, a further probe is necessary. Instead of selecting a forecasting technique by using whatever seems applicable, decision makers should determine what is appropriate. Some of the techniques are quite simple and rather inexpensive to develop and use, whereas others are extremely complex, require significant amounts of time to develop, and may be quite expensive. Some are best suited for short-term projections, whereas others are better prepared for intermediate- or long-term forecasts.

What technique or techniques to select depends on the following criteria:

1. What is the cost associated with developing the forecasting model compared with potential gains resulting from its use? The choice is one of benefit-cost trade-off.

2. How complicated are the relationships that are being forecasted?

3. Is it for short-run or long-run purposes?

4. How much accuracy is desired?

5. Is there a minimum tolerance level of errors?

6. How much data are available? Techniques vary in the amount of data they require.

The Qualitative Approach

The qualitative (or judgmental) approach can be useful in formulating short-term forecasts and also can supplement the projections based on the use of any of the quantitative methods. Four of the better known qualitative forecasting methods are Executive Opinions, the Delphi Method, Sales Force Polling, and Consumer Surveys.

Executive Opinions

The subjective views of executives or experts from sales, production, finance, purchasing and administration are averaged to generate a forecast about future sales. Usually this method is used in conjunction with some quantitative method such as trend extrapolation. The management team modifies the resulting forecast based on their expectations.

The advantage of this approach is that the forecasting is done quickly and easily, without need of elaborate statistics. Also, the jury of executive opinions may be the only feasible means of forecasting in the absence of adequate data. The disadvantage, however, is that of "group think." This is a set of problems inherent to those who meet as a group. Foremost among these problems are high cohesiveness, strong leadership, and insulation of the group. With high cohesiveness, the group becomes increasingly conforming through group pressure which helps stifle dissension and critical thought. Strong leadership fosters group pressure for unanimous opinion. Insulation of the group tends to separate the group from outside opinions, if given.

The Delphi Method

It is a group technique in which a panel of experts is individually questioned about their perceptions of future events. The experts do not meet as a group in order to reduce the possibility that consensus is reached because of dominant personality factors. Instead, the forecasts and accompanying arguments are summarized by an outside party and returned to the experts along with further questions. This continues until a consensus is reached by the group, especially after only a few rounds. This type of method is useful and quite effective for long-range forecasting.

The technique is done by "questionnaire" format and thus it eliminates the disadvantages of groupthink. There is no committee or debate. The experts are not influenced by peer pressure to forecast a certain way, as the answer is not intended to be reached by consensus or unanimity. Low reliability is cited as the main disadvantage of the Delphi Method, as well as lack of consensus from the returns.

Sales-Force Polling

Some companies use as a forecast source sales people who have continual contacts with customers. They believe that the sales force that is closest to the ultimate customers may have significant insights regarding the state of the future market. Forecasts based on sales-force polling may be averaged to develop a future forecast. Or they may be used to modify other quantitative and/or qualitative forecasts that have been generated internally in the company. The advantages to this way of forecast are that (1) it is simple to use and understand, (2) it uses the specialized knowledge of those closest to the action, (3) it can place responsibility for attaining the forecast in the hands of those who most affect the actual results, and (4) the information can be easily broken down by territory, product, customer or salesperson.

The disadvantages include salespeople being overly optimistic or pessimistic regarding their predictions, and inaccuracies due to broader economic events that are largely beyond their control.

Consumer Surveys

Some companies conduct their own market surveys regarding specific consumer purchases. Surveys may consist of telephone contacts, personal interviews, or questionnaires as a means of obtaining data. Extensive statistical analysis is usually applied to survey results in order to test hypotheses regarding consumer behavior.

A Word of Caution

Forecasting is not an exact science like mathematics; it is an art. The quality of forecasts tends to improve over time as the forecaster gains more experience. Evidence, however, shows that forecasts using qualitative techniques are not as accurate as those using quantitative techniques. Therefore, a forecaster must use both qualitative as well as quantitative techniques to create a reasonable forecast.

Common Features and Assumptions Inherent in Forecasting

As pointed out, forecasting techniques are quite different from each other. But there are certain features and assumptions that underlie the business of forecasting. They are:

1. Forecasting techniques generally assume that the same underlying causal relationship that existed in the past will continue to prevail in the future. In other words, most of our techniques are based on historical data.
2. Forecasts are very rarely perfect. Therefore, for planning purposes, allowances should be made for inaccuracies. For example, the company should always maintain a safety stock in anticipation of stockouts.
3. Forecast accuracy decreases as the time period covered by the forecast (that is, the time horizon) increases. Generally speaking, a long-term forecast tends to be more inaccurate than a short-term forecast because of the greater uncertainty.
4. Forecasts for groups of items tend to be more accurate than forecasts for individual items, since forecasting errors among items in a group tend to cancel each other out. For example, industry forecasting is more accurate than individual firm forecasting.

Steps in the Forecasting Process

There are six basic steps in the forecasting process (see Figure 1.3). They are:

1. Determine the what and why of the forecast and what will be needed. This will indicate the level of detail required in the forecast (for example, forecast by region, forecast by product, etc.), the amount of resources (for example, computer hardware and software, manpower, etc.) that can be justified, and the level of accuracy desired.

2. Establish a time horizon, short-term or long-term. More specifically, project for the next year or next 5 years, etc.

3. Select a forecasting technique. Refer to the criteria discussed before.

4. Gather the data and develop a forecast.

5. Identify any assumptions that had to be made in preparing the forecast and using it.

6. Monitor the forecast to see if it is performing in a manner desired. Develop an evaluation system for this purpose. If not, go to step 1.

Figure 1.3: The Forecasting Process

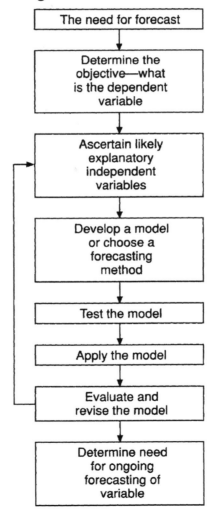

Chapter 2

Forecasting, Budgeting, and Business Valuation

Each company has a hierarchy of forecasts and their corollary budgets. Normally, all of these emanate from the sales forecast. This chapter describes the format and the use of the various budgets that are frequent in most organizations.

The sales forecast is the first step in the preparation of a budget and a master plan of the company. A (master) budget is a formal statement of management's expectation regarding sales, expenses, volume, and other financial transactions of an organization for the coming period. Simply put, a budget is a set of *pro forma* (projected or planned) financial statements. It consists basically of a pro forma income statement, pro forma balance sheet, and cash budget.

A budget is a tool for both planning and control. At the beginning of the period, the budget is a plan or standard; at the end of the period it serves as a control device to help management measure its performance against the plan so that future performance may be improved. The major objectives of any budget system are to foster the planning of operations, provide a framework for performance evaluation, and promote communication and coordination among organization segments.

The major steps in preparing the budget are:

1. Prepare a sales forecast.
2. Determine expected production volume.
3. Estimate manufacturing costs and operating expenses.
4. Determine cash flow and other financial effects.
5. Formulate projected financial statements.

Figure 2.1 summarizes the relation of forecasting among the various parts of the comprehensive (master) budget, the master plan of the company.

Figure 2.1 : Comprehensive (Master) Budget

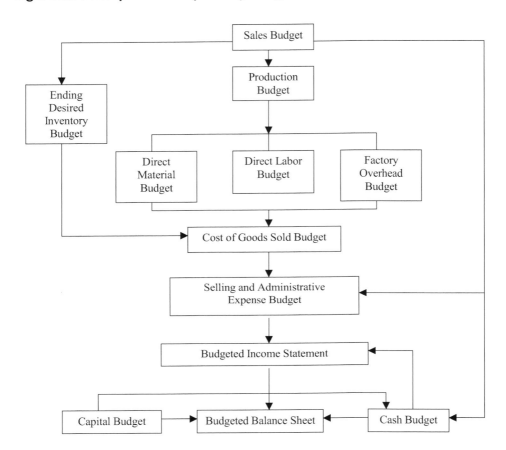

The Sales Budget

The outcome of the sales forecast is a sales budget. The sales budget is the starting point in preparing the master budget, since estimated sales volume influences nearly all other items appearing throughout the master budget. The sales budget ordinarily indicates the quantity of each product expected to be sold. After sales volume has been estimated, the sales budget is constructed by multiplying the expected sales in units by the expected unit selling price.

Table 2.1 is an example of a relatively uncomplicated sales budget. Of course, the budget becomes more complicated as the number of products, sales regions, and other subdivisions increases. Generally, the sales budget includes a projection of expected cash collections from credit sales, which will be used later for cash budgeting.

Table 2.1: Sales budget

Product	Volume Forecast	Price	Sale Forecast
Calculator X	100,000	$50	$5,000,000
Calculator Y	20,000	300	6,000,000
			$11,000,000

The Production Budget

Once the sales budget has been prepared the production budget can be generated. Its function is to indicate the number of units, which must be produced during the time period under consideration to meet forecast sales needs. Inventory-policies of the firm have an impact on production. The latter increases as a result of planned end-of-period finished-goods inventory and decreases as a result of beginning-of-period finished- goods inventory. Table 2.2 illustrates the format of the production budget, using the calculations of Table 2.1. From the production budget, the manager prepares the direct-labor budget and the direct-material budget.

Table 2.2: Production budget

	Calculator X	Calculator Y
Sale volume forecast	100,000	20,000
Planned end of period finished goods inventory	4,500	1,000
Total needs	104,500	21,000
Minus beginning of period finished good inventory	1,000	400
Expected production volume	103,500	20,600

The Direct Material Budget

The direct-material budget indicates the number and cost of the direct materials needed to fulfill production requirement. Some or all of the direct materials used may be produced by the firm, or they may be purchased from suppliers. The latter case is assumed here. Basically, direct-material needs are a function of planned end-of-period inventory, production requirements, beginning-of-period inventory, and cost per unit. Table 2.3 illustrates this budget.

Table 2.3: The Direct Material Budget

	Material X	Material Y
Production needs	30,000	40,000
Planned end of period direct material inventory (in units)	2,000	3,000
Total requirement	32,000	43,000
Minus beginning of period direct material inventory (in units)	2,000	2,000
Number of units to purchase or produce	30,000	41,000
Cost per unit	$1.20	$4.00
Total cost	$36,000	$164,000

The Direct Labor Budget

Like the direct-material budget, the direct-labor budget is based on levels of output set forth in the production budget. In addition, the direct-labor budget is influenced by wage scales and by the manufacturing process, as reflected in the number of labor hours needed for each unit of finished product. The output of the direct-labor budget is a statement of the total costs expected for labor in producing each product as well as total direct-labor costs. Other labor costs, those that cannot be assigned to particular products, appear in the factory overhead budget. These are termed *indirect labor costs*. Table 2.4 illustrates a direct-labor budget.

Table 2.4: The Direct Labor Budget

Product	Production Requirements	Direct-Labor Hour per unit of finished goods	Total Hours	Total Budget At $6 per hours
Calculator X	103,500	7	724,500	$4,347,000
Calculator Y	20,600	20	412,000	$2,472,000
				$6,819,000

The Factory Overhead Budget

The expenses listed here are based on the level of factory capacity use dictated by the production requirements (Table 2.2). Some expenses, such as supplies, can be expected to increase as production levels increase. Others, such as depreciation, are not affected by changes in the level of production. The net output of the factory overhead budget is an accounting of indirect costs. These are expenses that cannot be assigned to particular products.

Table 2.5: The Factory Overhead Budget

Depreciation	$15,000
Taxes	2,000
Insurance	500
Maintenance	3,000
Supplies	20,000
Indirect labor	14,000
Power	9,000
Total Budget	$63,500

The Cost of Goods Sold Budget

This budget (Table 2.6) is based primarily on data appearing in previously mentioned budgets. Its output is expected costs of increasing the level of inventory during the time period under consideration.

Table 2.6: The Cost of Goods Sold Budget

Direct-material (Table 2.3)	200,000
Direct-labor (from Table 2.4)	6,819,000
Factory overhead (from Table 2.5)	63,500
Total production costs	$7,082,500
Plus finished-goods inventory, beginning of period (costs per unit of inventory determined by accounting department)	380,000
	$7,462,500
Minus finished-goods inventory, end of period (costs per unit of inventory determined by accounting department)	100,000
Cost of goods sold	$7,362,500

The Selling and Administration Budget

Business concerns differ as to the specific way in which they budget such functions as selling and advertising. In many cases, individual budgets are prepared for each function. Another practice is to merge selling and advertising costs with others, such as administration, into composite budgets. That practice is exemplified in Table 2.7.

Table 2.7: The Selling and Administration Budget

Advertising	30,000	
Salesman compensation	200,000	
Travel	60,000	
Sales promotion	10,000	
Total selling expenses		$300,000
Executive compensation	200,000	
Clerical compensation	80,000	
Supplies	10,000	
Miscellaneous	5,000	
Total administrative expenses		295,000
Total selling and administrative expenses		$595,000

The Budgeted Income Statement

The budgeted income (profit and loss) statement summarizes the various component projections of revenue and expenses for the budgeting period. However, for control purposes the budget can be divided into quarters or even months depending on the need. This indicates the expected profitability of the firm in the upcoming year. Table 2.8 illustrates this process.

Table 2.8: The Budgeted Income Statement

Sales (from Table 2.1)	11,000,000	
Cost of goods sold (from Table 2.6)	7,362,500	
Gross margin		$3,637,500
Selling and administrative expense (from Table 2.7)	595,000	
Interest expenses (given)	50,000	
Total expenses		645,000
Net income before income tax		2,992,500
Income tax (30%)		897,750
Net income after income tax		$2,094,750

The Cash Budget

The cash budget is prepared for the purpose of cash planning and control. It presents the expected cash inflow and outflow for a designated time period. The cash budget helps management keep cash balances in reasonable relationship to its needs. It aids in avoiding unnecessary idle cash and possible cash shortages.

A sample cash budget is presented in Table 2.9.

The Budgeted Balance Sheet

The budgeted balance sheet is developed by beginning with the balance sheet for the year just ended and adjusting it, using all the activities that are expected to take place during the budgeting period. It indicates expected levels of assets, liability, and equity items in light of the developments predicted by the other budgets. From the budgeted balance sheet, management visualizes the probable status of each account at the end of the period under consideration.

Some of the reasons why the budgeted balance sheet must be prepared are:

(1) It could disclose some unfavorable financial conditions that management might want to avoid.

(2) It helps management perform a variety of ratio calculations.

(3) It highlights future resources and obligations.

Company-Wide and Departmental Budgets

So far we have emphasized company-wide budgeting. That is, each of the budgets described encompassed the entire firm, include its various divisions, departments, offices, branches, and other; subdivisions. It is important to recognize, however, that firms having subdivisions often develop budgets for the individual subdivision. A frequently employed process is to develop the individual budgets, and then to sum them into composite company-wide budgets. Another approach is to generate the composite budgets first and then to allocate these to individual subdivisions. Both methods require considerable skill and diligence, but produce documents that are essential for effective management of the total company and its subdivisions.

"What-If" Scenarios And Computer Simulation

It is important to realize that with the aid of computer technology, budgeting can be used as an effective device for evaluation of "what-if" scenarios. This way management should be able to move toward finding the best course of action among various alternatives through simulation. If management does not like what they see on the budgeted financial statements in terms of various financial ratios such as liquidity, activity (turnover), leverage, profit margin, and market value ratios, they can always alter their contemplated decision and planning set.

Using an Electronic Spreadsheet to Develop a Budget Plan

In practice a short-cut approach to budgeting is quite common using computer technology. You can develop a budget using a spreadsheet such as *Excel*. Using the spreadsheet program, you will be able to evaluate various "what-if" scenarios.

Table 2.9: The Monthly Cash Budget

		October (actual)	November (actual)	December (actual)	January	February	March	April
Expected Sales		$ 375,000	$ 457,500	$ 510,000	$ 410,000	$ 385,000	$ 580,000	$ 600,000
Cash receipts:								
Cash sales	10%				41,000	38,500	58,000	60,000
Collection from sales:								
One month ago	75%				344,250	276,750	259,875	391,500
Two months ago	15%				61,763	68,850	55,350	51,975
Three months ago	8%				27,000	32,940	36,720	29,520
Bad debts	2%							
	100%				474,013	417,040	409,945	532,995
Other cash receipts					11,000	7,600	18,500	12,000
Beginning of month cash					80,000	(18,988)	(97,748)	(106,003)
Total available cash					565,013	405,653	330,698	438,993
Cash disbursements:								
Material					138,000	145,000	150,000	125,000
Labor and wages					182,000	110,000	169,000	105,000
Selling costs					175,000	169,000	181,000	168,500
General and administrative costs					46,000	49,500	48,000	47,000
Income taxes						28,500		
Capital equipment					28,000	5,200	21,200	
Interest expense					15,000	16,200	17,500	16,900
Total cash disbursements					584,000	523,400	586,700	462,400
Ending cash balance (deficiency) before additional borrowings/(repayments) or (investments)/redemptions					(18,988)	(117,748)	(256,003)	(23,408)
Bank borrowings/(repayments) (Investments)/redemptions						20,000	150,000	-
Ending cash balance					$ (18,988)	$ (97,748)	$ (106,003)	$ (23,408)

Forecasting and business valuation

Forecasting has never been an exact science and never will be. The reason is that crystalballing the future is always a challenge in anybody's life. It is something every human being strives to achieve---or, something you and I will always to try to minimize—uncertainty or risk. The fact of the matter is if you can make a decent forecast about something in your life, you can easily make a fortune overnight. Here are a few simple examples which nobody can argue with. It can be a stock price, interest rate, foreign exchange rate, or even a lottery. Imagine you are able to pick the winning six numbers. You become an instant millionaire. Picking a right stock. How about predicting where an interest rate or a foreign exchange rate is heading and when. You can easily make fortune going into options, forward contracts, and so forth.

For buying and selling a business, a valuation might be important for establishing an asking or offering price. From a business standpoint, prediction and business valuation have a lot to do with each other. Business valuation is such an important issue that relates to determining the value you put on an asset, such as stock, bond, real estate, a business, or a targeted business to be acquired, to name a few. A question that comes up all the time is: How much are you willing to pay for a piece of real estate, a business, etc?

The process of determining business valuation involves finding the present value of an asset's *expected future* cash flows using the investor's required rate of return. The basic valuation model can be defined mathematically as follows:

$$V = \sum_{t=1}^{n} \frac{C_t}{(1+r)^t}$$

where V = intrinsic value or present value of an asset

           C_t = expected future cash flows or earnings in period $t = 1, ..., n$

           r = investor's required rate of return

For example, the value of a common stock is the present value of all *expected future* cash inflows expected to be received by the investor comprising of dividends and future selling price. At least in theory, the price you are willing to pay to buy a stock, for example, is the present worth of *expected future* earning power of the stock. The classical *discounted cash flow (DCF)* model is used for this purpose. In short, sound forecast of future cash flows or earning power is a vital for business valuations.

Note: Popular software such as *Corporate Valuation* (www.moneysoft.com/valuation; 800-966-7797) features a forecasting and discounted cash flow model to efficiently analyze and value a company.

Example 2.1

XYZ Company has the following year-end expected profits in each of the next three years: $30,000, $90,000, and $120,000. Then it shuts down. Assuming a 10 percent interest rate, we can determine the value of the firm as follows:

The present value of this series of profits is calculated as follows:

Year	Cash inflows	$1/(1+0.10)^n$	Present Value
1	$30,000	0.909	$27,270
2	90,000	0.826	74,340
3	120,000	0.751	90,120
			$191,730

Note: Present value calculations can be done using:

(a)   Financial calculators

(b)   Present value tables

(c)   Present value function keys in spreadsheet software such as *Excel* or *Lotus 1-2-3*.

Conclusion

Forecasting is an essential element of planning and budgeting. It is needed where the future financing needs are being estimated. Basically, forecasts of future sales and their related expenses provide the firm with the information needed to plan other activities of the business.

This chapter has emphasized budgets -- basic tool for planning and controlling the activities of the enterprise. The process involves developing a sales forecast and, based on its magnitude, generating those budgets needed by a specific firm. Once developed, the budgeting system provides management with a means of controlling their activities and of monitoring actual performance and comparing it to budget goals.

Budgeting can be done with ease with the aid of electronic spreadsheet software and was illustrated in this chapter, but there are many specialized software for budgeting available in the market.

Also discussed was the relationship between forecasting and business valuations. The key point is that how much you are willing to pay for a business, stock, or real estate is essentially the present worth of expected future (forecasted) earnings derived thereto.

Part 2

Forecasting Methods

Chapter 3

Moving Averages and Smoothing Methods

This chapter discusses several forecasting methods that fall in the quantitative approach category. The discussion includes naive models, moving averages, and exponential smoothing methods. Time series analysis and regressions are covered in future chapters. The qualitative methods were described in the previous chapter.

Naive Models

Naive forecasting models are based exclusively on historical observation of sales or other variables such as earnings and cash flows being forecast. They do not attempt to explain the underlying causal relationships which produce the variable being forecast.

Naive models may be classified into two groups. One group consists of simple projection models. These models require inputs of data from recent observations, but no statistical analysis is performed. The second group are made up of models, while naive, are complex enough to require a computer. Traditional methods such as classical decomposition, moving average, and exponential smoothing models are some examples.

Advantages: It is inexpensive to develop, store data, and operate.

Disadvantages: It does not consider any possible causal relationships that underlie the forecasted variable.

1.   A simplest example of a naive model type would be to use the actual sales of the current period as the forecast for the next period. Let us use the symbol Y'_{t+1} as the forecast value and the symbol Y_t as the actual value. Then, $Y'_{t+1} = Y_t$

2. If you consider trends, then $Y'_{t+1} = Y_t + (Y_t - Y_{t-1})$

This model adds the latest observed absolute period-to-period change to the most recent observed level of the variable.

3. If you want to incorporate the rate of change rather than the absolute amount, then

$$Y'_{t+1} = Y_t \left(\frac{Y_t}{Y_{t-1}} \right)$$

Example 3.1

Consider the following sales data

Month	20X1 Monthly Sales of Product
1	$3,050
2	2,980
3	3,670
4	2,910
5	3,340
6	4,060
7	4,750
8	5,510
9	5,280
10	5,504
11	5,810
12	6,100

We will develop forecasts for January 20X2 based on the aforementioned three models:

1. $Y'_{t+1} = Y_t = \$6,100$
2. $Y'_{t+1} = Y_t + (Y_t - Y_{t-1}) = \$6,100 + (\$6,100 - \$5,810) = \$6,100 + \$290 = \$6,390$
3. $Y'_{t+1} = Y_t \left(\frac{Y_t}{Y_{t-1}} \right)$

$$= \$6,100 \times \frac{\$6,100}{\$5,810} = \$6,100 \,(1.05) = \$6,405$$

The naive models can be applied, with very little need of a computer, to develop forecasts for sales, earnings, and cash flows. They must be compared with more sophisticated models such as the regression method for forecasting efficiency.

Smoothing Techniques

Smoothing techniques are a higher form of naive models. There are two typical forms: moving average and exponential smoothing. Moving averages are the simpler of the two.

Moving Averages

Moving averages are averages that are updated as new information is received. With the moving average, a manager simply employs the most recent observations to calculate an average, which is used as the forecast for the next period.

Example 3.2

Assume that the marketing manager has the following sales data.

Date		Actual Sales (Y_t)
Jan.	1	46
	2	54
	3	53
	4	46
	5	58
	6	49
	7	54

In order to predict the sales for the seventh and eighth days of January, the manager has to pick the number of observations for averaging purposes. Let us consider two cases: one is a six-day moving average and the other is a three-day average.

Case 1

$$Y'_7 = \frac{46 + 54 + 53 + 46 + 58 + 49}{6} = 51$$

$$Y'_8 = \frac{54 + 53 + 46 + 58 + 49 + 54}{6} = 52.3$$

where Y' = predicted

Case 2

$$Y'_7 = \frac{46 + 58 + 49}{3} = 51$$

$$Y'_8 = \frac{58 + 49 + 54}{3} = 53.6$$

Figure 3.1 summarizes the results of Cases 1 and 2 above.

In terms of weights given to observations, in case 1, the old data received a weight of 5/6, and the current observation got a weight of 1/6. In case 2, the old data received a weight of only 2/3 while the current observation received a weight of 1/3.

Figure 3.1: Moving Average Calculations

			Predicted Sales(Y'_t)	
	Date	Actual Sales	Case 1	Case 2
Jan.	1	46		
	2	54		
	3	53		
	4	46		
	5	58		51
	6	49	53.6	
	7	54	51	
	8		52.3	

Note:

1. You can choose the number of periods to use on the basis of the relative importance to be attached to old versus current data. In order to pick the right number, you may have to experiment with different moving average periods. Measures of forecasting accuracy such as the mean squared error (MSE) (to be discussed later) can be used to pick the optimal number of periods.

2. To utilize Excel for moving average, the following procedure needs to be followed:

    ◆ Click the *Tools* menu.

    ◆ Click *Data Analysis*.

    ◆ Click *Moving Average*.

    To obtain a graph, use Excel's Chart Wizard.

Advantages and Disadvantages

The moving average is simple to use and easy to understand. However, there are two shortcomings.

◆ It requires you to retain a great deal of data and carry it along with you from forecast period to forecast period.

◆ All data in the sample are weighted equally. If more recent data are more valid than older data, why not give it greater weight?

The forecasting method known as exponential smoothing gets around these disadvantages.

Exponential Smoothing

Exponential smoothing is a popular technique for short-run forecasting by financial managers. It uses a weighted average of past data as the basis for a forecast. The procedure gives heaviest weight to more recent information and smaller weights to observations in the more distant past. The reason for this is that the future is more dependent upon the recent past than on the distant past. The method is known to be effective when there is randomness and no seasonal fluctuations in the data. One disadvantage of the method, however, is that it does not include industrial or economic factors such as market conditions, prices, or the effects of competitors' actions.

The Model

The formula for exponential smoothing is:

$$Y'_{t+1} = \alpha Y_t + (1 - \alpha) Y'_t$$

or in words,

$$Y'_{new} = \alpha Y_{old} + (1 - \alpha) Y'_{old}$$

where Y'_{new} = Exponentially smoothed average to be used as the forecast.

Y_{old} = Most recent actual data.

Y'_{old} = Most recent smoothed forecast.

α = Smoothing constant.

The higher the α, the higher the weight given to the more recent information.

Example 3.3

The following data on sales are given below.

Time Period(t)	Actual sales (1000)(Y_t)
1	$60
2	64
3	58
4	66
5	70
6	60
7	70
8	74
9	62
10	74
11	68
12	66
13	60
14	66
15	62

To initialize the exponential smoothing process, we must have the initial forecast. The first smoothed forecast to be used can be

   1. First actual observations.

   2. An average of the actual data for a few periods

For illustrative purposes, let us use a six-period average as the initial forecast Y'_7 with a smoothing constant of $= 0.40$.

$$\text{Then } Y'_7 = (Y_1 + Y_2 + Y_3 + Y_4 + Y_5 + Y_6)/6$$

$$= (60 + 64 + 58 + 66 + 70 + 60)/6 = 63$$

Note that $Y_7 = 70$. Then Y'_8 is computed as follows:

$$Y'_8 = \alpha Y_7 + (1 - \alpha) Y'_7$$

$$= (0.40)(70) + (0.60)(63)$$

$$= 28.0 + 37.80 = 65.80$$

Similarly,

$$Y'_9 = \alpha Y_8 + (1 - \alpha) Y'_8$$

$$= (0.40)(74) + (0.60)(65.80)$$

$$= 29.60 + 39.48 = 69.08$$

and

$$Y'_{10} = \alpha Y_9 + (1 - \alpha)Y'_9$$
$$= (0.40)(62) + (0.60)(69.08)$$
$$= 24.80 + 41.45 = 66.25$$

By using the same procedure, the values of Y'_{11}, Y'_{12}, Y'_{13}, Y'_{14}, and Y'_{15} can be calculated. The following table shows a comparison between the actual sales and predicted sales by the exponential smoothing method.

Due to the negative and positive differences between actual sales and predicted sales, the forecaster can use a higher or lower smoothing constant (α), in order to adjust his/her prediction as quickly as possible to large fluctuations in the data series. For example, if the forecast is slow in reacting to increased sales, (that is to say, if the difference is negative), he/she might want to try a higher value. For practical purposes, the optimal α may be picked by minimizing what is known as the *mean squared error* (MSE), which will be discussed in more detail in a later chapter.

$$MSE = \Sigma \ (Y_t - Y'_t)^2 / \ (n - i)$$

where i = the number of observations used to determine the initial forecast (in our example, i=6).

Table 3.1: Comparison of Actual Sales and Predicted Sales

Time period (t)	Actual sales (Y_t)	Predicted Sales (Y'_t)	Difference $(Y_t - Y'_t)$	Difference^2 $(Y_t - Y'_t)^2$
1	$60			
2	64			
3	58			
4	66			
5	70			
6	60			
7	70	63.00	7.00	49.00
8	74	65.8	8.20	67.24
9	62	69.08	-7.08	50.13
10	74	66.25	7.75	60.06
11	68	69.35	-1.35	1.82
12	66	68.81	-2.81	7.90
13	60	67.69	-7.69	59.14
14	66	64.61	1.39	1.93
15	62	65.17	-3.17	10.05
				307.27

In our example,

$$MSE = 307.27 / (15 - 6) = 307.27 / 9 = 34.14$$

The Computer and Exponential Smoothing

As a manager, you will be confronted with complex problems requiring large sample data. You will also need to try different values of α for exponential smoothing. The idea is to select the a that minimizes MSE, which is the average sum of the variations between the historical sales data and the forecast values for the corresponding periods. Virtually all forecasting software has an exponential smoothing routine.

Note:

1. To utilize Excel for exponential smoothing, the following procedure needs to be followed:

    ◆ Click the *Tools* menu.

    ◆ Click *Data Analysis*.

    ◆ Click *Exponential Smoothing*

2. To obtain a scattergraph, use Excel's Chart Wizard.

Exponential Smoothing Adjusted for Trend

When data shows a sign of trend, we can add a trend factor to account for this. This situation can be handled by using another weighting (smoothing) constant. Thus, it involves two smoothings. First, the original data are smoothed as in single smoothing. Then the resulting values are smoothed as if they are original values.

These double-smoothed values have two useful properties.

1. They are smoother than the single-smoothed values, which means they will provide a clearer indication of the trend.

2. The double-smoothed values lag the single-smoothed values by about as much as the single-smoothed values lag the original data.

Consequently, by adding the difference between single-and double-smoothed values to the single-smoothed values, the resulting series will approximate the original series. Finally, by including an allowance for trend in the forecast, the forecasts will give a fairly good indication of future values. The smoothing and double lagging can be seen in the graph in Figure 3.3.

The exponentially smoothed forecast adjusted for trend is:

$$Y'_{t+1} = \begin{matrix} \text{Single} \\ \text{smoothed} \end{matrix} + \begin{bmatrix} \begin{matrix} \text{Single} \\ \text{smoothed} \end{matrix} - \begin{matrix} \text{Double} \\ \text{smoothed} \end{matrix} \end{bmatrix} + \begin{matrix} \text{Trend} \\ \text{adjustment} \end{matrix}$$

$$= \quad Y'_t + (Y'_t - S''_t) + b_t$$

where $\quad Y'_t = aY_{t-1} + (1 - \alpha) Y'_{t-1}$,

and the trend adjustment, bt, can be approximated by the amount of change each period in S". that is:

$$bt = S''_t - S''_{t-1}$$

Figure 3.2: Data, forecasts, and smoothed values

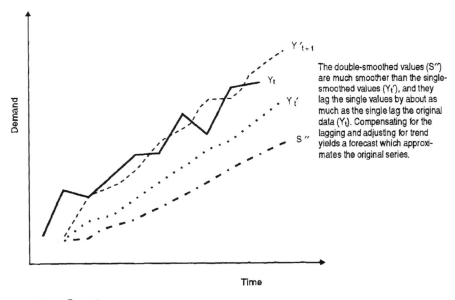

The double-smoothed values (S") are much smoother than the single-smoothed values (Y$_t$'), and they lag the single values by about as much as the single lag the original data (Y$_t$). Compensating for the lagging and adjusting for trend yields a forecast which approximates the original series.

Y'_{t+1} = Forecast
Y_t = Actual Data
Y_t' = Single Smoothed Values
S'' = Double Smoothed Values

Example 3.4

PC computer sales for a New York-based store over the past 10 years are shown below. Using trend-adjusted exponential smoothing with a single smoothing constant of $\alpha_1 = .4$ and a double smoothing constant of $\alpha_2 = .3$, prepare a forecast for period 11.

Period	Unit Sales
I	700
2	724
3	720
4	728
5	740
6	742
7	758
8	750
9	770
10	775

Calculations are shown, step by step.

Step 1: Smooth the data using the equation $Y'_t = (.4) Y_{t-1} + (1 - .4) Y'_{t-1}$. Using the first data point, 700, as the beginning forecast, the results are shown below under the Y'_t column.

Step 2: Smooth the Y'_t values using the equation $S''_t = Y_{t-1} + .3(Y_t - S''_{t-1})$, with 700 as the first value. The results are shown under the S''_t column.

Step 3: Compute the trend adjustment, bt, using the equation $bt = S''_t - S''_{t-1}$. The results are shown in Table 3.2 under column b_t.

Step 4: Determine the forecast for each period using the equation $Y'_t + (Y'_t - S''_t) + b_t$. The forecasts are shown in the last column of Table 3.2.

Table 3.2: Calculations for Trend-Adjusted Forecast

t	Y_t (data)	Y'_t (single)	S''_t (double)	$S''_t - S''_{t-1}$ (b_t)	Forecast
I	700	700.00	700.00		
2	724	709.60	702.88	2.88	700.00
3	720	713.76	706.14	3.26	719.2
4	728	719.46	710.14	3.99	724.64
5	740	727.67	715.40	5.26	732.77
6	742	733.40	720.80	5.40	745.21
7	758	743.24	727.53	6.73	751.41
8	750	745.95	733.06	5.52	765.68
9	770	755.57	739.81	6.75	764.36
10	775	763.34	746.87	7.06	778.08
11					786.87

The data, forecasts, and smoothed values are plotted in Figure 3.3.

Note: Again, virtually all forecasting software calculate forecasts based on exponential smoothing with trends.

Figure 3.3: Data, forecasts, and smoothed values

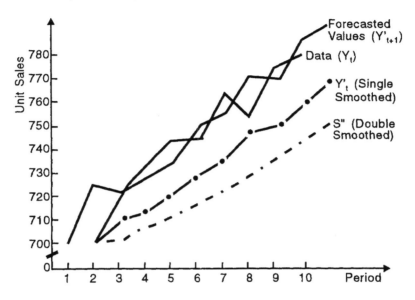

Conclusion

Various quantitative forecasting methods exist. Naive techniques are based solely on previous experience. Smoothing approaches include moving average and exponential smoothing. Moving averages and exponential smoothing employs a weighted average of past data as the means of deriving the forecast.

Chapter 4

Regression Analysis

Regression analysis is a statistical procedure for estimating mathematically the average relationship between the dependent variable and the independent variable(s). Simple regression involves one independent variable, price or advertising in a demand function, whereas multiple regression involves two or more variables, that is price and advertising together. Other applications of simple regression are:

1. Total manufacturing costs is explained by only one activity variable (such as either production volume or machine hours), i.e., $TC = a + bQ$.

2. A security's return is a function of the return on a market portfolio (such as Standard & Poor's 500), i.e., $r_j = a + \beta r_m$ where β = beta, a measure of uncontrollable risk.

3. Consumption is a function of disposable income, i.e., $C = a + bY_d$ where b = marginal propensity to consume.

4. Demand is a function of price, i.e., $Q_d = a - bP$.

5. Average time to be taken is a function of cumulative production, i.e., $Y = aX^{-b}$ where b represents a learning rate in the learning curve phenomenon.

6. Trend analysis that attempts to detect a growing or declining trend of time series data, i.e., $Y = a + bt$ where t = time.

In this chapter, we will discuss *simple (linear) regression* to illustrate the *least-squares method*.

We will assume the $Y = a + bX$ relationship, where a = intercept and b = slope.

The Least-Squares Method

The least-squares method is widely used in regression analysis for estimating the parameter values in a regression equation. The regression method includes all the observed data and attempts to find a line of best fit. To find this line, a technique called the least-squares method is used.

To explain the least-squares method, we define the error as the difference between the observed value and the estimated one and denote it with u. Symbolically,

$$u = Y - Y'$$

where   Y = observed value of the dependent variable

Y' = estimated value based on Y' = a + bX

The least-squares criterion requires that the line of best fit be such that the sum of the squares of the errors (or the vertical distance in Figure 1 from the observed data points to the line) is a minimum, i.e.,

$$\text{Minimum: } \Sigma u^2 = \Sigma(Y-a-bX)^2$$

Figure 4.1: Y and Y'

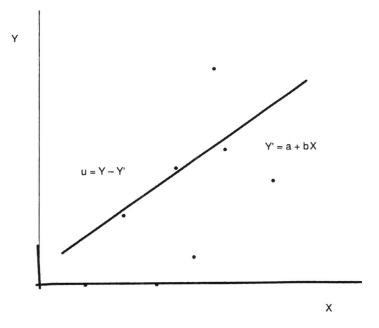

Using differential calculus we obtain the following equations, called normal equations:

$$\Sigma Y = na + b\Sigma X$$

$$\Sigma XY = a\Sigma X + b\Sigma X^2$$

Solving the equations for b and a yields

$$b = \frac{n\sum XY - (\sum X)(\sum Y)}{n\sum X^2 - (\sum X)^2}$$

$$a = \overline{Y} - b\overline{X}$$

$$\text{where } \overline{Y} = \frac{\sum Y}{n} \text{ and } \overline{X} = \frac{\sum X}{n}$$

Example 4.1

To illustrate the computations of b and a, we will refer to the data in Table 4.1. All the sums required are computed and shown below.

Table 4.1: Computed Sums

Adv. (X) (in $000s)	Sales (Y) (in $000s)	XY	X2	Y2
9	15	135	81	225
19	20	380	361	400
11	14	154	121	196
14	16	224	196	256
23	25	575	529	625
12	20	240	144	400
12	20	240	144	400
22	23	506	484	529
7	14	98	49	196
13	22	286	169	484
15	18	270	225	324
17	18	306	289	324
174	225	3414	2792	4359

From the table above:

$\Sigma X = 174$; $\Sigma Y = 225$; $\Sigma XY = 3,414$; $\Sigma X^2 = 2,792$.

$\overline{X} = \Sigma X/n = 174/12 = 14.5$; $\overline{Y} = \Sigma Y/n = 225/12 = 18.75$.

Substituting these values into the formula for b first:

$$b = \frac{n\sum XY - (\sum X)(\sum Y)}{n\sum X^2 - (\sum X)^2} = \frac{(12)(3,414) - (174)(225)}{(12)(2,792) - (174)^2} = \frac{1,818}{3,228} = 0.5632$$

$a = \overline{Y} - b\overline{X} = 18.75 - (0.5632)(14.5) = 18.75 - 8.1664 = 10.5836$

Thus, $Y' = 10.5836 + 0.5632\,X$

Example 4.2

Assume that the advertising of $10 is to be expended for next year; the projected sales for the next year would be computed as follows:

$$Y' = 10.5836 + 0.5632\,X$$
$$= 10.5836 + 0.5632\,(10)$$
$$= \$16.2156$$

Note that ΣY^2 is not used here but rather is computed for r-squared (R^2).

Use of Spreadsheet for Regression

Spreadsheet programs such as *Excel* has a regression routine which you can use without any difficulty. As a matter of fact, in reality, you do not compute the parameter values a and b manually. We will show it later in the chapter.

A Word of Caution

Before attempting a least-squares regression approach, it is extremely important to plot the observed data on a diagram, called the scattergraph (See Figure 4.2). The reason is that you might want to make sure that a linear (straight-line) relationship existed between Y and X in the past sample.

If for any reason there was a nonlinear relationship detected in the sample, the linear relationship we assumed – Y = a + bX – would not give us a good fit.

In order to obtain a good fit and achieve a high degree of accuracy, you should be familiar with statistics relating to regression such as r-squared (R^2) and t-value, which are discussed later.

Figure 4.2: Scatter diagram

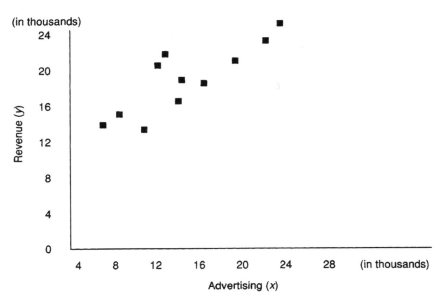

Regression Statistics

Regression analysis is a statistical method. Hence, it uses a variety of statistics to tell about the accuracy and reliability of the regression results. They include:

1. Correlation coefficient (R) and coefficient of determination(R^2)

2. Standard error of the estimate (S_e) and prediction confidence interval

3. Standard error of the regression coefficient (S_b) and t-statistic

Each of these statistics is explained below.

1. Correlation coefficient (R) and coefficient of determination (R^2)

The correlation coefficient R measures the degree of correlation between Y and X. The range of values it takes on is between -1 and +1. More widely used, however, is the coefficient of determination, designated R^2 (read as r-squared). Simply put, R^2 tells us how good the estimated regression equation is. In other words, it is a measure of "goodness of fit" in the regression. Therefore, the higher the R^2, the more confidence we have in our estimated equation.

More specifically, the coefficient of determination represents the proportion of the total variation in Y that is explained by the regression equation. It has the range of values between 0 and 1.

Example 4.3

The statement "Sales is a function of advertising expenditure with $R^2 = 70$ percent," can be interpreted as "70 percent of the total variation of sales is explained by the regression equation or the change in advertising and the remaining 30 percent is accounted for by something other than advertising, such as price and income."

The coefficient of determination is computed as

$$R^2 = \frac{\sum(Y - Y')^2}{\sum(Y - \overline{Y})^2}$$

In a simple regression situation, however, there is a short-cut method available:

$$R^2 = \frac{[n\sum XY - (\sum X)(\sum Y)]^2}{[n\sum X^2 - (\sum X)^2][n\sum Y^2 - (\sum Y)^2]}$$

Comparing this formula with the one for b, we see that the only additional information we need to compute R^2 is ΣY^2.

Example 4.4

To illustrate the computations of various regression statistics, we will refer to the data in Table 4.1.

Using the shortcut method for R_2,

$$R^2 = \frac{(1,818)^2}{[3,228][(12)(4,359) - (225)^2]} = \frac{3,305,124}{[3,228][52,308 - 50,625]} = \frac{3,305,124}{(3,228)(1,683)}$$

$$= \frac{3,305,124}{5,432,724} = 0.6084 = 60.84\%$$

This means that about 60.84 percent of the total variation in sales is explained by advertising and the remaining 39.16 percent is still unexplained. A relatively low R^2 indicates that there is a lot of room for improvement in our estimated forecasting formula (Y' = \$10.5836 + \$0.5632X). Price or a combination of advertising and price might improve R2.

2. Standard Error of the Estimate (S_e) and Prediction Confidence Interval

The standard error of the estimate, designated S_e, is defined as the standard deviation of the regression. It is computed as:

$$Se = \sqrt{\frac{\sum(Y - Y')^2}{n - 2}} = \sqrt{\frac{\sum Y^2 - a\sum Y - b\sum XY}{n - 2}}$$

This statistic can be used to gain some idea of the accuracy of our predictions.

Example 4.5

Going back to our example data, S_e is calculated as :

$$S_e \sqrt{\frac{\sum Y^2 - a\sum Y - b\sum XY}{n-2}} = \sqrt{\frac{4,359 - (10.5836)(225) - (0.5632)(3,414)}{12-2}} = \sqrt{\frac{54.9252}{10}}$$

$$= \quad 2.3436$$

Suppose you wish to make a prediction regarding an individual Y value--such as a prediction about the sales when an advertising expense $= \$10$. Usually, we would like to have some objective measure of the confidence we can place in our prediction, and one such measure is a *confidence (or prediction) interval* constructed for Y.

A confidence interval for a predicted Y, *given a value for* X, can be constructed in the following manner.

$$Y' \pm t\, S_e \sqrt{1 + \frac{1}{n} + \frac{(X_p - X)^2}{\sum X^2 - \frac{(\sum X)^2}{n}}}$$

where Y' = the predicted value of Y given a value for X;

X_p = the value of independent variable used as the basis for prediction;

Note: t is the critical value for the level of significance employed. For example, for a significant level of 0.025 (which is equivalent to a 95% confidence level in a two-tailed test), the critical value of t for 10 degrees of freedom is 2.228 (See Table A.2 in the Appendix). As can be seen, the confidence interval is the linear distance bounded by limits on either side of the prediction.

Example 4.6

If you want to have a 95 percent confidence interval of your prediction, the range for the prediction, given an advertising expense of $10 would be between $10,595.10 and $21,836.10, as determined as follows: Note that from Example 4.2, Y' = $16.2156

The confidence interval is therefore established as follows:

$$\$16.2156 \pm (2.228)(2.3436) \sqrt{1 + \frac{1}{12} + \frac{(10 - 14.5)^2}{2,792 - \frac{(174)^2}{12}}}$$

$$= \$16.2156 \pm (2.228)(2.3436)\ (1.0764)$$

$$= \$16.2156 \pm 5.6205$$

which means the range for the prediction, given an advertising expense of $10 would be between $10.5951 and $21.8361. Note that $10.5951 = $16.2156 - 5.6205 and $21.8361 =$16.2156 + 5.6205.

3. Standard Error of the Regression Coefficient (S_b) and t-Statistic

The standard error of the regression coefficient, designated Sb, and the t-statistic are closely related.

Sb is calculated as:

$$S_b = \frac{S_e}{\sqrt{(X - \overline{X})^2}}$$

or in short-cut form

$$Sb = \frac{S_e}{\sqrt{X^2 - \overline{X}\sum X)}}$$

S_b gives an estimate of the range where the true coefficient will "actually" fall.

t-statistics (or t-value) is a measure of the statistical significance of an independent variable X in explaining the dependent variable Y. It is determined by dividing the estimated regression coefficient b by its standard error S_b. It is then compared with the table t-value (See Table 2 in the Appendix). Thus, the t-statistic measures how many standard errors the coefficient is away from zero.

Rule of thumb: Any t-value greater than +2 or less than -2 is acceptable. The higher the t-value, the greater the confidence we have in the coefficient as a predictor. Low t-values are indications of low reliability of the predictive power of that coefficient.

Example 4.7

The S_b for our example is:

$$Sb = \frac{S_e}{\sqrt{X^2 - \overline{X}\sum X)}} = \frac{2.3436}{\sqrt{2,792 - (14.5)(174)}} = \frac{2.3436}{\sqrt{2,792 - 2,523}} = 0.143$$

Thus, t-statistic $= \dfrac{b}{S_b} = \dfrac{0.5632}{0.143} = 3.94$

Since, t = 3.94 > 2, we conclude that the b coefficient is statistically significant. As was indicated previously, the table's critical value (cut-off value) for 10 degrees of freedom is 2.228 (from Table A.2 in the Appendix).

To review:

(1)   t-statistic is more relevant to multiple regressions which have more than one b's.

(2) R^2 tells you how good the forest (overall fit) is while t-statistic tells you how good an individual tree (an independent variable) is.

In summary, the table t value, based on a degree of freedom and a level of significance, is used:

1.   To set the prediction range—upper and lower limits—for the predicted value of the dependent variable.

2.   To set the confidence range for regression coefficients.

3.   As a cutoff value for the t-test.

Using Regression on Excel

To utilize Excel for regression, the following procedure needs to be followed:

◆ Click the *Tools* menu.

◆ Click *Data Analysis*.

◆ Click *Regression*.

To obtain a scattergraph, use Excel's Chart Wizard.

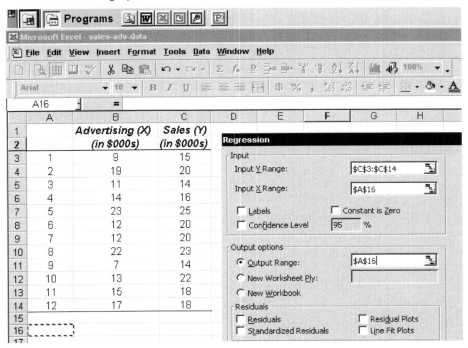

Excel Regression Output

Figure 4.3 shows an Excel regression output that contains the statistics we discussed so far

Figure 4.3: Excel Regression Output

SUMMARY OUTPUT

Regression Statistics	
Multiple R	0.77998
R Square	0.60837 (R^2)
Adjusted R Square	0.56921
Standard Error	2.34362 (S_e)
Observations	12

ANOVA

	df	SS	MS	Significance F
Regression	1	85.32434944	85.3243	0.002769
Residual	10	54.92565056	5.49257	
Total	11	140.25		

	Coefficients	Standard Error (S_b)	t Stat	Lower 95%	Upper 95%
Intercept	10.5836	2.17960878	4.85575	5.727171	15.4401
Advertising	0.5632	0.142893168	3.94139	0.244811	0.88158

(1)   R-squared (R^2) = .608373 = 60.84%

(2)   Standard error of the estimate (S_e) = 2.343622

(3)   Standard error of the coefficient (S_b) = 0.142893

(4)   t-value = 3.94

All of the above are the same as the ones manually obtained.

Figure 4.4 is the regression output from popular statistical software, *Minitab*.

Figure 4.4: Minitab Regression Output

```
Regression Analysis


The regression equation is
FO = 10.6 + 0.563 DLH

Predictor        Coef        Stdev      t-ratio        p
Constant        10.584       2.180         4.86     0.000
DLH              0.5632      0.1429         3.94     0.003

s = 2.344       R-sq = 60.8%      R-sq(adj) = 56.9%

Analysis of Variance

SOURCE         DF           SS          MS         F         p
Regression      1        85.324      85.324     15.53     0.003
Error          10        54.926       5.493
Total          11       140.250
```

Note: Regression analysis assumes:

1. **Normality**—The points around the regression line are normally distributed. That is, the error values are normally distributed--or at least t-distributed. This assumption is necessary concerning inferences about Y', a, and b. For example, the normality assumption is necessary to make probability statements using the standard error of the estimate.

2. **Constant variance (homoscedasticity)**—Also called homoscedasticity, the assumption is that the variance of the X's is constant for all X's, i.e., as X changes, the dispersion does not change. This indicates that there is uniform scatter or dispersion of points about the regression line. If the constant variance assumption does not hold, the accuracy of the b coefficient is open to question. It will ruin the validity of important statistical tests associated with regression analysis.

3. **Independence**—   It is further assumed that the errors are independent of each other, i.e., the occurrence of an error of one magnitude does not cause an error of another size. If the errors are not independent, the problem of *serial correlation* (also called *autocorrelation*) is present. When autocorrelation exists, the standard errors of the regression coefficients are seriously underestimated. As a result, the use of a t-statistic may yield incorrect conclusions concerning the significance of the individual predictor (i.e., independent) variables.

Conclusion

Regression analysis is the examination of the effect of a change in independent variables on the dependent variable. It is a popularly used method to forecast sales.

This chapter discussed the well-known estimation technique, called the *least-squares method*.

To illustrate the method, we assume a simple regression, which involves one independent variable in the form of $Y = a + bX$. In an attempt to obtain a good fit, we discussed various regression statistics. These statistics tell you how good and reliable your estimated equation is and help you set the confidence interval for your prediction.

Most importantly, we discussed how to utilize spreadsheet programs such as Lotus 1-2-3 to perform regressions, step by step. The program calculates not only the regression equation, but also all the regression statistics discussed in this chapter.

Chapter 5
Multiple Regression

Multiple regression analysis is a powerful statistical technique that is perhaps the most widely used one by forecasters. Multiple regression attempts to estimate statistically the average relationship between the dependent variable (e.g., sales) and two or more independent variables (e.g., price, advertising, income, etc.).

In reality, forecasters will face more multiple regression situations than simple regression. In order to obtain a good fit and achieve a high degree of accuracy, they should be familiar with statistics relating to regression such as R-squared (R^2) and t-value. *Note*: Look beyond the statistics we discussed here. Furthermore, forecasters will have to perform additional tests unique to multiple regression.

Applications

Applications of multiple regression are numerous. Multiple regression analysis is used to do the following:

1. To find the overall association between the dependent variable and a host of explanatory variables. For example, overhead costs are explained by volume, productivity, and technology.

2. To attempt to identify the factors that influence the dependent variable. For example,

   (a) Factors critical in affecting sales include price levels, advertising expenditures, consumer take-home income, taste, and competition.

   (b) Financial analysts might seek causes of a change in stock prices or price-earnings (P-E) ratios by analyzing growth in earnings, variability of earnings, stock splits, inflation rates, beta, and dividend yields.

(c)   Advertising directors wish to study the impact on consumer buying of advertising budgets, advertising frequency, media selection, and the like.

(d)   Personnel managers attempt to determine the relationship between employee salary levels and a host of factors such as industry type, union leadership, competitive salaries, unemployment, skill levels, and geographical location.

3.   To use it as a basis for providing sound forecasts of the dependent variable. For example, sometimes cash collections from customers are forecasted from credit sales of prior months since cash collections lag behind sales.

The Model

The multiple regression model takes the following form:

$$Y = b_o + b_1 X_1 + b_2 X_2 ... + b_k X_k + u$$

where Y = dependent variable, X's = independent (explanatory) variables, b's = regression coefficients, u = error term.

Example 5.1

When a simple regression is not good enough to provide a satisfactory fit (as indicated typically by a low R-squared), the manager should use multiple regression. Presented below is an example of both simple and multiple regressions and their spreadsheet printout. The sales manager is trying to develop a model for forecasting annual sales for toothpaste using advertising budgets for the current year and for two previous years.

Assuming the data in Table 5.1, Figure 5.1 presents two regression results:

Table 5.1: Annual Data for Toothpaste Sales With Current and Previous Advertising Budgets (in $ millions)

Year	Sales(Yt)	Advertising Budget(Xt)	Xt-1	Xt-2
1999	113.750	15.000		
2000	124.150	14.000	15.000	
2001	133.000	15.400	14.000	15.000

continued

Year	Sales(Yt)	Advertising Budget(Xt)	Xt-1	Xt-2
2002	126.000	18.250	15.400	14.000
2003	162.000	17.300	18.250	15.400
2004	191.625	23.000	17.300	18.250
2005	189.000	19.250	23.000	17.300
2006	210.000	23.056	19.250	23.000
2007	224.250	26.000	23.056	19.250
2008	245.000	28.000	26.000	23.056

The simple regression model shows:

$$Y_t = -9.59 + 9.11\, X_t \qquad\qquad R^2 = 89.46\%$$
$$(1.11)*$$

* Standard error of regression coefficient S_b.

The multiple regression model with advertising budgets for two previous years is:

$$Y_t = -37.88 + 4.97\, X_{t-1} + 6.93\, X_{t-2} \quad R^2 = 94.1\%$$
$$(1.52) \qquad (1.82)$$

This model has two advantages:

1. The explanatory power has increased from 89.46% to 94.1%
2. From the forecaster's point of view, using only lagged variables does not require any assumptions about actual future budgets.

Figure 5.1: Excel Regression Output

SUMMARY OUTPUT

Regression Statistics	
Multiple R	0.94582068
R Square	0.894576758
Adjusted R Square	0.881398853
Standard Error	16.06997067
Observations	10

ANOVA

	df	SS	MS	F
Regression	1	17530.7864	17530.7864	67.88459479
Residual	8	2065.951659	258.2439574	
Total	9	19596.73806		

	Coefficients	Standard Error	t Stat	P-value
Intercept	-9.59129596	22.60367164	-0.42432469	0.682509532
X Variable 1	9.107319025	1.10536303	8.239210811	3.53015E-05

SUMMARY OUTPUT

Regression Statistics	
Multiple R	0.970047934
R Square	0.940992994
Adjusted R Square	0.917390191
Standard Error	12.16478478
Observations	8

ANOVA

	df	SS	MS	F
Regression	2	11799.44748	5899.723739	39.86785007
Residual	5	739.9099436	147.9819887	
Total	7	12539.35742		

	Coefficients	Standard Error	t Stat	P-value
Intercept	-37.87704146	25.43926526	-1.488920418	0.196681922
X Variable 1	4.970408737	1.522161365	3.265362563	0.022312771
X Variable 2	6.934206808	1.821730969	3.806383559	0.01254633

Example 5.2

The Los Alamitos Equipment Company wants to identify trends in demand for its heavy equipment so that funds available for investment, and related expenditures, can be efficiently allocated. The company collected data on real GDP and the Treasury-bill rate, as given in Table 5.2. Using popular statistical software, MINITAB, the company obtained: (1) a trend equation and (2) a multiple regression model which incorporates explanatory factors besides trend.

The results from MINITAB (see Figure 5.2) are as follows:

Simple regression (trend) equation

$$Y = 821 + 4.07\ X_1 \qquad R^2 = 54.6\%$$

$$(0.7019)$$

Multiple regression equation

$$Y = 221.7 + 1.99\ X_1 + 0.504\ X_2 - 8.93\ X_3 \qquad R^2 = 78.0\%$$

$$(1.855) \quad (0.1308) \quad (2.821)$$

where X_1 = time, X_2 = real GDP, and X_3 = 90-day T-bill rate

Table 5.2: Los Alamitos Equipment Company

Year	Sales (Y)	Time (X_1)	GNP (X_2)	T-Bill (X_3)
1980	777.73	1	1206.3	5.75
1981	791.62	2	1221.0	5.39
1982	799.99	3	1248.4	6.33
1983	814.76	4	1259.7	5.63
1984	837.22	5	1287.2	4.92
1985	840.74	6	1295.8	5.16
1986	847.57	7	1303.3	5.15
1987	858.59	8	1315.4	4.67
1988	875.18	9	1341.3	4.63
1989	886.17	10	1363.3	4.84
1990	892.60	11	1385.8	5.50
1991	977.15	12	1388.4	6.11
1992	809.61	13	1400.0	6.39
1993	918.31	14	1437.0	6.48
1994	916.26	15	1448.8	7.31
1995	916.93	16	1468.4	8.57
1996	913.99	17	1472.6	9.38
1997	912.60	18	1469.2	9.38
1998	922.57	19	1486.6	9.67
1999	904.71	20	1489.3	11.84
2000	897.52	21	1496.2	13.35
2001	915.71	22	1461.4	9.62
2002	922.27	23	1464.2	9.15
2003	891.65	24	1477.9	13.61
2004	906.66	25	1510.1	14.39
2005	903.33	26	1512.5	14.90
2006	913.17	27	1525.8	15.05
2007	934.99	28	1506.9	11.75
2008	913.01	29	1485.8	12.81
2009	921.58	30	1489.3	12.42

Figure 5.2: Minitab results

Regression Analysis
1. Simple (trend) regression:
The regression equation is: Sales = 821 + 4.07 Time

Predictor	Coef	Stdev	t-ratio	p
Constant	821.32	12.46	65.91	0.000
Time	4.0744	0.7019	5.80	0.000

s = 33.27   R-sq = 54.6%   R-sq (adj) = 53.0%

Analysis of Variance

Source	DF	SS	MS	F	p
Regression	1	37310	37310	33.70	0.000
Error	28	31002	1107		
Total	29	68312			

Unusual Observations

Obs.	Time	Sales	Fit	Stddev Fit	Residual	St Resid
19	12.0	977.15	870.21	6.55	106.94	3.28R*

Durbin-Watson statistic = 1.65

2. Multiple regression:
The regression equation is: Sales = 222 + 1.99 Time + 0.504 GNP − 8.93 T-bill

Predictor	Coef	Stdev	t-ratio	p
Constant	221.7	164.3	1.35	0.189
Time	1.989	1.855	1.07	0.293
GNP	0.5041	0.1308	3.85	0.001
T-bill	-8.928	2.821	-3.16	0.004

s = 24.02   R-sq = 78.0%   R-sq (adj) = 75.5%

Analysis of Variance

Source	DF	SS	MS	F	p
Regression	3	53315	17772	30.81	0.00
Error	26	14997	577		
Total	29	68312			

Source	DF	SEQ SS
Time	1	37310
GNP	1	10228
T-bill	1	5777

Unusual Observations

Obs	Time	Sales	Fit	Stddev Fit	Residual	St Resid
18	13.0	809.61	896.21	6.34	-86.60	-3.74R*
19	12.0	977.15	890.87	6.30	86.28	3.72R*

Durbin-Watson statistic = 3.03

*R denotes an observation with a large standard residual.

Nonlinear Regression

Thus far we assumed a linear relationship. In some cases, however, a nonlinear form may be more appropriate. For example, in Example 5.1, it is sometimes difficult to assume that a linear relationship exists between lagged advertising budgets and sales, because of the diminishing returns effect of accumulated advertising.

In addition to the nonlinearity which might be associated with the decay it is frequently postulated that the sales-advertising relationship is S-shaped. That is, at lower levels of advertising the ability of the ads to reach the audience is at best limited. At moderate spending levels, the audience reach expands and sales grow at a relatively more rapid pace. At a higher and higher level, the sale response slows and eventually is oversaturated.

A popular formulation to account for this phenomenon is as follows:

$$Y_t = b_o + b_1 \, 1/X_{t-1} + b_2 \, 1/X_{t-2} \qquad\qquad b_1, b_2 < 0$$

This specification represents a hyperbola, and describes a S-shaped relationship. Example 5.3 illustrates this, using the data in Table 5.3.

Example 5.3

Using the nonlinear form specified above yields:

$$Y_t = 413.94 - 1614.35 \, 1/X_{t-1} - 2514.22 \, 1/X_{t-2} \qquad R^2 = 96.63\%$$

$$(45.45) \qquad\qquad\qquad (487.73)$$

Table 5.3: Annual Data for Toothpaste Sales With Current and Previous Advertising Budgets (in $ millions)

Year	Sales(Yt)	Advertising Budget(Xt)	X_{t-1}	X_{t-2}	$1/X_{t-1}$	$1/X_{t-2}$
2000	113.750	15.000				
2001	124.150	14.000	15.000		0.067	
2002	133.000	15.400	14.000	15.000	0.071	0.067
2003	126.000	18.250	15.400	14.000	0.065	0.071
2004	162.000	17.300	18.250	15.400	0.055	0.065
2005	191.625	23.000	17.300	18.250	0.058	0.055
2006	189.000	19.250	23.000	17.300	0.043	0.058
2007	210.000	23.056	19.250	23.000	0.052	0.043
2008	224.250	26.000	23.056	19.250	0.043	0.052
2009	245.000	28.000	26.000	23.056	0.038	0.043

SUMMARY OUTPUT

Regression Statistics	
Multiple R	0.983016313
R Square	0.966321072
Adjusted R Square	0.952849501
Standard Error	9.190343964
Observations	8

ANOVA

	df	SS	MS	F	Significance F
Regression	2	12117.04531	6058.52266	71.730392	0.00020816
Residual	5	422.3121109	84.4624222		
Total	7	12539.35742			

	Coefficients	Standard Error	t Stat	P-value	Lower 95%	Upper 95%
Intercept	413.9353029	19.50573694	21.2212081	4.307E-06	363.794292	464.076314
X Variable 1	-1614.354723	448.4473008	-3.5998761	0.01554529	-2767.1233	-461.58612
X Variable 2	-2514.227913	487.7338655	-5.1549177	0.00360002	-3767.9857	-1260.4701

Using Qualitative Factors – Dummy Variables

Forecasting with qualitative (or dummy) variables can help in many practical business situations. Suppose you need to predict monthly sales based on advertising expenditures and variables such as indicators of the local economy or sales of a complementary product. Then your company makes a price change. Add a qualitative-variable column containing 0s for all months before the price change and 1s for all months thereafter. The X coefficient for this variable estimates the effect of the price change on sales.

Dummy variables can be used to represent:

1. Temporal effects such as shifts in relations between:

    a. wartime and peace time years

    b. different seasons

2.   qualitative (or categorical) variables such as

    a.   sex

    b.   marital status

    c.   occupational or social status

    d.   age

    e.   location

    f.   product features

    g.   race

Adding these qualitative variables to regression models can improve accuracy whenever nonnumeric factors affect the outcomes. Thus far, we have assumed that any independent variable that is to be used in an estimating equation has values that can be measured on at least a cardinal scale (e.g., 1, 2, 3, etc.). However, there are many instances where a relationship may not be described on such a refined measurement scale.

For example, we may believe that sex can influence the level of salary. Sex may be treated as a dummy variable that has only two values assigned to it -- a 1 when its influence is to be included in the estimating equation, and a 0 otherwise. To illustrate, suppose our salary equation is

$$Y = b_0 + b_1 X_1 + b_2 X_2$$

where X_1 = experience in years

$$X_2 = \begin{cases} 1 \text{ for males} \\ 0 \text{ for females} \end{cases} = \text{dummy variable}$$

That is, X_2 is a dummy variable representing the gender. Note that this dummy variable merely shifts the intercept of our estimating equation by the amount of its coefficient, b_2, whenever $X_2 = 1$.

The single equation is equivalent to the following two equations:

$$Y = b_0 + b_1 X_1 + b_2 \quad \text{for males}$$
$$Y = b_0 + b_2 X_2 \quad\quad \text{for females}$$

Note that b_2 represents the effect of a male on salary and b1 represents the effect of experience differences (the b_2 value is assumed to be the same for males and females). The important point is that one multiple regression equation will yield the two estimated lines. One line is the estimate for males and the other is the estimate for females. Dummy variables provide a useful technique for including the influence of unusual factors.

Example 5.4

Assume the following data.

Salary (Y)	Experience (X_1)	Gender (X_2)
$50,000	5	1
45,000	4	1
52,000	8	0
35,000	2	0
55,000	12	1
38,000	2	1
25,000	1	0
40,000	2	1
43,000	6	0
36,000	2	0
26,000	1	0

Figure 5.4 (over the page) shows the *MicroTSP* input procedure and a variety of regression output. The estimated multiple regression equation is shown as follows.

$$Y = 28692 + 2243\,X_1 + 5696\,X_2 \qquad R^2 = 83.02\%$$

$$(429) \qquad (2835)$$

The explanatory power of the model (R^2) is 83.02%, which suggests that both experience and gender makes a contribution to the salary level. The computed t values, 5.22 (2243/429) and 2.01 (5695/2835), respectively, indicates that both variables are statistically significant at the 10% significance level. *Note:* Again, in multiple regressions, look beyond these statistics (R^2 and t values), which will be discussed in detail later.

For the two values (0 and 1) of X_2, the equation provides

$$Y = 28692 + 2243\,X_1 + 5696\,(1)$$

$$= 34388 + 2243\,X_1 \qquad \text{for males}$$

and

$$Y = 28692 + 2243\,X_1 + 5696\,(0)$$

$$= 28692 + 2243\,X_1 \qquad \text{for females}$$

Figure 5.4 : MicroTSP Data Input and Regression Output

Running Least-Squares Regression on MicroTSP:

>LS
Dependent variable//SALARY
List may include D, AR, SAR, MA, SMA, and PDL items.
Independent variable List ? c experien sex

Descriptive Statistics and Correlative Matrix:

SMPL range: 1 - 11   Number of observations: 11

Variable	Mean	SD	Maximum	Minimum
SALARY	40454.545	9832.2290	55000.000	25000.000
EXPERIEN	4.0909091	3.4483197	12.000000	1.0000000
SEX	0.4545455	0.5222330	1.0000000	0.0000000

	Covariance	Correlation
SALARY, SALARY	87884298.000	1.0000000
SALARY, EXPERIEN	26595.041	0.8628471
SALARY, SEX	2338.8430	0.5010459
EXPERIEN, EXPERIEN	10.809917	1.0000000
EXPERIEN, SEX	0.4132231	0.2524094
SEX, SEX	0.2479339	1.0000000

Regression Output:

LS / / Dependent variable is SALARY
Date: 1-11-1998 / Time: 23.07
SMPL range: 1 - 11
Number of observations: 11

Variable	Coefficient	Std. Error	T-STst.	2-Tail Sig.
C	28691.617	2338.2987	12.270296	0.0000
EXPERIEN	2242.5150	429.30467	5.2235979	0.0008
SEX	5695.8084	2834.7115	2.0093080	0.0794

R-squared	0.830198	Mean of dependent variable	40454.55
Adjusted R-squared	0.787748	SD of dependent variable	9832.229
SE of regression	4529.792	Sum of dependent variable	1.64E+08
Log likelihood	-106.4596	F-statistic	19.55687
Durbin-Watson statistic	1.639067	Probability (F-statistic)	0.000831

These two equations may be interpreted as follows:

1. The regression coefficient, b_1 = 2243, which is the slope of each of the regression lines, represents the estimated increase in salary for each year in experience. This value applies to both males and females.

2. The other regression coefficient value, b_2 = 5696, applies only to males. This means that males receive $5,696 more in salary than females for the same years of experience.

Weighted (or Discounted) Regression

The problem with using the ordinary least-squares model is that the line fits the early data points more closely than it fits the later ones. The so-called *weighted (or discounted) least squares model* gets around this problem. Under this method, we use the weights decline from recent data to older data.

With standard regression, the computed line minimizes the squared distances from the points to the line. In discounted regression, the line minimizes weighted squared distances. Because earlier values are discounted, they have less influence on the final forecast. By the same token, the more weight that is placed on particular data, the more the line reflects that data.

The table below shows the four sets of weights for eight periods ($t = 0,...7$) you get by using four different discount factors. Weights are computed using the following formula:

$$W_t = \sqrt{(\text{discount factor})^t}$$

Table 5.4: Discount Factor

t	0.70	0.80	0.90	1.00
7	0.29	0.46	0.69	1.00
6	0.34	0.51	0.73	1.00
5	0.41	0.57	0.77	1.00
4	0.49	0.64	0.81	1.00
3	0.59	0.72	0.85	1.00
2	0.70	0.80	0.90	1.00
1	0.84	0.89	0.95	1.00
0	1.00	1.00	1.00	1.00

Note: When the discount factor is 1.00, all data get equal weight and the result is the same as with the traditional least squares. As the discount factor is reduced, the weights on older data fall off substantially.

Example 5.5

To illustrate the method, we use quarterly data of sales and the number of warranty claims of a refrigerator maker which is given in Table 5.5. The company believes that warranty claims in a given quarter (C_t) are closely related to sales from the previous quarter (S_{t-1}).

Without proof, using the discounted data, the multiple regression equation to be fitted becomes:

$$Y_t = aX_1 + bX_2$$

where $Y_t = W_t \times C_t$, $X_1 = W_t$, and $X_2 = W_t \times S_t$

The bottom portion of Table 5.5 reveals regression output (from *Lotus 1-2-3*) with predicted warranty claims:

$$Y = -5.95 \, X_1 + 0.11 \, X2 \qquad R^2 = 0.99$$

$$(9.40) \quad (0.02)$$

Figure 5.5 reveals that the solid line, labeled "Discounted," fits later data points more closely than the broken line, and it better reflects the changes in claims experience. As you can see from Figure 5.5, the discounted prediction for the fourth quarter of 2006 is lower than the standard prediction for the same quarter.

Table 5.5: Discounted Least-Squares Regression Discount factor 0.80

Year	Qtr	T	Weight Wt	Prv Qtr Sales X	Claims Y	Weight X_1	Sales x Wt X_2	Claims x Wt Y	Pred Claims Y
				Actual Data		*Discounted Data*			
2007	4	7	0.46	397.00	33.00	0.46	182.62	15.18	36.48
2008	1	6	0.51	408.00	36.00	0.51	208.08	18.36	37.66
	2	5	0.57	427.00	38.00	0.57	243.39	21.66	39.69
	3	4	0.64	430.00	39.00	0.64	275.20	24.96	40.01
	4	3	0.72	433.00	42.00	0.72	311.76	30.24	40.33
2009	1	2	0.80	445.00	44.00	0.80	356.00	35.20	41.62
	2	1	0.89	465.00	45.00	0.89	413.85	40.05	43.75
	3	0	1.00	507.00	47.00	1.00	507.00	47.00	48.24
	4			520.00					49.63

Regression Output:		
Constant		0.00
Std Err of Y Est		1.44
R Squared		0.99
No. of Observations		8.00
Degrees of Freedom		6.00
X Coefficient(s)	-5.95	0.11
Std Err of Coef.	9.40	0.02

Figure 5.5 : Regression Model Comparisons

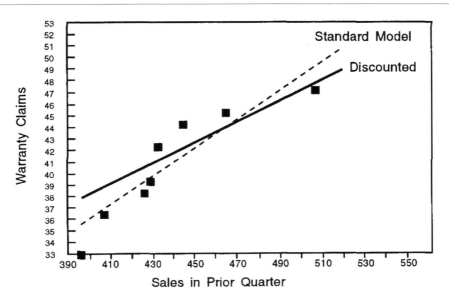

Statistics to Look for in Multiple Regressions

In multiple regressions that involve more then one independent (explanatory) variable, managers must look for the following statistics:

◆ t-statistics
◆ R-bar squared ($\overline{R}^2$) and F-statistic
◆ Multicollinearity
◆ Autocorrelation (or serial correlation)

t-statistics

The t-statistic was discussed earlier, but is taken up again here since it is more valid in multiple regressions than in simple regressions. The t-statistic shows the significance of each explanatory variable in predicting the dependent variable. It is desirable to have as large (either positive or negative) a t-statistic as possible for each independent variable. Generally, a t-statistic greater than +2.0 or less than -2.0 is acceptable. Explanatory variables with low t-value can usually be eliminated from the regression without substantially decreasing R^2 or increasing the standard error of the regression. In a multiple regression situation, the t-statistic is defined as

$$\text{t-statistic} = \frac{b_i}{S_{b_i}}$$

where $i = i_{th}$ independent variable

R-Bar Squared ($\overline{R}^2$) and F-Statistic

A more appropriate test for goodness of fit for multiple regressions is R-bar squared ($\overline{R}^2$):

$$\overline{R}^2 = 1 - (1 - R^2)\, \frac{n-1}{n-k}$$

where   n = the number of observations

k = the number of coefficients to be estimated

An alternative test of the overall significance of a regression equation is the F-test. Virtually all computer programs for regression analysis show an F-statistic.

The F-statistic is defined as

$$F = \frac{(Y'-\overline{Y})^2 / k}{(Y - Y')^2 / (n-k-1)} = \frac{\text{Explained variation} / k}{\text{Unexplained variation} / (n - k - 1)}$$

If the F-statistic is greater than the table value, it is concluded that the regression equation is statistically significant in overall terms.

Multicollinearity

When using more than one independent variable in a regression equation, there is sometimes a high correlation between the independent variables themselves. Multicollinearity occurs when these variables interfere with each other. It is a pitfall because the equations with multicollinearity may produce spurious forecasts.

Multicollinearity can be recognized when

◆ The t-statistics of two seemingly important independent variables are low

◆ The estimated coefficients on explanatory variables have the opposite sign from that which would logically be expected

There are two ways to get around the problem of multicollinearity:

◆ One of the highly correlated variables may be dropped from the regression

◆ The structure of the equation may be changed using one of the following methods:

● Divide both the left and right-hand side variables by some series that will leave the basic economic logic but remove multicollinearity

● Estimate the equation on a first-difference basis

● Combine the collinear variables into a new variable, which is their weighted sum

Autocorrelation (Serial Correlation)

Autocorrelation is another major pitfall often encountered in regression analysis. It occurs where there is a correlation between successive errors. The Durbin-Watson statistic provides the standard test for autocorrelation. Table 4 in the Appendix provides the values of the Durbin-Watson statistic for specified sample sizes and explanatory variables. The table gives the significance points for d_L and dU for tests on the autocorrelation of residuals (when no explanatory variable is a lagged endogenous variable). The number of explanatory variables, K excludes the constant term.

Generally speaking,

Durbin-Watson Statistic	Autocorrelation
Between 1.5 and 2.5	No autocorrelation
Below 1.5	Positive Autocorrelation
Above 2.5	Negative Autocorrelation

Autocorrelation usually indicates that an important part of the variation of the dependent variable has not been explained. *Recommendation*: The best solution to this problem is to search for other explanatory variables to include in the regression equation.

Checklists: How to Choose the Best Forecasting Equation

Choosing among alternative forecasting equations basically involves two steps. The first step is to eliminate the obvious losers. The second is to select the winner among the remaining contenders.

How to Eliminate Losers

1. Does the equation make sense? Equations that do not make sense intuitively or from a theoretical standpoint must be eliminated.

2. Does the equation have explanatory variables with low t-statistics? These equations should be reestimated or dropped in favor of equations in which all independent variables are significant. This test will eliminate equations where multicollinearity is a problem.

3. How about a low $\overline{R}^2$? The can be used to rank the remaining equations in order to select the best candidates. A low $\overline{R}^2$ could mean:

◆ A wrong functional was fitted
◆ An important explanatory variable is missing
◆ Other combinations of explanatory variables might be more desirable

How to Choose the Best Equation

1. *Best Durbin-Watson statistic.* Given equations that survive all previous tests, the equation with the Durbin-Watson statistic closest to 2.0 can be a basis for selection.

2. *Best forecasting accuracy.* Examining the forecasting performance of the equations is essential for selecting one equation from those that have not been eliminated. The equation whose prediction accuracy is best in terms of measures of forecasting errors, such as MAD, MSE, RMSE, or MPE (to be discussed in detail in a later chapter) generally provides the best basis for forecasting.

Note: Excel does not provide Durbin-Watson statistic. You have to go to stand-alone software packages such as *Statistical Analysis System (SAS)*, *Minitab*, and *Statistical Packages for Social Scientists (SPSS)*, to name a few.

Use of a Computer Statistical Package for Multiple Regression

Example 5.6

Stanton Consumer Products Corporation wishes to develop a forecasting model for its dryer sale by using multiple regression analysis. The marketing department has prepared the following sample data.

	Sales of Washers X_1 (000s)	Disposable Income X_2 (000s)	Savings X_3 (000s)	Sales of Dryers Y (000s)
January	45	16	71	29
February	42	14	70	24
March	44	15	72	27
April	45	13	71	25
May	43	13	75	26
June	46	14	74	28
July	44	16	76	30
August	45	16	69	28
September	44	15	74	28
October	43	15	73	27

The computer statistical package called SPSS was employed to develop the regression model. Figure 5.6 contains the input data and output that results using three explanatory variables. To help you understand the listing, illustrative comments are added whenever applicable.

Figure 5.6: SPSS Regression Output

Model Summary[b]

Model	R	R Square	Adjusted R Square	Std. Error of the Estimate	Durbin-Watson
1	.992[a]	.983	.975	286.1281	2.094

a. Predictors: (Constant), SAVINGS, sales, INCOME

b. Dependent Variable: SALESDRY

Coefficients[a]

Model		Unstandardized Coefficients		Standardized Coefficients	t	Sig.
		B	Std. Error	Beta		
1	(Constant)	-45796.3	4877.651		-9.389	.000
	sales	.597	.081	.394	7.359	.000
	INCOME	1.177	.084	.752	13.998	.000
	SAVINGS	.405	.042	.508	9.592	.000

a. Dependent Variable: SALESDRY

ANOVA[b]

Model		Sum of Squares	df	Mean Square	F	Sig.
1	Regression	29108784	3	9702928.0	118.517	.000[a]
	Residual	491215.904	6	81869.317		
	Total	29600000	9			

a. Predictors: (Constant), SAVINGS, sales, INCOME

b. Dependent Variable: SALESDRY

Coefficient Correlations[a]

Model			SAVINGS	sales	INCOME
1	Correlations	SAVINGS	1.000	.043	.096
		sales	.043	1.000	-.179
		INCOME	.096	-.179	1.000
	Covariances	SAVINGS	1.784E-03	1.467E-04	3.406E-04
		sales	1.467E-04	6.581E-03	-1.22E-03
		INCOME	3.406E-04	-1.22E-03	7.068E-03

a. Dependent Variable: SALESDRY

1. *The forecasting equation.* From the SPSS output we see that

    $Y' = -45,796.35 + 0.597X_1 + 1.177X_2 + 0.405X_3$

    Suppose that in November the company expects

    X_1 = sales of washers = \$43,000

    X_2 = disposable income = \$15,000

    X_3 = savings = \$75,000

    Then the forecast sales for the month of November would be

    Y' = $-45,796.35 + 0.597(43,000) + 1.177(15,000) + 0.405(75,000)$

    = $-45,796 + 25,671 + 17,655 + 30,375$

    = \$27,905.35

2. *The coefficient of determination.* Note that the SPSS output gives the value of R, R^2, and R^2 adjusted. In our example, R = 0.992 and R^2 = 0.983. In the case of multiple regression, is more appropriate, as was discussed previously.

    $$\bar{R}^2 = 0.975$$

    This tells us that 97.5 percent of total variation in sales of dryers is explained by the three explanatory variables. The remaining 2.5 percent was unexplained by the estimated equation.

3. *The standard error of the estimate* (S_e). This is a measure of dispersion of actual sales around the estimated equation. The output shows S_e = 286.1281.

4. *Durbin-Watson test.* The output shows 2.094. Since it is between 1.5 and 2.5, no autocorrelation exists.

5. *Computed t.* We read from the output

	t-Statistic
X_1	7.359
X_2	13.998
X_3	9.592

All t values are greater than a rule-of-thumb table t value of 2.0. (Strictly speaking, with n - k - 1 = 10 - 3 - 1 = 6 degrees of freedom and a level of significance of, say, 0.01, we see from Table A.2 that the table t value is 3.707.) For a two-sided test, the level of significance to look up was .005. In any case, we conclude that all three explanatory variables we have selected were statistically significant.

6. *F-test.* From the output, we see that

$$F = 118.517$$

At a significance level of 0.01, our F-value is far above the value of 9.78 (which is from Table A.3), so we conclude that the regression as a whole is highly significant.

7. *Multicollinearity.* The output shows low correlation coefficients among the explanatory variables, which indicates no multicollinearity problems.

8. *Conclusion.* Based on statistical considerations, we see that:
   - ◆ The estimated equation had a good fit
   - ◆ All three variables are significant explanatory variables
   - ◆ The regression as a whole is highly significant
   - ◆ No serial correlation and multicollinearity problems are detected.
   - ◆ The model developed can be used as a forecasting equation with a great degree of confidence

Conclusion

Multiple regression analysis is the examination of the effect of a change in explanatory variables on the dependent variable. For example, various financial ratios bear on a firm's market price of stock. Many important statistics that are unique to multiple regression analysis were explained with computer illustrations. An emphasis was placed on how to pick the best forecasting equation.

Chapter 6

Time Series Analysis and Classical Decomposition

A time series is a sequence of data points at constant time intervals such as a week, month, quarter, and year. Time series analysis breaks data into components and projects them into the future. The four commonly recognized components are trend, seasonal, cycle, and irregular variation:

1.   The *trend component* (T) is the general upward or downward movement of the average over time. These movements may require many years of data to determine or describe them. The basic forces underlying the trend include technological advances, productivity changes, inflation, and population change.

2.   The *seasonal component* (S) is a recurring fluctuation of data points above or below the trend value that repeats with a usual frequency of one year, e.g., Christmas sales.

3.   *Cyclical components* (C) are recurrent upward and downward movements that repeat with a frequency that is longer than a year. This movement is attributed to business cycles (such as recession, inflation, unemployment, and prosperity), so the periodicity (recurrent rate) of such cycles does not have to be constant.

4.   The *irregular (or random) component* (R) is a series of short, erratic movements that follow no discernible pattern. It is caused by unpredictable or nonrecurring events such as floods, wars, strikes, elections, environmental changes, and the passage of legislation.

Trend Analysis

Trends are the general upward or downward movements of the average over time. These movements may require many years of data to determine or describe them. They can be described by a straight line or a curve. The basic forces underlying the trend include technological advances, productivity changes, inflation, and population change.

Trend analysis is a special type of simple regression. This method involves a regression whereby a trend line is fitted to a time series of data. In practice, however, one typically finds linear and nonlinear curves used for business forecasting.

Linear Trend

The *linear* trend line equation can be shown as

$$Y = a + b t$$

where t = time.

The formula for the coefficients a and b are essentially the same as the cases for simple regression. However, for regression purposes, a time period can be given a number so that $\Sigma t = 0$. When there is an odd number of periods, the period in the middle is assigned a zero value. If there is an even number, then -1 and +1 are assigned the two periods in the middle, so that again $\Sigma t = 0$.

With $\Sigma t = 0$, the formula for b and a reduces to the following:

$$b = \frac{n \sum tY}{n \sum t^2}$$

$$a = \frac{\sum Y}{n}$$

Example 6.1

Case 1 (odd number)

t =	20X1	20X2	20X3	20X4	20X5
	-2	-1	0	1	2

Case 2 (even number)

t =	20X1	20X2	20X3	20X4	20X5	20X6
	-3	-2	-1	1	2	3

In each case $\Sigma t = 0$.

Example 6.2

Consider ABC Company, whose historical sales follows.

Year	Sales (in millions)
20X1	$10
20X2	12
20X3	13
20X4	16
20X5	17

Since the company has five years' data, which is an odd number, the year in the middle is assigned a zero value.

Year	t	Sales (in millions) (Y)	tY	t^2	Y^2
20X1	-2	$10	-20	4	100
20X2	-1	12	-12	1	144
20X3	0	13	0	0	169
20X4	1	16	16	1	256
20X5	2	17	34	4	289
	0	68	18	10	958

$$b = \frac{(5)(18)}{5(10)} = 90/50 = 1.8$$

$$a = \frac{68}{5} = 13.6$$

Therefore, the estimated trend equation is

$$Y' = \$13.6 + \$1.8\,t$$

To project 20X6 sales, we assign +3 to the t value for the year 20X6.

$$Y' = \$13.6 + \$1.8\,(3)$$
$$= \$19$$

Nonlinear Trend

A typical example of nonlinear trend is a constant growth model. A model structure that captures the increasing growth pattern described in Table 6.1 Los Al sales data shows the constant growth rate, or constant rate of change over time, by a proportional rather than constant amount. Other common nonlinear trends described by the *modified exponential growth curve* and the *logistic growth curve* are discussed in a later chapter.

Note: The right hand column in the table is the logarithmic values of sales.

Table 6.1: Total Sales Revenue for Los Al, Inc. (1998-2007)

Year	Sales	Time	in (Sales)
1998	2000.1	1	7.600952458
1999	2308.9	2	7.7445265
2000	2645.0	3	7.880426344
2001	2909.4	4	7.975702153
2002	3243.0	5	8.084254106
2003	3745.0	6	8.228176896
2004	4170.3	7	8.335743255
2005	4852.4	8	8.487228707
2006	5312.1	9	8.577742516
2007	5550.8	10	8.62169734

Regression Output:	
Constant	7.511069229
Std Err of Y Est	0.029150173
R Squared	0.993999587
No. of Observations	10
Degrees of Freedom	8

X Coefficient(s)	0.116832	
Std Err of Coef.	0.0032093	

The constant rate of change, or proportional change model, involves determining the average historical rate of change in a variable and projecting that rate into the future. This is essentially identical to the compounding of value model used in finance. For example, if a firm is projecting its sales for five years into the future and if it has determined that sales are increasing at an annual rate of 10 percent, the projection would simply involve multiplying the 10 percent compound value interest factor for five years times current sales. Assuming current sales are $1 million, the forecast of sales five years from now would be:

$$\text{Sales in Year 5} = \text{Current Sales} \times (1 + \text{Growth Rate})^5$$
$$= \$1,000,000 \times (1.10)^5$$
$$= \$1,000,000 \times 1.61$$
$$= \$1,610,000.$$

More generally, the constant rate of change projection model can be stated as follows:

$$\text{Value t Years in the Future} = \text{Current Value} \times (1 + \text{Rate of Change})^t.$$

Just as one can estimate the constant annual change in a business time series by fitting historical data to a linear regression model of the form $Y = a + bt$, so, too, can one estimate the annual growth rate in a constant rate of change projection model using the same technique. In this case, the growth rate is estimated using linear regression by fitting historical data to the logarithmic transformation of the basic model. For example, if one were to formulate a constant growth rate model for firm sales it would take the form:

$$S_t = S_0 (1 + g)^t. \qquad\qquad (1)$$

Here sales t years in the future (S_t) is assumed to be equal to current sales, S_0, compounded at a growth rate, g, for a period of t years. Taking logarithms of both sides of Equation (1) results in the expression:

$$\ln S_t = \ln S_0 + \ln (1 + g) \times t \qquad\qquad (2)$$

Note that Equation (2) is an expression of the form:

$$Y_t = a + bt,$$

where $Y_t = \ln S_t$, $a = \ln S_0$, and $b = \ln (1 + g)$; hence, its coefficients, $\ln S_0$ and $\ln (1 + g)$, can be estimated using the least squares regression technique.

Applying this technique to the Los Al sales data in table 6.1 for the 1998-2007 period results in the regression (standard error in parenthesis)

$$\ln S_t = 7.51 + 0.117t \quad R_2 = 99.4\%,$$

$$(0.003)$$

or, equivalently, by transforming this estimated equation back to its original form:

$$S_t = [\text{Antilog } 7.51] \times [\text{Antilog } 0.117]^t = 1,826.21 \, (1.124)^t$$

Note: Most scientific calculators have a key to antilog.

In this model, $1,826.21 million is the adjusted sales for $t = 0$ (which would be 1997, since the first year of data used in the regression estimation [t=1] was 1998); and

1.124 is equal to one plus the average annual rate of growth, meaning that Los Al's sales increased by 12.4 percent annually over the 1999-2007 period.

To forecast sales in any future year using this model, we subtract 1997 from the year being forecast to determine t. Thus, a constant growth model forecast of sales in 2008 is:

$$t = 2008 - 1997 = 11$$
$$S_{2006} = 1,826.21 \ (1.124)^{11}$$
$$= \$7,425.85$$

Forecasting Using Decomposition of Time Series

When sales exhibit seasonal or cyclical fluctuation, we use a method called *classical decomposition*, for dealing with seasonal, trend, and cyclical components together. Note that the classical decomposition model is a time series model. This means that the method can only be used to fit the time series data, whether it is monthly, quarterly, or annually. The types of time series data the company deals with include sales, earnings, cash flows, market share, and costs.

We assume that a time series is combined into a model that consists of the four components - trend (T), cyclical (C), seasonal (S), and random (R). We assume the model is of a multiplicative type, i.e.,

$$Y_t = T \times C \times S \times R$$

In this section, we illustrate, step by step, the classical decomposition method by working with the quarterly sales data.

The approach basically involves the following four steps:

1. Determine seasonal indices, using a four-quarter moving average.
2. Deseasonalize the data.
3. Develop the linear least squares equation in order to identify the trend component of the forecast.
4. Forecast the sales for each of the four quarters of the coming year.

The data we are going to use are the quarterly sales data for the video set over the past four years. (See Table 6.2) We begin our analysis by showing how to identify the seasonal component of the time series.

Step 1: Use moving average to measure the combined trend-cyclical (TC) components of the time series. This way we eliminate the seasonal and random components, S and R.

More specifically, Step 1 involves the following sequences of steps:

Table 6.2: Quarterly Sales Data for DVDs over the Past 4 Years

Year	Quarter	Sales
1	1	5.8
	2	5.1
	3	7.0
	4	7.5
2	1	6.8
	2	6.2
	3	7.8
	4	8.4
3	1	7.0
	2	6.6
	3	8.5
	4	8.8
4	1	7.3
	2	6.9
	3	9.0
	4	9.4

a)   Calculate the 4-quarter moving average for the time series, which we discussed in the above. However, the moving average values computed do not correspond directly to the original quarters of the time series.

b)   We resolve this difficulty by using the midpoints between successive moving-average values. For example, since 6.35 corresponds to the first half of quarter 3 and 6.6 corresponds to the last half of quarter 3, we use $(6.35+6.6)/2 = 6.475$ as the moving average value of quarter 3. Similarly, we associate $(6.6+6.875)/2 = 6.7375$ with quarter 4. A complete summary of the moving-average calculation is shown in Table 6.3.

Table 6.3: Moving Average Calculations for the DVD Sales Time Series

Year	Quarter	Sales	Four-Quarter Mov. Av.	Centred Mov. Ave.
1	1	5.8		
	2	5.1		
			6.35	
	3	7.0		6.475
			6.6	
	4	7.5		6.7375
			6.875	
2	1	6.8		6.975
			7.075	
	2	6.2		7.1875
			7.3	
	3	7.8		7.325
			7.35	
	4	8.4		7.4
			7.45	
3	1	7.0		7.5375
			7.625	
	2	6.6		7.675
			7.725	
	3	8.5		7.7625
			7.8	
	4	8.8		7.8375
			7.875	
4	1	7.3		7.9375
			8	
	2	6.9		8.075
			8.15	
	3	9.0		
	4	9.4		

c) Next, we calculate the ratio of the actual value to the moving average value for each quarter in the time series having a 4-quarter moving average entry. This ratio in effect represents the seasonal-random component, SR=Y/TC. The ratios calculated this way appear in Table 6.4.

Table 6.4: Seasonal Random Factors for the Series

Year	Quarter	Sales	Four-Quarter Mov. Av.	Centered Mov. Av. TC	Sea.-Rand SR=Y/TC
1	1	5.8			
	2	5.1			
			6.35		
	3	7.0		6.475	1.081
			6.6		
	4	7.5		6.738	1.113
			6.875		
2	1	6.8		6.975	0.975
			7.075		
	2	6.2		7.188	0.863
			7.3		
	3	7.8		7.325	1.065
			7.35		
	4	8.4		7.400	1.135
			7.45		
3	1	7.0		7.538	0.929
			7.625		
	2	6.6		7.675	0.860
			7.725		
	3	8.5		7.763	1.095
			7.8		
	4	8.8		7.838	1.123
			7.875		
4	1	7.3		7.938	0.920
			8		
	2	6.9		8.075	0.854
			8.15		
	3	9.0			
	4	9.4			

d)   Arrange the ratios by quarter and then calculate the average ratio by quarter in order to eliminate the random influence.

For example, for quarter 1

(0.975+0.929+0.920)/3=0.941

e)   The final step, shown below, adjusts the average ratio slightly (for example, for quarter 1, 0.941 becomes 0.940), which will be the *seasonal index*.

Step 2: After obtaining the seasonal index, we must first remove the effect of season from the original time series. This process is referred to as deseasonalizing the time series. For this, we must divide the original series by the seasonal index for that quarter. This is shown in Table 6.5.

Step 3: Looking at the graph in Figure 6.1, we see the time series seem to have an upward linear trend. To identify this trend, we develop the least squares trend equation. This procedure is shown in Table 6.6, which was discussed in a previous chapter.

Table 6.5: Seasonal Component Calculations

Quarter	Sea. Rand. SR	Seasonal Factor S	Adjusted S
1	0.975		
	0.929		
	0.920	0.941	0.940
2	0.863		
	0.860		
	0.854	0.859	0.858
3	1.081		
	1.065		
	1.095	1.080	1.079
4	1.113		
	1.135		
	1.123	1.124	1.123
		4.004	4.000

Table 6.6: Deseasonalized Data

Year	Quarter	Sales	Seas. S	Des. Data	t	tY	t^2
1	1	5.8	0.940	6.17	1	6.17	1
	2	5.1	0.858	5.94	2	11.89	4
	3	7.0	1.079	6.49	3	19.46	9
	4	7.5	1.123	6.68	4	26.72	16
2	1	6.8	0.940	7.23	5	36.17	25
	2	6.2	0.858	7.23	6	43.35	36
	3	7.8	1.079	7.23	7	50.59	49
	4	8.4	1.123	7.48	8	59.86	64
3	1	7.0	0.940	7.45	9	67.01	81
	2	6.6	0.858	7.69	10	76.91	100
	3	8.5	1.079	7.88	11	86.64	121
	4	8.8	1.123	7.84	12	94.07	144
4	1	7.3	0.940	7.76	13	100.94	169
	2	6.9	0.858	8.04	14	112.57	196
	3	9.0	1.079	8.34	15	125.09	225
	4	9.4	1.123	8.37	16	133.98	256
				117.82	136	1051.43	1496

t-bar = 8.5   y-bar = 7.3638

b =   0.1469

a =   6.1147

which means y = 6.1147 + 0.1469 t for the forecast periods:

t=   17

18

19

20

Table 6.7: Quarter-To-Quarter Sales Forecasts for Year 5

Year	Quarter	Trend Forecast	Seasonal Factor	Quarterly Forecast
5	1	8.6128 (a)	0.940	8.0971
	2	8.7598	0.858	7.5170
	3	8.9067	1.079	9.6121
	4	9.0537	1.123	10.1632

Note: (a) y = 6.1147 + 0.1469 t = 6.1147 + 0.1469 (17) = 8.6128

Step 4: Develop the forecast using the trend equation and adjust these forecasts to account for the effect of season. The quarterly forecast, as shown in Table 6.7, can be obtained by multiplying the forecast based on trend times the seasonal factor.

Figure 6.1: Actual versus Deseasonalized Data

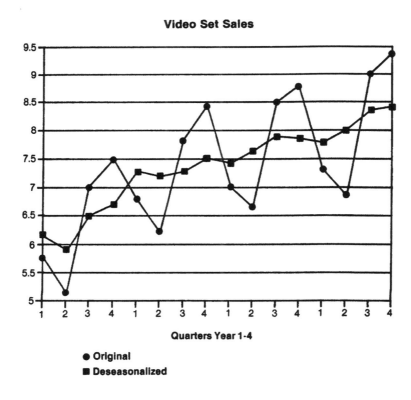

Video Set Sales

Quarters Year 1-4

● Original
■ Deseasonalized

Conclusion

A time-series is a chronologically arranged sequence of data on a particular variable. Several methods are available to analyze the time-series data. Trend analysis and decomposition of time series are such models. Trend analysis - linear and curvilinear -can effectively be used when the company has no data. The classical decomposition method is utilized for seasonal and cyclical situations.

Chapter 7
Forecasting with No Data

An electronics manufacturer develops a new DVD player. A pharmaceutical firm targets AIDS patients for the first time in an ad campaign for its vaccine. The life cycle of a typical new product is divided into four major stages: introduction, growth, maturity, and saturation.

How can these firms forecast future sales of their new products? Most quantitative forecasting models are designed to detect patterns (trends, cycles, seasonality, etc.) in past time-series data and to project those patterns into the future.

If you have no such data available, you should consider (1) using the A-T-A-R concept (awareness-trial-availability-repeat) or (2) developing a model that projects future growth without data.

The A-T-A-R- Model

THE A-T-A-R- MODEL originates from what is called *diffusion of innovation*, explained this way: for a person or a firm to become a regular buyer/user of an innovation, there must first be awareness that it exists, then there must be a decision to try that innovation, then the person must find the item available to them, and finally there must be the type of happiness with it that leads to adoption, or repeat usage.

The model can be used to calculate all the way to profit, so we expand it to include target market size (potential adopters), units purchased by each adopter, and the economics of the operation. The formula is:

Units sold = Number of buying units

x Percentage who become aware of the product

x Percentage who opt to try the product if they can get it

x Percentage of intended triers who can get the product (it is available to them)

x Percentage of triers who like the item enough to repeat their purchase

x Number of units that repeaters will buy in a year

Profit per unit = Revenue per unit (unit list price less trade margins, promotional allowances, freight, etc.) - Costs per unit (usually cost of goods sold plus direct marketing costs)

Therefore:

Profits = Buying units x Percent aware x Percent trial x Percent availability x Percent repeat x Annual units bought x (Revenue per unit - Costs per unit)

Example 7.1

Assume a new device developed to replace the security bars owners attach to steering wheels in expensive sports cars. It is built on an electronic principle of metal adherence. To determine sales and profit forecasts, we assume the following data:

◆ Number of owners of such sports cars: 3 million.

◆ Percentage of target owners who we think we can make aware of our new device the first year on the market: 40 percent.

◆ Percentage of "aware" owners who will decide to try the device during the first year and set out to find it: 20 percent.

◆ Percentage of customary auto parts and mass retailers whom we can convince to stock the new device during the market introduction period: (To keep it simple for this demonstration, assume that potential buyers are busy and probably will not seek beyond one store if they cannot find it there.) 40 percent.

◆ Percentage of the actual triers who will like the product and buy one for a second car: 50 percent.

◆ Number of devices a typical user will buy in the first year of ownership: 1.5

◆ Dollar revenue at the factory, per device, after trade margins and promotion discounts: $25.

◆ Unit cost of a device, at the intended volume: $12.50.

The sales forecast is:

3 million x 0.40 x 0.20 x 0.40 x 0.50 x 1.5 = 0.072 million

The profit contribution forecast would be 3 million x 0.40 x 0.20 x 0.40 x 0.50 x 1.5 x ($25 - $12.50) = $900,000.

Growth Models

Trend models fall into this category. Long-range forecasting typically involves a projection of future growth. There is no doubt that forecasting with such a model involves a certain amount of guesswork. At best, the model projects long-term trends based on reasonable assumptions about the immediate future. Fortunately, trend analysis (linear or nonlinear) and spreadsheet models such as *Microsoft's Excel*, *Lotus 1-2-3*, and *Quattro Pro* are handy tools for analyzing those assumptions.

The basic idea is to assume data values for the first period in the future and for some later period, usually the time when you think the market will stabilize. Then you use forecasting models to fill in the data between these two periods, using a variety of possible growth patterns. Once you have some actual data, you'll be able to arrive at a final forecast. Although not as reliable as forecasts based on historical data, this procedure makes the forecasting process more objective than operating with no model.

Popular growth models widely in use include:

1.   The linear model - constant change growth

2.   The exponential model - constant percentage growth

3.   The logistic growth model

4.   The modified exponential model

We will illustrate each of the four models using the Peters Company as an example. The company is about to introduce a new DVD player, Model 310. Using its years of experience with other DVD players (including other companies' products), the company

♦ Predicts that it will have sold 1.05 million units by the end of 2008.

♦ Expects annual sales to hit 3.15 million units in 10 years.

♦ Foresee a saturation level of 6.5 million units sold each year.

Table 7.1 calculates forecasts using the four models. Figure 7.1 plots and compares predictions by these models.

As can be seen from Figure 7.1, all the growth curves start at the same point, the first-year data assumption of 1.05 million, and run through the target value of 3.15 million in the year 2017. Their routes to that target, however, differ significantly.

Table 7.1: Sales of New VCRDVD – Growth Pattern Comparisons

INPUTS

First-period data	1050
Saturation level	6500
Target sales	3150
Target period	10

Model parameters

	Constant Change – Growth Linear	Constant Percentage – Growth Exponential	Optimistic Growth – Modified Exponential	Average Growth – Logistic	(Logistic)
a =	816.667		929	6500	0.0002
b =	233.333		#N/A	5753	-0.0010
g =	#N/A		0.1298	0.9474	0.8385

Year	Constant Change – Growth Linear			Constant Percentage – Growth Exponential			Optimistic Growth – Modified Exponential			Average Growth – Logistic					
	Forecast	Growth Amount	Growth Percent	Forecast	Growth Amount	Growth Percent	Forecast	Growth Amount	Growth Percent	Forecast	Growth Amount	Growth Percent	Forecast	Growth Amount	Growth Percent
2008	1050	–	–				1050	–	–	1050	–	–	1050	–	–
2009	1283	233.33	22.22%				1186	136.32	12.98%	1337	286.87	27.32%	1214	164.45	15.66%
2010	1517	233.33	18.18%				1340	154.02	12.98%	1609	271.77	20.33%	1398	183.60	15.12%
2011	1750	233.33	15.38%				1514	174.02	12.98%	1866	257.47	16.01%	1601	202.95	14.52%
2012	1983	233.33	13.33%				1711	196.61	12.98%	2110	243.91	13.07%	1823	221.88	13.86%
2013	2217	233.33	11.76%				1933	222.14	12.98%	2341	231.07	10.95%	2063	239.69	13.15%
2014	2450	233.33	10.53%				2184	250.98	12.98%	2560	218.91	9.35%	2318	255.58	12.39%
2015	2683	233.33	9.52%				2468	283.56	12.98%	2767	207.39	8.10%	2587	268.79	11.60%
2016	2917	233.33	8.70%				2788	320.38	12.98%	2964	196.47	7.10%	2866	278.60	10.77%
2017	3150	233.33	8.00%				3150	361.97	12.98%	3150	186.13	6.28%	3150	284.45	9.93%
2018	3383	233.33	7.41%				3559	408.97	12.98%	3326	176.33	5.60%	3436	285.99	9.08%
2019	3617	233.33	6.90%				4021	462.06	12.98%	3493	167.05	5.02%	3719	283.13	8.24%
2020	3850	233.33	6.45%				4543	522.05	12.98%	3652	158.26	4.53%	3995	276.04	7.42%
2021	4083	233.33	6.06%				5133	589.83	12.98%	3802	149.93	4.11%	4260	265.14	6.64%
2022	4317	233.33	5.71%				5799	666.41	12.98%	3944	142.04	3.74%	4511	251.05	5.89%

Figure 7.1: Growth Pattern Comparison

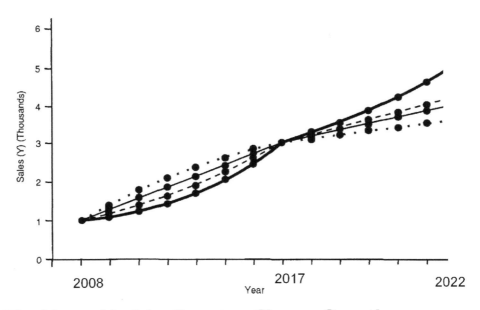

The Linear Model – Constant Change Growth

The linear (constant change growth) model assumes that growth is constant.

The *linear* trend line equation can be shown as

$$Y = a + b\,t$$

where t = time.

As was discussed in Chapter 6 (Time Series Analysis), the formula for the coefficients and b are essentially the same as the cases for simple regression. The linear trend equation used in this example is:

$$Y = 816.667 + 233.333\,t$$

In Table 7.1, we see that the linear model predicts that sales of Model 310 will increase by some 233,333 units each year. Even though unit growth remains fixed, percentage growth declines more rapidly than in the other models (to be discussed later).

The Exponential Model – Constant Percentage Growth

A typical example of nonlinear trend is a constant percentage growth model. A model structure here is the constant growth rate, or constant rate of change over time by a proportional rather than constant amount. Other common nonlinear trends described by the *S-type curves* such as *modified exponential growth curve* and the *logistic growth curve* are discussed later.

As discussed in Chapter 6, the growth rate is estimated using linear regression by fitting historical data to the logarithmic transformation of the basic model. The exponential model takes the following form:

$$S_t = a (1 + g)^t.$$

where a is the starting point for the growth curve, the point at which the straight line that represents this growth pattern intersects the Y axis of the graph and g is the rate of growth.

In this example, the model used is $S_t = 929 (1 + 0.1298)^t$.

Note that the value of a (929) is multiplied by 1.1298 for the first-period forecast, by $(1.1298)^2 = 1.2764$ for the second-period forecast, by $(1.1298)^3 = 1.4421$ for the third-period forecast, and so forth. Thus, the forecasts become larger until they exceed the target sales level.

The exponential model projects a 12.98% increase in sales of DVD each year, which means that the number of units will increase by a larger amount each year.

Many people mistakenly believe that the simple exponential model is too optimistic because it predicts constant percentage growth. How, they ask, can sales of any product consistently grow at a certain percent year after year?

Admittedly, exponential growth gets out of hand and reaches impossible saturation levels after passing the target level. Note, however, that since it takes time for exponential growth to build up steam, its predictions of early growth are actually pessimistic compared with other models.

Modified Exponential Growth

The modified exponential model is the most optimistic. It projects early growth of about 27.32% from 2007 to 2008.

The modified exponential curve runs well above the other curves for every year until it reaches the target value. After that, growth slows dramatically as sales approach the saturation level.

Of the four models in Table 7.1, the modified exponential model always produces the most optimistic growth pattern between any two data values. If you expect your data to show strong early growth, you should use the modified exponential model as a planning tool.

The modified exponential growth model takes the following form:

$$Y_t = a - b\,g^t$$

In this equation, a is the saturation level (SL), and b and g are parameters that determine the shape of the growth curve. Note that

(1) g is computed by subtracting a from the target level, dividing that difference between a and the first period forecast, then raising that ratio to the power of 1 over the target period minus 1. g is always less than 1.

(2) b is simply the difference between a and the first-period forecast divided by g. When multiplied by g, it is the difference between a and the first-period forecast.

In the example, a is 6,500, b is 5,753, and g is 0.9474. For the first period, the forecast value is the same as the first period data, because 0.9474 to the first power is 0.9474. Therefore, b x g is 5,450, and a - (b x g) is 1,050. For the second period, $g^2 = (0.9474)^2 = 0.8976$, so b x g^2 is 5,163, and a - (b x g^2) is 1,337. In subsequent periods, g is raised to larger powers and therefore decreases, so smaller and smaller amounts are subtracted from a, and the forecast gets closer to the saturation level.

Logistic Growth

The logistic model should be used when you expect growth to follow an S-shaped curve. That is, you expect slow growth at first, followed by a period of rapid expansion, then a decline in growth as sales approach the saturation level.

This type of forecasting model is used to typically fit the life cycle of a new product. Examples were Sony's DVD and Texas instrument's electronic calculator. The logistic curve is a middle-ground assumption falling between the exponential curve and the modified exponential curve.

The logistic-curve growth model is determined with the following equation:

$$Y_t = 1/(a - b\,g^t)$$

where a = 1/SL. The behavior of this fraction is more complicated than you'd expect. In Figure 1, notice that the amount of growth each period increases for a time and then begins to decrease. In terms of percentage growth, the logistic curve always starts out somewhere below the modified exponential curve. It gradually catches up as the data approach the saturation point.

A Word of Caution

Forecasting with no data can be a problem. If you choose too pessimistic a model, you may underestimate early sales and fail to meet customer demand. If you bank on too optimistic a model, initial revenues may not meet expectations and the entire project could sour.

Nevertheless, it's better than going forward with no model of the future. The trend and growth models presented here should at least give you a starting point.

Checklists – Choosing the Right Growth Model

The big question, however, is choosing the right model. The following checklists of questions can be helpful:

1. You can think of the area between the exponential and the modified exponential curves as the range of likely values for actual data. The modified exponential model generates the best-case scenario, while the exponential model generates the worst-case scenario. The linear and logistic models represent middle-ground possibilities.

2. Examine your assumptions about the first-period data, target sales data, and saturation level. The size of the range among the models depends on these assumptions.

3. Developing a good estimate of these numbers and do "what-if" on the effects of alternative values.

4. Combine your marketing experience with these models. Computer models are useful for testing hypotheses. *Note:* In a new product environment, models must work hand-in-hand with solid marketing experience and expert judgment. Before basing business plans on any forecasting model, compare the models projected growth patterns against the growths of products that you believe would receive a similar reception in the marketplace.

Chapter 8

Indirect Methods

The forecasting methods we have discussed to date were, for the most part, based on the use of historical data. They did not consider aspects of consumer behavior in making purchase decisions in the marketplace. In this section, we will present a model based on learned behavior, called the *Markov model*, and indirect methods of sales forecasting--the use of economic indicators (barometric forecasting), input-output analysis, survey techniques, and econometric forecasting.

Forecasting Sales with the Markov Model

We operate on the thesis that consumption is a form of learned behavior. That is, consumers tend to repeat their past consumption activities. Some consumers become loyal to certain product types as well as specific brands. Others seek other brands and products. In general, there is a great degree of regularity about such behavior. The Markov model is developed so as to predict market share by considering consumer brand loyalty and switching behaviors.

The model has the following objectives:

1. To predict the market share that a firm will have at some point in the future.

2. To predict whether some constant or level market share will be obtained in the future. Most Markov models will result in a final constant market share where changes in market share will no longer result with the passage of time.

3. To investigate the impact of the company's marketing strategies and promotional efforts, such as advertising, on gain or loss in market share.

To answer these questions, we need to compute what is called transition probabilities for all the companies involved in the market. Transition probabilities are nothing more than the probabilities that a certain seller will retain, gain, and lose customers.

To develop this, we need sample data of past consumer behavior. Let us assume that there are three battery manufacturers, A, B, and C. Each of the firms know that consumers switch from one firm to another over time because of advertising, dissatisfaction with service, and other sales promotion efforts. We assume that each firm maintains records of consumer movements for a specified time period, like one month. We further assume that no new customers enter and no old customers leave the market during this period.

Table 8.1 provides data on the flows among all the firms.

Table 8.1: Flow of Customers

Firms	Jan. 1 Customers	From	Gains A	B	C	To	Losses A	B	C	Feb. 1 Customers
A	300		0	45	35		0	30	30	320
B	600		30	0	20		45	0	15	590
C	400		30	15	0		35	20	0	390

This table can be converted into a matrix form as shown in Table 8.2.

Table 8.2: Retention, Gain, and Loss

	Firms	Retention and Loss to A	B	C	Total
Retention	A	240	30	30	300
And	B	45	540	15	600
Gain	C	35	20	345	400
	Total	320	590	390	1300

Table 8.3 is a matrix of the same sizes as the one in Table 8.2 illustrating exactly how each probability was determined

Table 8.3: Transition Probability Matrix

Probability of Customers being Retained or gained	Firms	Probability of Customers Being Retained or Lost A	B	C
	A	240/300=.80	30/300=.10	30/300=.10
	B	45/600=.075	540/600=.9	15/600=.025
	C	35/400=.0875	20/400=.05	345/400=.8625

The rows in this matrix show the probability of the retention of customers and the loss of customers; the columns represent the probability of retention of customers and the gain of customers. For example, row 1 indicates that A retains .8 of its customers (30) to C. Also, column 1, for example, indicates that A retains .8 of its customers (240), gains .075 of B's customers (45), and gains .0875 of C's customers (35).

The original market share of January 1 was:

(300A 600B 400C)=(.2308A .4615B .3077C)

With this, we will be able to calculate market share, using the transition matrix we developed in Table 8.3.

To illustrate, Company A held 23.08 percent of the market at January 1. Of this, 80 percent was retained, Company A gained 10 percent of Company B's 46.15 percent of the market, and another 10 percent of Company C's 30.77 percent.

The February 1 market share of Company A is, therefore, calculated to be:

Retention	.8 x .2308=.1846
Gain from B	.1 x .4615=.0462
Gain from C	.1 x .3077=.0308
	.2616 *

Similarly, Company B's market share is as follows:

Gain from A	.075 x .2308=.0173
Retention	.9 x .4615=.4154
Gain from C	.025 x .3077=.0077
	.4404 *

Company C's market share is:

Gain from A	.0875 x .2308=.0202
Gain from B	.05 x .4615=.0231
Retention	.8625 x .3077=.2654
	.3087 *

*These numbers do not add up to exactly 100 percent due to rounding.

In summary, the February I market share came out to be approximately:

26% for Company A

44% for Company B

30% for Company C

The market share forecasts may then be used to generate a specific forecast of sales. For example, if industry sales are forecast to be, say, $10 million, obtained through regression analysis, input-output analysis, or some other technique, the forecast of sales for A is $2.6 million ($10 million x .26).

If the company wishes to forecast the market share for March, then, the procedure is exactly the same as before, except using the February I forecasted market share as a basis. The forecaster must be careful when using the Markov casting market shares in the near future. Distant forecasts, after many time periods, generally are not very reliable forecasts by this method. Even in short-term forecasts, constant updating of the transition matrix is needed for accuracy of projection.

At least in theory, most Markov models will result in a final constant market share in which market share will no longer change with the passage of time. However, this market share and its derivation will not be discussed here. In effect, this model has very little practical application because the constant or level condition assumes no changes in competitive efforts of the firms within the industry.

Indirect Methods

Indirect methods include techniques in which forecasts can be based on projections of national or regional economic activity (such as GDP or leading economic indicators), industry sales, or market surveys.

Typically, the indirect method involves the following three steps:

1. Forecast the level of economic indicators such as GDP.
2. Translate the forecast into an industry forecast.
3. Translate the industry sales forecast into a company forecast.

Barometric Forecasting – Indexes of Economic Indicators

Economists use a variety of economic indicators to forecast turns in the business cycle. Economic indicators are variables that in the past have had a high correlation with aggregate economic activity. Indicators may lead, lag, or coincide with economic activity.

1. Leading Indicators

The Index of Leading Economic Indicators is the economic series of indicators that tend to predict future changes in economic activity; officially called *Composite Index of 11 Leading Indicators*. This index was designed to reveal the direction of the economy in the next six to nine months. *Note*: If the Index is consistently rising, even only slightly, the economy is chugging along and a setback is unlikely. If the indicator drops for three or more consecutive months, look for an economic slowdown and possibly a recession in the next year or so.

The Index consists of 11 indicators, and is subject to revision. For example, petroleum and natural gas prices were found to distort the data from crude material prices and were subsequently dropped from that category

This series is the government's main barometer for forecasting business trends. Each of the series has shown a tendency to change before the economy makes a major turn--hence, the term "leading indicators." The Index is designed to forecast economic activity six to nine months ahead (1982=100). This series is published monthly by the U.S. Department of Commerce, consisting of:

1. *Average workweek of production workers in manufacturing*. Employers find it a lot easier to increase the number of hours worked in a week than to hire more employees.

2. *Initial claims for unemployment insurance*. The number of people who sign up for unemployment benefits signals changes in present and future economic activity.

3. *Change in consumer confidence*. It is based on the University of Michigan's survey of consumer expectations. The index measures consumers' optimism regarding the present and future state of the economy (1966=100). *Note*: Consumer spending buys two-thirds of GDP (all goods and services produced in the economy), so any sharp change could be an important factor in an overall turnaround.

4. *Percent change in prices of sensitive crude materials*. Rises in prices of such critical materials as steel and iron usually mean factory demands are going up, which means factories plan to step up production.

5. *Contracts and orders for plant and equipment*. Heavier contracting and ordering usually lead economic upswings.

6. *Vendor performance*. Vendor performance represents the percentage of companies reporting slower deliveries. As the economy grows, firms have more trouble filling orders.

7. *Stock prices*. A rise in the common stock index indicates expected profits and lower interest rates. Stock market advances usually precede business upturns by three to eight months.

8. *Money supply.* A rising money supply means easy money that sparks brisk economic activity. This usually leads recoveries by as much as fourteen months.

9. *New orders for manufacturers of consumer goods and materials.* New orders mean more workers hired, more materials and supplies purchased, and increased output. Gains in this series usually lead recoveries by as much as four months.

10. *Residential building permits for private housing.* Gains in building permits signal business upturns.

11. *Factory backlogs of unfilled durable goods orders.* Backlogs signify business upswings.

These eleven components of the Index are adjusted for inflation. Rarely do these components all go in the same direction at once. Each factor is weighted. The composite figure is designed to tell only in which direction business will go. It is not intended to forecast the magnitude of future ups and downs.

2. Coincident Indicators

Coincident indicators are the types of economic indicator series that tend to move up and down in line with the aggregate economy and therefore are measures of current economic activity. They are intended to gauge current economic conditions. Examples are gross domestic product (GDP), employment, retail sales, and industrial production.

3. Lagging Indicators

Lagging indicators are the ones that follow or trail behind aggregate economic activity. There are currently six lagging indicators published by the government, including unemployment rate, labor cost per unit, loans outstanding, average prime rate charged by banks, ratio of consumer Installment credit outstanding to personal income, and ratio of manufacturing and trade inventories to sales.

Figure 8.1 depicts the Index of Leading Economic Indicators.

Figure 8.1: Leading Economic Indicators

Index of Leading Indicators, % Chg.

Input-Output Analysis

Another indirect method is input-output analysis. This method of analysis is concerned with the inter-industry or inter-departmental flows of goods or services in the economy or a company and its markets.

Input-output analysis focuses on the sales of each industry to firms in that industry, other industries, and other sectors such as governmental units and foreign purchasers. The data are set forth in a matrix table that depicts each industry as a row and a column. Each industry's row indicates its sales to firms in that industry to other industries, and to other sections of the economy, such as governmental units and foreign firms. Some tables set forth the dollar volume or percent of total sales of the industry to the other sectors. The table most applicable to business sales forecasting presents indexes representing expected increases in sales of the companies in the industries. The tables that have been prepared to date depict a larger number of industries.

For an illustrative purpose, Table 8.4 presents an abridged, hypothetical input-output table involving only four industries. The coefficients reflect the impact of a dollar increase in sales in each industry on the expected sales of the industries in row 1. For instance, a one-dollar increase in sales of paper and allied products (column 3) is expected to produce a six-cent increase in sales of lumber and wood products. Thus, it indicates to firms in the lumber and wood products industry the impact of changes in sales in the paper and allied products industry Similar conclusions can be drawn from data in the various other rows.

Note: Forecasts are limited, however, to industrial products and to very large companies with broad product groupings.

Table 8.4: Input-Output Table

	Lumber and Wood Products	Household Furniture	Paper and Allied Products	Plastics and Synthetic Materials
Lumber and Wood Products	1.00	0.08	0.06	0.001
Household Furniture	0.002	1.00	0.001	0.002
Paper and Allied Products	0.04	0.002	1.00	0.001
Plastic and Synthetic Male/lab	0.003	0.008	0.02	1.00

Market Survey Techniques

Market survey techniques constitute another important forecasting tool, especially for short-term projections. Designing surveys that provide unbiased and reliable information is a costly and difficult task. When properly carried out, however, survey research can provide managers with valuable information that would be unobtainable otherwise.

Surveys generally involve the use of interviews or mailed questionnaires asking business firms, government agencies, and individuals about their future plans. Business firms plan and budget virtually all their expenditures in advance of actual purchases. Budgets can thus provide much useful information for forecasting. Government units also prepare formal budgets well before the actual spending is done, and surveys of budget material, congressional appropriations hearings, and the like can provide a wealth of information to the forecaster. Finally, even individual consumers usually plan expenditures for such major items as automobiles, furniture, housing, vacations, and education well ahead of the purchase date, so surveys of consumer intentions often accurately predict future spending on consumer goods.

While surveys provide an alternative to quantitative forecasting techniques (survey information may be all that is obtainable in certain forecasting situations, for example, when a firm is attempting to project the demand for a new product), they are frequently used to supplement rather than replace quantitative analysis. The value of survey techniques as a supplement to quantitative methods stems from two factors.

First, a nonquantifiable psychological element is inherent in most economic behavior, and surveys and other qualitative methods are especially well suited to picking up this phenomenon. Second, quantitative models generally assume stable consumer tastes and, if these are actually changing, survey data may reveal such changes.

Econometric Forecasting

This approach develops a system of simultaneous equations (mainly through regression) to describe the operation of the economy--of a nation or the particular market within which a company operates--and the relationships among them. The equations are then solved simultaneously to obtain a forecast for the key variables such as GDP and consumer spending.

For example, assume that sales are a function of price, advertising, disposable income, and GDP. While variables such as disposable income and GDP are exogenous to (determined outside) the forecasting system, others are interdependent. For example, the advertising budget will affect the price of the product, since manufacturing and selling expenses influence the per-unit price. The price, in turn, is influenced by the size of sales, which can also affect the level of advertising. All of this points to the interdependence of all variables in the system, which justifies a system of simultaneous equations, as follows:

(1)   Sales = f (price, advertising, disposable income, GDP)

(2)   Manufacturing costs = f (volume, technology)

(3)   Selling expenses = f (advertising, sales, and others)

(4)   Price = f (manufacturing costs, selling expenses)

As in regression analysis, the forecaster must (1) determine the functional form of each of the equations, (2) estimate the values of their coefficients, and (3) test for the statistical significance of the results and the validity of the assumptions.

Keep in mind that econometric models are usually quite complex and expensive to construct, but can give very accurate forecasts.

Conclusion

This chapter has been concerned with forecasting based on consumer behavior--the Markov model--and several popular indirect forecasting methods, those that begin with analysis of an aggregate economic variable, such as GDP, and produce industry or company sales as a component of that aggregate. The breakdown approach requires forecasts of a broad measure of economic performance such as GDP. In many cases, this forecast is conducted by an outside source, such as a private consultant or a governmental agency. The forecaster then translates this forecast into one for the industry and then into company sales forecasts.

Chapter 9
Evaluation of Forecasts

The cost of a prediction error can be substantial. The forecaster must always find the ways to improve his forecasts. That means that he might want to examine some objective evaluations of alternative forecasting techniques. This chapter presents the guidelines needed. Two evaluation techniques are presented here. The first is in the form of a checklist. A forecaster could use it to evaluate either a new model he or she is in the process of developing or an existing model. The second is a statistical technique for evaluating a model.

Cost of Prediction Errors

There is always a cost involved with a failure to predict a certain variable accurately. It is important to determine the cost of the prediction error in order to minimize the potential detrimental effect on future profitability of the company. The cost of the prediction error can be substantial, depending upon the circumstances. For example, failure to make an accurate projection on sales could result in poor production planning, too much or too little purchase of labor, and so on, thereby causing potentially huge financial losses.

The cost of the prediction error is basically the contribution or profit lost on an inaccurate prediction. It can be measured in terms of lost sales, disgruntled customers, and idle machines.

Example 9.1

Assume that a company has been selling a toy doll having a cost of $.60 for $1.00 each. The fixed cost is $300. The company has no privilege of returning any unsold dolls. It has predicted sales of 2,000 units. However, unforeseen competition has reduced sales to 1,500 units. Then the cost of its prediction error--that is, its failure of predict demand accurately would be calculated as follows:

1. Initial predicted sales = 2,000 units.

    Optimal decision: purchase 2,000 units.

    Expected net income = $500 [(2,000 units x $.40 contribution) - $300 fixed costs]

2. Alternative parameter value = 1,500 units.

    Optimal decision: purchase 1,500 units.

    Expected net income = $300 [(1,500 units x $.40 contribution) - $300 fixed costs]

3. Results of original decision under alternative parameter value.

    Expected net income:

    Revenue (1,500 units x $1.00) - Cost of dolls (2,000 units x $.60) - $300 fixed costs

    = $1,500 - $1,200 - $300 = $0.

4. Cost of prediction error, (2) - (3) = $300.

Checklist

Two main items to be checked are the data and the model with its accompanying assumptions. The questions to be raised are the following:

1. Is the source reliable and accurate?

2. In the case of use of more than one source that is reliable and accurate, is the source used the best?

3. Are the data the most recent available?

4. If the answer to question 3 is yes, are the data subject to subsequent revision?

5. Is there any known systematic bias in the data with which to deal?

The model and its accompanying assumptions should be similarly examined. Among other things, the model has to make sense from a theoretical standpoint. The assumptions should be clearly stated and tested as well.

Measuring Accuracy of Forecasts

The performance of a forecast should be checked against its own record or against that of other forecasts. There are various statistical measures that can be used to measure performance of the model. Of course, the performance is measured in terms of forecasting error, where error is defined as the difference between a predicted value and the actual result.

Error (e) = Actual (A) - Forecast (F)

MAD, MSE, RMSE, and MAPE

The commonly used measures for summarizing historical errors include the *mean absolute deviation* (MAD), the *mean squared error* (MSE), the *root mean squared error* (RMSE), and the *mean absolute percentage error* (MAPE). The formulas used to calculate MAD, MSE, and RMSE are

MAD $= \Sigma \, |e| \, / \, n$

MSE $= \Sigma \, e^2 / (n - 1)$

RMSE $= \sqrt{(e^2 / n)}$

Sometimes it is more useful to compute the forecasting errors in percentages rather than in amounts. The MAPE is calculated by finding the absolute error in each period, dividing this by the actual value of that period, and then averaging these absolute percentage errors, as shown below.

MAPE $= \Sigma \, |e|/A \, / \, n$

The following example illustrates the computation of MAD, MSE, and RMSE, and MAPE.

Example 9.2

Sales data of a microwave oven manufacturer are given in Table 9.1.

Table 9.1: Calculation of Errors

Period	Actual(A)	Forecast(F)	e(A-F)	|e|	e^2	Absolute Percent Error |e|/A
1	217	215	2	2	4	0.0092
2	213	216	-3	3	9	0.0014
3	216	215	1	1	1	0.0046
4	210	214	-4	4	16	0.0190
5	213	211	2	2	4	0.0094
6	219	214	5	5	25	0.0023
7	216	217	-1	1	1	0.0046
8	212	216	-4	4	16	0.0019
			-2	22	76	0.0524

Using the figures,

$$MAD = \Sigma \ |e| \ /n = 22/8 = 2.75$$

$$MSE = \Sigma \ e^2 / (n - 1) = 76/7 = 10.86$$

$$RMSE = \sqrt{(e^2 / n)} = \sqrt{76/8} = 3.08$$

$$MAPE = \Sigma \ |e|/A \ / n = .0524/8 = .0066$$

One way these measures are used is to evaluate forecasting ability of alternative forecasting methods. For example, using either MAD or MSE, a forecaster could compare the results of exponential smoothing with alphas and elect the one that performed best in terms of the lowest MAD or MSE for a given set of data. Also, it can help select the best initial forecast value for exponential smoothing.

The U Statistic and Turning Point Errors

There are still a number of statistical measures for measuring accuracy of the forecast. Two standards may be identified. First, one could compare the forecast being evaluated with a naive forecast to see if there are vast differences. The naive forecast can be anything like the same as last year, moving average, or the output of an exponential smoothing technique. In the second case, the forecast may be compared against the outcome when there is enough to do so. The comparison may be against the actual level of the variable forecasted, or the change observed may be compared with the change forecast.

The Theil U Statistic is based upon a comparison of the predicted change with the observed change. It is calculated as:

$$U = \frac{(1/n)\sum (F - A)^2}{(1/n)\sum F^2 + (1/n)\sum A^2}$$

As can be seen, U=0 is a perfect forecast, since the forecast would equal actual and F - A = 0 for all observations. At the other extreme, U=1 would be a case of all incorrect forecasts. The smaller the value of U, the more accurate are the forecasts. If U is greater than or equal to 1, the predictive ability of the model is lower than a naive no-change extrapolation. *Note*: Many computer software packages routinely compute the U Statistic.

Still other evaluation techniques consider the number of *turning point* errors which is based on the total number of reversals of trends. The turning point error is also known as "error in the direction of prediction." In a certain case, such as interest rate forecasts, the turning point error is more serious than the accuracy of the forecast. For example, the ability of forecasters to anticipated reversals of interest rate trends is more important -- perhaps substantially more important -- than the precise accuracy of the forecast. Substantial gains or losses may arise from a move from generally upward moving rates to downward rate trends (or vice versa) but gains or losses from incorrectly forecasting the extent of a continued increase or decrease in rates may be much more limited.

Control of Forecasts

It is important to monitor forecast errors to insure that the forecast is performing well. If the model is performing poorly based on some criteria, the forecaster might reconsider the use of the existing model or switch to another forecasting model or technique. The forecasting control can be accomplished by comparing forecasting errors to predetermined values, or limits. Errors that fall within the limits would be judged acceptable while errors outside of the limits would signal that corrective action is desirable (See Figure 9.1).

Figure 9.1: Monitoring Forecast Errors

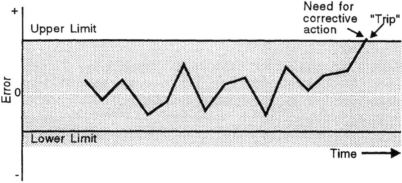

Forecasts can be monitored using either tracking signals or control charts.

Tracking Signals

A tracking signal is based on the ratio of cumulative forecast error to the corresponding value of MAD.

$$\text{Tracking signal} = \Sigma(A - F) / MAD$$

The resulting tracking signal values are compared to predetermined limits. These are based on experience and judgment and often range from plus or minus 3 to plus or minus 8. Values within the limits suggest that the forecast is performing adequately. By the same token, when the signal goes beyond this range, corrective action is appropriate.

Example 9.3

Going back to Example 9.1, the deviation and cumulative deviation have already been computed:

$$MAD = \Sigma \, |A - F| \, / \, n = 22 \, / \, 8 = 2.75$$

Tracking signal $= \Sigma \, (A - F) \, / \, MAD = -2 \, / \, 2.75 = -0.73$

A tracking signal is as low as - 0.73, which is substantially below the limit (-3 to -8). It would not suggest any action at this time.

Note: After an initial value of MAD has been computed, the estimate of the MAD can be continually updated using exponential smoothing.

$$MADt = \alpha(A - F) + (1 - \alpha) \, MAD_{t-1}$$

Control Charts

The control chart approach involves setting upper and lower limits for individual forecasting errors instead of cumulative errors. The limits are multiples of the estimated standard deviation of forecast, S_f, which is the square root of MSE. Frequently, control limits are set at 2 or 3 standard deviations.

$$\pm \, 2(\text{or } 3) \, S_f$$

Note: Plot the errors and see if all errors are within the limits, so that the forecaster can visualize the process and determine if the method being used is in control.

Example 9.4

For the sales data in Table 9.2, using the naive forecast, we will determine if the forecast is in control. For illustrative purposes, we will use 2 sigma control limits.

Table 9.2: Error Calculations

Year	Sales	Forecasts	Error	Error$_2$
1	320			
2	326	320	6	36
3	310	326	-16	256
4	317	310	7	49
5	315	317	-2	4
6	318	315	3	9
7	310	318	-8	64
8	316	310	6	36
9	314	316	-2	4
10	317	314	3	9
			-3	467

First, compute the standard deviation of forecast errors

$$Sf = \sqrt{e^2 / (n - 1)} = \sqrt{467/(9 - 1)} = 7.64$$

Two sigma limits are then plus or minus $2(7.64) = -15.28$ to $+15.28$

Note: The forecast error for year 3 is below the lower bound, so the forecast is not in control (See Figure 9.2). The use of other methods such as moving average, exponential smoothing, or regression would possibly achieve a better forecast.

Figure 9.2: Control Charts for Forecasting Errors

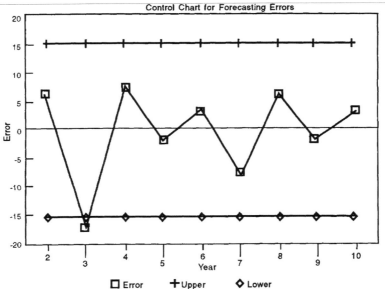

Note: A system of monitoring forecasts needs to be developed. The computer may be programmed to print a report showing the past history when the tracking signal "trips" a limit. For example, when a type of exponential smoothing is used, the system may try a different value of a (so the forecast will be more responsive) and to continue forecasting.

Conclusion

There is always a cost associated with a failure to predict a certain variable accurately. Because all forecasts tend to be off the mark, it is important to provide a measure of accuracy for each forecast. Several measures of forecast accuracy and a measure of turning point error can be calculated.

These quite often are used to help managers evaluate the performance of a given method as well as to choose among alternative forecasting techniques. Control of forecasts involves deciding whether a forecast is performing adequately, using either a control chart or a tracking signal. Selection of a forecasting method involves choosing a technique that will serve its intended purpose at an acceptable level of cost and accuracy.

Chapter 10

What is the Right Forecasting Tool and Software for You?

The life cycle of a typical new product is divided into four major stages: introduction, growth, maturity, and saturation (decline). The proper choice of forecasting methodology depends on the nature of the market. Figure 10.1 shows life cycle effects on forecasting methodologies. Table 10.1 shows life cycle effects upon forecasting methodology. Table 10.2 summarizes the forecasting methods that have been discussed in this book. It is organized in the following format:

1. Description
2. Accuracy
3. Identification of turning point
4. Typical application
5. Data required
6. Cost
7. Time required to develop an application and make forecasts

Furthermore, in an effort to aid forecasters in choosing the right methodology, Figure 10.2 provides rankings of forecasting methodology by:

1. Accuracy: Why do you need the forecast?
2. Cost: How much money is involved?
3. Timing: When will the forecast be used?
4. Form: Who will use the forecast?
5. Data: How much data are available?

Figure 10.1: Life Cycle Effects on Forecasting Methodology

Introduction

Data:	No data available; Rely on qualitative methods.
Time:	Need long horizon.
Methods:	Qualitative (judgement) such as market surveys and Delphi.

Growth

Data:	Some data available for analysis.
Time:	Still need long horizon; trends and cause-effect relationships important.
Methods:	Market surveys still useful. Regression, time series and growth models justified.

Maturity

Data:	Considerable data available.
Time:	More uses of short-term forecasts; still need long-term projections, but trends change only gradually.
Methods:	Quantitative methods more useful. Time series helpful for trend, seasonal. Regression and exponential smoothing very useful.

Decline

Data:	Abundant data.
Time:	Shorter horizon.
Methods:	Continue use of maturity methods as applicable. Judgement and market surveys may signal changes.

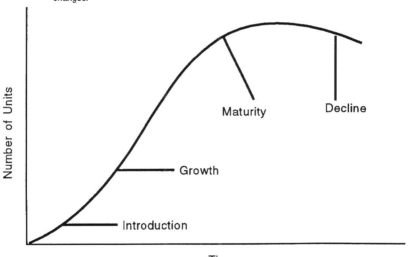

Table 10.1: Summary of Commonly Used Qualitative (Judgmental) Forecasting Techniques

Technique	Delphi Method	Expert Opinions
Description	A panel of experts is interrogated by a sequence of questionnaires in which the responses to one questionnaire are used to produce the next questionnaire. Any set of information available to some experts and not to the others is thus passed on to the others, enabling all the experts to have access to all the information for forecasting.	Based on the assumption that several experts can arrive at a better forecast than can one person. There is no secrecy, and communication is encouraged. Forecasts are sometimes influenced by social factors and may not reflect a true consensus.
Accuracy:		
Short-term (0–3 mon)	Fair to very good	Poor to fair
Medium-term (3 mon–2 yr)	Fair to very good	Poor to fair
Long-term (2 yr and over)	Fair to very good	Poor
Identification of turning point	Fair to good	Poor to fair
Typical application	Forecasts of long-range and new product sales; technological forecasting.	Forecasts of long-range and new product sales; technological forecasting.
Data required	A coordinator issues the sequence of questionnaires, editing and consolidating the responses.	Information from a panel of experts is presented openly in group meetings to arrive at a consensus forecast. Minimum is two sets of reports over time.
Cost of forecasting with a computer	Expensive	Minimal
Time required to develop an application and make forecasts	1 month	Two weeks

Technique	PERT-Derived	Sales Force Polling	Consumer Surveys
Description	Based on three estimates provided by experts: pessimistic, most likely, and optimistic.	Based on sales force opinions; tend to be too optimistic.	Based on market surveys regarding specific consumer purchases.
Accuracy:			
Short-term (0–3 mon)	Fair	Fair to good	Fair to good
Medium-term (3 mon–2 yr)	Poor	Poor	Poor
Long-term (2 yr and over)	Poor	Poor	Poor
Identification of turning point	Poor to fair	Poor to good	Poor
Typical application	Same as expert opinions.	Forecasts of short-term sales forecasts.	Forecasts of short-term sales forecasts.
Data required	Same as expert opinions.	Data by regional and product line breakdowns.	Telephone contacts, personal interviews or questionnaires.
Cost of forecasting with a computer	Minimal	Minimal	Expensive
Time required to develop an application and make fore- casts	Two weeks	Two weeks	More than a month

Summary of commonly used indirect methods

Technique	Input-Output Model	Leading Indicator	Lifecycle Analysis
Description	A method of analysis concerned with the interindustry or interdepartmental flow of goods or services in the economy or a company and its markets. It shows what flow of inputs must occur to obtain outputs.	Time series of an economic activity whose movement in a given direction precedes the movement of some other time series in the same direction.	Analysis and forecasting new product growth rates based on S-curves.
Accuracy:			
Short-term (0–3 mon)	Not applicable	Poor to good	Poor
Medium-term (3 mon–2 yr)	Good to very good	Poor to good	Poor to good
Long-term (2 yr and over)	Good to very good	Very poor	Poor to good
Identification of turning point	Fair	Good	Poor to good
Typical application	Forecasts of company sales and division sales for industrial sectors and subsectors.	Forecasts of sales by product class.	Forecasts of new product sales.
Data application	Ten or fifteen years' history. Considerable amounts of information on product and service flows within a corporation (or economy) for each year for which an input-output analysis is desired.	The same as an intention-to-buy survey plus 5 to 10 years' history.	As a minimum, the annual sales of the product being considered or of a similar product are sometimes necessary.
Cost of forecasting with a computer	Expensive	Varies with application	Varies with application
Time required to develop an application and make forecasts	More than a month	One month	One month

Summary of commonly used quantitative forecasting techniques

Technique	Regression Analysis	Econometric Model	Markov Analysis
Description	Functionally relates sales to other economic, competitive, or internal variables and estimates an equation using the least-squares technique.	A system of interdependent regression equations that describes some sector of economic sales or profit activity. The parameters of the regression equations are usually estimated simultaneously.	Models based on learned behavior: Consumers tend to repeat their part brand loyalty.
Accuracy:			
Short-term (0–3 mon)	Good to very good	Good to very good	Excellent
Medium-term (3 mon–2 yr)	Good to very good	Very good to excellent	Poor
Long-term (2 yr and over)	Poor	Good	Poor
Identification of turning point	Good	Excellent	Good
Typical application	Forecasts of sales by product classes, forecasts of earnings, and other financial data.	Forecasts of sales by product classes, forecasts of earnings.	Forecasts of sales and cash collections.
Data required	At least 30 observations are recommended for acceptable results.	The same as for regression.	Data required for transaction probabilities.
Cost of forecasting with a computer	Varies with application	Expensive	Expensive
Time required to develop an application and make forecasts	Depends on ability to identify relationships	More than a month	More than a month

Summary of commonly used time series forecasting methods

Technique	Moving Average	Exponential Smoothing	Trend Analysis
Description	Averages are updated as the latest information is received; weighted average of a number of consecutive points of the series.	Similar to moving average, except that more recent data points are given more weight. Effective when there is random demand and no seasonal fluctuation in the data series.	Fits a trend line to time-series data. There are two variations: the linear and nonlinear methods.
Accuracy:			
Short-term (0–3 mon)	Poor to good	Fair to very good	Very good
Medium-term (3 mon–2 yr)	Poor	Poor to good	Good
Long-term (2 yr and over)	Very poor	Very poor	Good
Identification of turning point	Poor	Poor	Poor
Typical application	Inventory control for low-volume items and sales with no data.	Production and inventory control, forecasts of sales, and financial data.	New product forecasts and products in the growth and maturity stages of the life cycle; inventory control.
Data required	A minimum of two years of sales history if seasonals are present. Otherwise, fewer data. (Of course, the more history the better.) The moving average must be specific.	The same as for a moving average.	Varies with the technique used. However, a good rule of thumb is to use a minimum of five years' annual data to start. Thereafter, the complete history.
Cost of forecasting with a computer	Very minimal	Minimal	Varies with application
Time required to develop an application and make forecasts	One day	One day	One day

Technique	Classical Decomposition
Description	Decomposes a time series into seasonals, trend cycles, and irregular elements. Primarily used for detailed time-series analysis (including) estimating seasonals).
Accuracy:	
Short-term (0–3 mon)	Very good to excellent
Medium-term (3 mon–2 yr)	Good
Long-term (2 yr and over)	Very poor
Identification of turning point	Very good
Typical application	Tracking and warning, forecasts of sales and financial data.
Data required	A minimum of three years' history to start. Thereafter, the complete history.
Cost of forecasting with a computer	Minimal
Time required to develop an application and make forecasts	One day

Figure 10.2: The Forecasting Decisionmatrix

Techniques	Accuracy: Why Do You Need the Forecast?	Rankings
Qualitative or Judgmental	High Accuracy ↑ ↓ Low Accuracy	Delphi Market Surveys Consensus Opinion Sales Force Polling Expert Oninion
Time Series	High Accuracy ↑ ↓ Low Accuracy	Box-Jenkins Classical Decomposition Exponential Smoothing Moving Average Trend Analysis
Causal, Markov, and Indirect	High Accuracy ↑ ↓ Low Accuracy	Input-Output Analysis Ecometric Leading Indicator Regression Surveys Life Cycle Analysis

Techniques	Cost: How Much Money Is Involved?	Rankings
Qualitative or Judgmental	Low Cost ↓ High Cost	Expert Opinion Sales Force Polling Market Surveys
Time Series	Low Cost ↑ ↓ High Cost	Trend Analysis Moving Average Exponential Smoothing Classical Decomposition Box-Jenkins
Causal, Markov, and Indirect	Low Cost ↑ ↓ High Cost	Regression Leading Indicator Life Cycle Analysis Econometric Input-Output Analysis

123

Techniques	Timing: When Will the Forecast Be Used?	Rankings
Qualitative or Judgmental	Short Lead Time ↕ Long Lead Time	Expert Opinion Consensus Opinion Sales Force Polling Market Surveys Delphi
Time Series	Short Lead Time ↕ Long Lead Time	Trend Analysis Moving Average Exponential Smoothing Classical Decomposition Box-Jenkins
Causal, Markov, and Indirect	Short Lead Time ↕ Long Lead Time	Markov Regression Leading Indicator Life Cycle Analysis Surveys Econometric Input-Output Analysis

Techniques	Form: Who Will Use the Forecast?	Rankings
Qualitative or Judgmental	Precise Forecast ↕ Imprecise Forecast	Market Surveys Expert Opinion Sales Force Polling Delphi
Time Series	Precise Forecast ↕ Imprecise Forecast	All Similar, Giving Precise Forecasts.
Causal, Markov, and Indirect	Precise Forecast ↕ Imprecise Forecast	All Similar, Giving Precise Forecasts.

Techniques	Data: How Much Are Available?	Rankings
Qualitative or Judgmental	Considerable Data Required ↕ Little Data Required	Generally All Similar; Little Historical Data Needed
Time Series	Considerable Data Required ↕ Little Data Required	All Similar; At Least Two Years' Data Usually Required
Causal, Markov, and Indirect	Considerable Data Required ↕ Little Data Required	Input-Out Analysis Econometric Life Cycle Analysis Markov Leading Indicator Regression Surveys

Forecasting and Statistical Software

There are numerous computer software that are used for forecasting purposes. They are broadly divided into two major categories: forecasting software and general purpose statistical software. Some programs are stand-alone, while others are spreadsheet add-ins. Still others are templates. A brief summary of some popular programs follows.

1. Forecast Pro

Forecast Pro, stand-alone forecasting software, is the business software that uses artificial intelligence. A built-in expert system examines your data. Then it guides you to state-of-the-art forecasting techniques (exponential smoothing, Box-Jenkins, dynamic regression, Croston's model, event models, and multiple level models) - whichever method suits the data best.

Business Forecast Systems, Inc.
68 Leonard Street
Belmont, MA 02478
Tel: (617) 484-5050
Fax: (617) 484-9219
www.forecastpro.com

2. Easy Forecaster Plus I and II

Easy Forecaster Plus I and II is a *stand-alone* forecasting software, developed by the Institute of Business Forecasting. The software's features include the following models: naïve, moving averages, exponential smoothing (single, double, and Holt's), linear trend line, and multiple regression. The program selects optimal model automatically and prepares monthly/quarterly forecasts using seasonal indices.

Institute of Business Forecasting
P. O. Box 670159, Station C
Flushing, NY 11367-9086
Tel: (718) 463-3914
Fax: (718) 544-9086
www.ibf.org

3. Autobox 5.0

This is the software utilizing Box-Jenkins forecasting methodology.

Automatic Forecasting Systems
PO Box 563
Hatboro, Pennsylvania 19040
Tel: (215) 675-0652
Fax: (215) 672-2534
www.autobox.com

4. DS FM (Demand Solutions Forecast Management)

This system delivers detailed information to front-line inventory managers, as well as top-level sales forecasts to front-office executives. It is the forecasting engine and data warehouse of choice for effective supply chain management. Key benefits include:

◆ Forecast at any level of data - item, item/customer, item/country/customer, or however you need it

◆ Quantify market intelligence, promotions and other variables

◆ Create production and purchase plans

◆ Meet your inventory and sales objectives. Continuously analyze a comprehensive and accurate view of your inventory and production

◆ Features the new Service Level Optimizer

◆ Microsoft SQL Server ODBC-compliant

Demand Management, Inc.
165 North Meramec Ave.,
Suite 300
St. Louis, MO 63105-3772 USA
Tel: (314) 727-4448
www.demandsolutions.com

5. Forecast Xpert Toolkit

The software provides:

◆ Full integration with Excel to eliminate the learning curve

◆ One Click business forecasting to pick the best method and generate award winning results

◆ Forecast one item or thousands of items with unlimited batch sales forecasting

◆ Clear, concise customizable reports to present results and collaborate with others

◆ Ad-Hoc planning and analysis with "what-if" scenarios

◆ Compelling charts and graphs that allow drag and drop adjustments

◆ Determine the effectiveness and timing of promotions with best/worst case analysis

John Galt Solutions, Inc.
125 South Clark Street, Suite 1950
Chicago, IL. 60603
Tel: (312)701-9026
Fax: (312) 701-9033
www.forecastxperttoolkit.com

6. Demandworks DP

The critical element in any supply chain plan is the demand forecast. *Demand Works DP*™ is a full-featured demand management solution that improves the entire business planning function by maximizing forecast accuracy. It leverages demand history, current sales orders, promotions, events, and user judgment to arrive at an optimal estimate of future demand and required safety stocks. Demand Works DP combines best-in-class forecasting, a powerful and highly flexible design, and a 100% web architecture for better deployment and enhanced teamwork.

Demand Works Co.
16 W. Market Street
West Chester, PA 19382
Tel:: (610) 701-9873
Fax: (610) 701-9875
www.demandworks.com

7. Roadmap Geneva Forecasting

Roadmap Geneva Forecasting uses advanced statistical techniques to forecast sales of new and established products and predict the effects of advertising, promotion, new products, pricing changes or competitive actions. Geneva Forecasting includes:

◆ Powerful statistical modeling.

◆ Collaborative planning between headquarters and field sales.

◆ Advanced data mining tools to uncover exceptions and trends.

◆ Support for remote and mobile users.

◆ Interfaces to SAP and Retail POS databases.

◆ Specialized modules for promotion analysis, sales planning and customer forecasting.

Roadmap Technologies
900 Cummings Center
Beverly, MA 01915
Tel: (978) 232-8901
Fax: (978) 232-8903
www.managingautomation.com

8. SmartForecasts

SmartForecasts Enterprise combines automatic forecasting with rapid batch processing to accurately forecast thousands or tens of thousands of items quickly and easily—more than 100,000 items per hour. Manufacturers, distributors, and retailers can easily create accurate demand forecasts for each product item in inventory, along with item-specific estimates of safety stock requirements that significantly reduce inventory costs. The Enterprise edition provides direct connectivity and easy integration with your corporate database (including major client/server systems such as Oracle, IBM DB2 and SQL Server), as well as ERP, DRP, Supply Chain and other planning systems.

Automatic Statistical Forecasting provides fast, accurate forecasts for hundreds or thousands of product items—at the click of your mouse.

SmartForecasts' expert system selects the best forecasting method for your data and handles all the math, easily incorporating trends, seasonal patterns and the effects of promotions and other special events. Interactive (Eyeball) Adjustments let you adjust your forecast results directly on-screen based on your business knowledge, for more realistic forecasts and informed planning decisions.

Multilevel (Multiseries) Forecasting makes it easy to obtain top-down and bottom-up forecasts, by product group/item or item/region, for large groups containing hundreds or thousands of items.

Smart Software, Inc.
Four Hill Road
Belmont, MA 02478
Tel: (617) 489-2743 or 1 (800) SMART-99
Fax: (617) 489-2748
www.smartcorp.com

9. EViews 6

EViews 6 is a *stand-alone* software that provides the tools most frequently used in practical econometric and forecasting work. It covers Estimation, forecasting, statistical analysis, graphics, simulation, data management, all in a powerful, graphical object-oriented interface.

Quantitative Micro Software
4521 Campus Drive, Suite 336
Irvine, CA 92715
Tel: (949) 856-3368
Fax: (949) 856-2044
www.eviews.com

11. Sibyl/Runner

Sibyl/Runner is an interactive, *stand-alone* forecasting system. In addition to allowing the usage of all major forecasting methods, the package permits analysis of the data, suggests available forecasting methods, compares results, and provides several accuracy measures in such a way that it is easier for the user to select an appropriate method and forecast needed data under different economic and environmental conditions.

What is the Right Package for You?

Since different software packages choose different techniques for many of the same tasks, it is a good idea to select a package that explains which method it is using and why, so you can eventually learn the most appropriate technique for your specific forecasting task. Figure 10.3 spells out your options in choosing the right package.

Figure 10.3: Which Forecasting Software is Right for You? Know Your Options

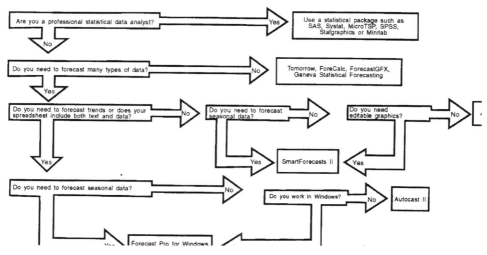

Conclusion

Today's managers have some powerful tools at hand to simplify the forecasting process and increase its accuracy. Several forecasting models are available, and the automated versions of these should be considered by any manager who is regularly called upon to provide forecasts. A personal computer with a spreadsheet is a good beginning, but the stand-alone packages currently available provide the most accurate forecasts and are the easiest to use. In addition, they make several forecasting models available and can automatically select the best one for a particular data set.

Part 3

Applications

Chapter 11
Sales and Revenue Forecasting

In all the field of business, probably no area is more challenging than sales forecasting for the individual company, nor of more direct relevance to policy formation. The challenge arises from the discreteness of the unit involved. It is more difficult to predict the responses of an individual than of a universe; the possibility of salvation through compensating errors declines as the size of the sample is reduced.

The relevance arises from the direct use of the sales forecast in formulating company policy. The direct use of an economic forecast is rare. Government economists may forecast, say, the gross domestic product with great accuracy, but it is not possible to base government economic policy upon this forecast. Policy must also consider a host of noneconomic factors, special interests, and sensitivities foreign and domestic, including the slowness with which a representative government changes its laws. An economic forecast in government may simply serve as a basis for exhortation—for example, that if Congress doesn't reduce taxes the economy will face a recession, or that if businessmen and labor unions price according to market potentials we will have inflation. The forecast itself can serve as a guide to policy to only a limited extent.

Similarly, an industry forecast can rarely be used directly for policy formation. A forecast for the general economy or for some particular industry is an abstract concept which cannot be used directly, as it stands, to formulate policy. By contrast, the sales forecast of a modern business corporation can be, and should be, a complete expression of the outlook for the particular company, and can constitute the complete frame of reference within which company policy is formulated. (In view of the difficulties of exact prediction, of course, the sales forecast is only a framework, not a straitjacket.)

It might be well to note a further difference between private sales forecasts prepared by individual companies and the public forecasts of general business or a particular industry. Published forecasts by government or by industry spokesmen must always keep in mind the "feedback" effect and are often designed not to guide policy which the forecaster may be able to control, but to influence the actions of others—for example, customers—over whom the forecaster has no control. Of course, individual businesses may also allow for the "feedback" effect; there are reportedly several companies with three sets of sales forecasts—a coldly realistic one for top management, a more favorable one for supervisory personnel, and a highly optimistic one for salesmen.'

Admittedly, there is wide skepticism on the entire question of forecasting. Many individuals are so keenly aware of the importance of the unpredictable in human events that they suggest that the forecasting effort should be abandoned. The professional economist is no more able to forecast the economic future than is the businessman or, for that matter the man on the street because:

(1)   The course of business is dictated, in large measure, by events that cannot be anticipated.

(2)   Our business indices, including especially Gross Domestic Product, are statistical horrors.

(3)   The professional economist is today unable to assign a statistical weight to each of the indices he employs in his folderol.

(4)   There is no scientifically valid formula for evaluating the significance of the available statistics.

Now there is, of course much merit in this argument. The unpredictable is frequently important—perhaps of overriding importance. Our economic measures, even if not statistical monstrosities, have many serious inadequacies, and are sometimes used in inadequate, if not monstrous ways. Problems of statistical discrepancies and intercorrelation of variables, along with serious gaps in our basic theories, make it easy to obtain fallacious parameters in econometric analysis and model-building. But all these points simply illustrate the difficulty of developing accurate forecasts, and the necessity to review past projections against current developments to check on the desirability of modifying future forecasts.

Despite all these difficulties, you have to forecast. Every action taken, every policy formed, is based on some implicit forecast of future results. The basic purpose of making the forecast explicit is simply to test the reasonableness of the fundamental assumptions and to quantify the hypotheses on which decisions are made. It is desirable to have an economist do the job, instead of having the businessman do it himself, partly to free the businessman for other activities and partly to assure the systematic, objective allowance for known factors for which the businessman— whose skills incline to more profitable directions—is rarely equipped by either training or temperament.

The business forecaster is not a shaman who can "look into the seeds of time and say which grain will grow and which will not," but simply a student attempting through the systematic analysis of inadequate data to determine probable outcomes. The function of the sales forecast is not to eliminate all odds so that gamblers can wager on sure things; it has the more realistic, if less ambitious, goal of narrowing the frame of reference within which management must decide. Business genius—an amalgam of instincts in buying, selling, producing, and investing—is the essential hallmark of management; and sales forecasting, like any other staff function, is only a supplement or support to managerial genius, not a substitute for it.

The future is necessarily uncertain, but its uncertainties transpire within a framework given by the certainties of the past (however uncertainly measured). By a careful review of the record of the past we can indicate a reasonable course of future developments and perhaps provide a standard for gauging the significance of the unexpected.

In any company sales forecast there are three basic factors, which may be considered explicitly, but which are necessarily implicit, even where no specific, systematic allowance is made for them. First, the outlook for the general economy, which determines the general environment within which operations will take place. Second, the outlook for the particular industry (or industries), which is conditioned by the general economic environment and which in turn determines the basic environment for the individual company. Third, the industry position or market share of the individual company, the part of the total demand for the particular industry which can be obtained by the specific company.

The extent to which these three separate factors are considered explicitly will depend upon many variables: the purpose of the forecast, the availability of data, the importance of general economic developments in the demand for the particular product (in technical terms, the elasticity of demand with respect to income), the nature of the company's particular market and the importance of forces other than the general economic situation in the demand for the products of the particular company, and a host of other factors. But implicitly or explicitly there must be either an allowance for these three separate values or an assumption, again implicit or explicit, that the demand for the company's product is independent of general economic developments, or independent of industry developments, or both.

An additional point should be made on the basic nature of sales forecasting, implied above. All sales forecasting is *demand forecasting*. If demand exceeds supply, if the market for a product is greater than the amount which can be produced, the sales forecast becomes an engineering estimate of maximum output, and "sales" become simply the optimum allocation of the maximum output to the more profitable customers. In such a case the engineer and the cost-accountant allot output to the salesman, who has become an order-taker. The "sales" forecast, as an analysis of potential demand, becomes only a statement of what might have been, and the business economist is left with the invidious assignment of warning that this delightful euphoria does not represent a permanent way of life.

In the usual course of events, however, capacity exceeds demand, and can, at least in the long run, always be expanded to exceed demand, and so usually the forecast of what can be sold is an essential and integral part of company policy; it is, in fact, the very basis of company policy.

The point is sometimes made that a sales forecast, through warning of potential dangers, can lead to corrective actions which invalidate the forecast. Such a situation, however, represents a failure to integrate the sales forecast into company policy. If, for example, a sales manager, warned by an otherwise valid forecast that sales will decline, adopts some new and effective policies to improve his sales position, he may cover himself with glory, and make the poor forecaster look an idiot. But a more effective approach, from the point of view of over-all company operations, would be to modify the forecast in the light of the new policies and practices, so that company planning generally can be adapted to the new program. An unexpectedly good sales record can pose problems for the manufacturing department, for example, and while these are the kinds of problems business likes to face, the effects of such problems can be reduced, and profits increased, if manufacturing is allowed to know the plans of the sales department, if the sales forecast is adjusted to reflect all significant known factors, and if company planning at all levels is based upon one cohesive, consistent plan.

Dependent and Independent Demand

Demand for a product or service is termed independent when it occurs independently of demand for any other product or service. Conversely, when demand for one product is linked to demand for another product, the demand is termed dependent. Dependency may occur when one item demand is derived from a second item (vertical dependency) or when one item relates in another manner to the second item (horizontal dependency). In a movie theater, for example, demand for film postage is independent of demand for popcorn. Vertical dependency might be the relationship between popcorn and theater ticket (patron) demand. Horizontal dependency might be the relationship between popcorn demand and popcorn box demand. Only independent demand needs forecasting; dependent demand can be derived from the independent demand to which it is linked.

Purposes, Concepts and Methods of Forecasts

Basically, we can distinguish three separate purposes of sales forecasts, each of which requires a separate type of forecast. First, the short-term forecast, which is used for planning current policy, assessing current developments. The concern of this forecast is limited; it covers a period of perhaps two to six months; its use is for planning current policy, on inventory, hiring, shutdowns, and similar day-to-day concerns of management. Second, the "budget" forecast, usually covering an entire fiscal year, which is used for setting standard costs and prices, for determining cash-flow, and generally for establishing basic policies for the coming year—policies which, of course, will require adjustment over the year to such extent as actual developments differ from the forecast. Both these types of forecasts are basically concerned with the most efficient use of a company's existing capital equipment and financial structure.

The third type, by contrast, is concerned with changes in these factors. This third type, the "long-term" forecast, covering any period from five to fifty years, is used primarily for planning capacity changes and other capital expenditures, for considering entry into new markets, for long-term financial planning, and for any other purposes involving a change in the company's capital equipment, financial structure, market areas, product-mix, and so on. By and large, the long-term forecast represents projections of secular trends, with no allowance for cyclical or other "non-trend" forces. The "short-term" and "budget" forecasts, however, attempt to predict actual sales, and to allow for all factors.

Basic Forecasting Methods

Along with these three basic types of forecasts we may distinguish three essentially different methods or techniques of sales forecasting. First, the informed estimates, or guesses, of line personnel, usually sales managers, occasionally corporate executives or customers. Second, the internal analysis of individual company data. Third, analysis of company data in relation to external standards of performance by the industry or the economy: regression analysis, econometric analysis, and others, which were discussed in the previous chapters, to focus the insight of line personnel, to narrow the area of managerial judgment.

Each of these various methods has its strengths, each its weaknesses. Ideally, a combination of these methods will be used, to such extent as permitted by the availability of time and of data, for each approach offers a useful supplement to the others. Before considering the use of these various methods, it is necessary to consider the question of availability of data, particularly on the company level.

The many elements of forecasting revenue include internal estimates and opinions, statistical analyses (including regression analysis), smoothing methods, previous sales volume and market history. Other economic indicators, including general economic indications and industry economic indicators, may also be used. Regardless of the methods used, the key concept is that a great deal of subjectivity enters into the budget process.

The use of regression analysis is illustrated below. The following example shows how to develop a forecasting model with the aid of Excel.

Example 11.1

A firm wishes to develop a sales forecasting model, by relating sales to price and advertising.

Month	Sales (Y) (000)	Advertising (X_1)(000)	Price (X_2)
1	25	4	75
2	26	5	82
3	32	6	94
4	30	6	95
5	32	7	98
6	37	7	110
7	38	8	110
8	41	8	99
9	46	9	95
10	48	10	97

SUMMARY OUTPUT

Regression Statistics	
Multiple R	0.97366474
R Square	0.94802302
Adjusted R Square	0.93317246
Standard Error	2.0400664
Observations	10

ANOVA

	df	SS	MS
Regression	2	531.3669036	265.6835
Residual	7	29.13309639	4.161871
Total	9	560.5	

	Coefficients	Standard Error	t Stat
Intercept	10.1734656	6.251683507	1.627316
Advertising	4.41923505	0.480669674	9.193913
Price	-0.0587237	0.081383757	-0.72157

The sales forecasting model then is:

Sales = 10.17 + 4.42 (Advertising) − 0.06 (Price)

Sales Forecasting: A Combined Process

Where industry data on shipments or production are available, it is possible to make use of a combined forecasting process which will maintain the objectivity of the ivory tower approach, while at the same time involving sales personnel, and their insight and knowledge, so that the forecasts are essentially forecasts developed by the sales departments rather than schedules imposed upon them by an outside group.

The first step in this process is to develop a forecast of the general economic outlook which receives the approval of top management. This is a necessary step for purposes of consistency. If one department is forecasting on the assumption of great prosperity and a second on the assumption of moderate recession, it is not feasible to develop a coherent over-all policy from a combination of the two forecasts. The differences will not reflect differences in sales potentials.

From a management-endorsed view of the general economic outlook, the economics department can develop forecasts of the specific aggregates of most significance to the industry, and forecasts of total industry shipments or production.

These forecasts, together with historical data showing both industry and company sales, and the company as a per cent of industry, are given to the sales manager (or whatever line position is involved), and his assignment is then, not to make a sales forecast—in a vacuum, as it were—but to forecast the share of the industry total which he feels his particular organization can achieve. He is also, of course, free to modify the industry forecast, perhaps even—if he dares—the general economic forecast which management has approved.

But whatever changes or modifications he chooses to make, the ideas influencing the sales forecast must be made explicit. It is no longer a question of "we sold one million pounds last year so I think this year we should be able to sell 1.05 million pounds," or whatever.

With this more systematic procedure, the sales manager is forced, in the first place, to accept or modify the objectively-made industry forecast—and this is in itself useful, since he knows industry details not available to the ivory tower statistician, although this knowledge is not immediately available in any organized fashion. Once agreement is reached on the industry outlook, the sales manager is asked to forecast not his own level of sales, in a vacuum, but what percentage of the total industry he expects his organization to achieve. Since the past record of market shares is a part of the forecasting work sheet, there is an immediate test of the reasonableness of the forecast. Any anticipated improvement in industry position must be justified in the light of special circumstances or techniques not available to the competition, or on the basis of other special situations or unique factors.

With a forecast of industry shipments or production, and a forecast of the industry position for the particular company, the company sales forecast is obtained automatically, with the major factors underlying this forecast stated explicitly, rather than being implicitly lumped in with other values in a forecast based at best on internal analysis of the company's own sales record.

The question of changes in industry position or market shares is one requiring close attention. It is very easy for a sales manager, planning a particular new intensive sales campaign, to overlook the fact that the same device may be open to every other company in the industry, and that there may be other firms working on even better campaigns.

It is very easy for a concern accounting for, say, 5 per cent of the output of an industry to assume it can grow to 6 per cent with a little extra effort, but this change of only one percentage point actually represents an improvement of 20 per cent for the particular company— a brilliant achievement, not a foregone conclusion.

Where industry data are not available, it may be useful to forecast simply from the relation between company sales and some appropriate economic aggregate such as industrial production or GDP or personal income. This is not nearly so satisfactory— particularly because of the difficulty of handling special industry situations such as inventory-building, liquidation, or changes in market shares— but it does offer some sort of yardstick to measure the reasonableness of the forecast.

This combination method of sales forecasting, even when industry data are readily available, is of limited value in short-term sales forecasting, partly because of the time required and partly because random factors may produce strong shifts from one month to the next which make it unprofitable to use this time-consuming approach, calling for frequent reappraisals because of factors not really representative. (For short-term forecasting, trend projection based on internal analysis is probably the most satisfactory approach.)

But for medium-term and long-term forecasting, the combined approach is extremely effective, and while special factors may limit its applicability in particular situations, the possibility of using this approach should always be explored.

Can You Manage Demand?

"Passive response to demand" and "active influence on demand" are two planning strategies. The passive response states that in some situations a firm would simply accept demand for its products or services as a given factor without making any attempt to change demand. Active influence on demand states that firms, in most situations, can take an active role both in influencing the environment (price cuts, managerial pressure on the sales force, incentives and campaigns) and in adapting themselves to the environment (contracyclical product mix, or creation of order backlogs).

A great deal of coordination is required to "manage" this demand on the firm's productive facilities since these demands originate from a variety of functional areas. For example, replacement parts for repair of previously sold products originate from the product service department; new products are sold through the sales department; restocking standard items may be handled by the factory warehouse; and in-process inventories and partially completed subassemblies are determined by the manufacturing function. The challenge of demand management is to blend all of these demands so that the productive system can be utilized efficiently and the products or services delivered on time.

Chapter 12

Forecasting the Economy

Economic forecasting is typically concerned with predicting future values of key economic variables such as gross domestic product, inflation, interest rates, and unemployment. These variables are called *exogenous* or input variables. They are outside the control of the decision maker.

Barometric Forecasting

Barometric methods involve the use of economic indicators such as leading indicators to predict turning points in economic activity. It is used primarily to identify potential future changes in general business conditions or conditions of a specific industry rather than conditions for a specific firm. The series chosen serve as barometers of economic change. Types of indicators, which were discussed in Chapter 8, are (1) coincident indicators, (2) lagging indicators, (3) leading indicators, more exactly known as *Index of Leading Economic Indicators (LEI)*.

As a further tool and aid to understanding business conditions, a series known as diffusion indexes are used. Unlike a composite index such as the LEI, a diffusion index indicates the percentage of economic series that experience increases over the time interval being measured. Often, the 50 percent mark is used as a guide. For example, if more than 50 percent of the leading indicators are rising, it might be plausible to predict an upturn in aggregate economic activity. In a more general sense, however, diffusion indexes can be employed to help measure and interpret the breadth and intensity of recessions and recoveries, the state of economic conditions, and the degree of optimism or pessimism on the part of businessmen.

Barometric models have the following limitations:

1.   No series accurately signals changes in other economic variables on a consistent basis.

2. It may still indicate only the direction of future change, little or nothing about the magnitude of the change.

Econometric Models

The approach employs statistically based models where relationships among economic variables are expressed in mathematical equations, single or simultaneous in nature and then estimated using such techniques as regression methods. The simplest kind of econometric models would be a single equation, expressing some dependent variable as a function of some other set of variables. For example, gross domestic product (GDP) might be expressed as a function of past GDP (GDP-t), construction activity (C), changes in the unemployment rate(DU), and the level of interest rates (I).

A linear model expressing this relation is:

$$GDP = a + bGDP\text{-}t + cC + d\Delta U + eI$$

Some models attempt to capture the complexity of the entire economy; they may contain hundreds of equations that must all be estimated simultaneously. *The Wharton model* is a good example. Multiple equation systems, however, are difficult and expensive to construct.

Example 12.1

Suppose that a major U.S automaker wishes to project GDP as a step toward forecasting the demand for autos. The company has developed the following econometric model:

$$GDP = C + I + G$$

$$C = 60 + 0.7Y$$

$$I = 200 + 0.3\pi_{t\text{-}1}$$

$$G = 800$$

$$Y = GDP - T$$

$$T = 0.3GDP$$

$$\pi_{t\text{-}1} = 900$$

where C = consumption, I = investment, G = government expenditure, Y = national income, T = tax receipts, and $\pi_{t\text{-}1}$ = prior year's corporate profit. (Figures are in billions of dollars).

We will calculate GDP, step by step, as follows:

(1) I = 200 + 0.3π_{t-1} = 200 + 0.3(900) = 470

(2) GDP = C + I + G = 60 + 0.7Y + 470 + 800 = 60 + 0.7(GDP - T) + 470 + 800

  = 60 + 0.7(GDP - 0.3GDP) + 470 + 800 = 60 + 0.49GDP + 470 + 800

  0.51 GDP = 1,330

  GDP = 2,608 (in billions of dollars)

Input-Output Analysis

Input-output analysis, also called *interindustry analysis* is the input-output approach to forecasting. It employs historical tabular data on intersectional output and material flows to predict demand and supply changes for individual industries. An input-output matrix table, which was discussed in Chapter 8, is the source of this method. The table is very useful in evaluating the effects of a change in demand in one industry on other industries (i.e., a change in oil prices and its resulting effect on demand for cars, then steel sales, then iron ore and limestone sales). The *total requirements* table prepared as a part of the input-output table shows the *direct*, as well as *indirect*, requirements of each industry listed in the left-hand column (supplying industry) in order to produce one dollar's worth of output for the industry identified at the top of each column (producing industry). This table makes it possible to compute the impacts on various industries in the economy which result from changes in the final demand for products of one or more industries.

Input-output analysis for forecasting, however, suffers from two major limitations:

1. The development of accurate and updated supplements to the original *Commerce Department* input-output table is prohibitively expensive.

2. The method is a *linear* approach to forecasting and thereby fails to capture some possible *nonlinear* relations.

Economic forecasting at AT&T

At AT&T, the economics function is handled by the Economic Analysis Section, which has a staff of nine people: the chief economist, four professional economists with training at the PhD level, and four support personnel. The Economic Analysis Section is located within the Tax Division of AT&T; however, according to AT&T's chief economist Dr. Ken Militzer, it doesn't matter where the economics function is located, what matters is the culture in which the chief economist operates.

Essentially, the culture in which the chief economist operates must provide access, visibility, independence, and adequate resources. In terms of access, the chief economist must have direct access to senior managers across the full spectrum of the corporation, all the way through to the chairman of the board. Otherwise, the message of the chief economist will become diluted or distorted, if it must travel through the layers of management, thereby making the message less useful. In terms of visibility the chief economist needs to be visible to everyone in the firm who may require his services. In this way, the chief economist is able to meet the diverse needs of the corporation. The chief economist must also be independent and free to make accurate forecasts, especially if the forecasts are unfavorable or unpopular. Therefore, all economic forecasts should be separate from the budget process. Finally, the chief economist must have adequate resources and must be positioned to compete for these resources among all the other needs of the corporation, despite the fact that the Economic Analysis Section brings no direct revenue to the corporation.

At AT&T, the Economic Analysis Section provides forecasts of the domestic economic climate, determines the impact of the economic climate on the firm's markets, analyzes public policy issues, performs international market analyses and forecasts, and provides support for departmental problems and activities.

Opinion Polling

This is a qualitative and subjective method of predicting economic activity or some particular phase of it. The surveys include:

1. Surveys of business executives' intentions on what to spend on plant and equipment, made independently by McGraw-Hill, Department of Commerce, Securities and Exchange Commission, and the Conference Board.

2. Surveys of consumers' finances, buying plans, and confidence, made independently by the University of Michigan and the Conference Board.

3. Surveys of business plans regarding inventory changes, made by the National Association of Purchasing Agents.

The surveys seem to do well in forecasting turning points of business, but are not that useful for predicting the magnitude of change.

Economic Forecasting Services

An examination of these economic variables will give a business a handy reference in interpreting the direction of the economy and the security market. This, along with expert economic opinion and projection in newspapers and newsletters, such as publications as *Blue Chip Consensus* (Figures 12-2 & 12-3) and *Kiplinger Washington Letter* should lead to the formulation of a sound investment policy. For example, the Blue Chip Economic Indicators are constructed based on a poll of 50 business

Figure 12-2

2 ■ BLUE CHIP ECONOMIC INDICATORS ■ MARCH 10, 2005

2005 Real GDP Consensus Forecast Rises To 3.7%

March 2005 Forecast For 2005 SOURCE:	Percent Change 2005 From 2004 (Year-Over-Year)									Average For 2005			Total Units-2005		2005-
	1 Real GDP (Chained) (2000 $)	2 GDP Price Index	3 Nominal GDP (Cur. $)	4 Consumer Price Index	5 Indust. Prod. (Total)	6 Dis. Pers. Income (2000 $)	7 Personal Cons. Exp (2000 $)	8 Non-Res. Fix Inv. (2000 $)	9 Corp. Profits (Cur. $)	10 Treas. Bills 3-mo.	11 Treas. Notes 10-Year	12 Unempl. Rate (Civ.)	13 Housing Starts (Mil.)	14 Auto/Truck Sales (Mil.)	15 Net Exports (2000 $)
Conference Board*	4.4 H	1.9	6.4 H	3.4 H	5.6 H	4.0	3.8	12.5	23.6	3.1	4.5	4.9 L	1.83	17.3	-600.8
Action Economics	4.2	2.4	6.7	2.6	3.9	4.0	3.7	11.2	12.8	3.1	4.6	5.2	2.06	17.2	-620.9
Classicalprinciples.com	4.2	1.9	6.1	2.4	3.9	2.5	na	na	7.5	3.4	4.9	5.1	na	16.9	na
Deutsche Bank Securities	4.0	2.1	6.2	2.5	3.1	4.6	3.7	10.7	na	3.5	4.9	5.1	na	na	-633.7
Macroeconomic Advisers, LLC**	4.0	1.9	6.1	2.3	4.3	3.7	3.7	11.0	25.2	3.1	4.6	5.2	1.90	17.3	-607.4
Eaton Corporation	4.0	1.8	5.8	2.6	4.8	3.3	3.1 L	10.4	9.0	3.1	4.4	5.3	1.87	17.1	-554.0 H
National City Corporation	4.0	1.7 L	5.7	2.2	3.9	3.6	3.6	13.1 H	6.9	2.9	4.6	5.1	1.87	17.3	-617.7
Bear, Stearns & Co., Inc.	3.9	2.4	6.4	2.9	4.1	3.1	4.1 H	9.6	7.6	3.5	4.9	5.0	1.85	17.0	-651.5
U.S. Chamber of Commerce	3.9	2.0	6.0	2.4	4.2	1.9 L	3.8	11.5	na	3.2	4.9	5.1	1.91	na	-642.2
Nomura Securities	3.9	2.0	6.0	2.3	4.1	3.0	3.5	11.8	12.0	3.1	4.7	5.2	1.81	17.4	-595.0
J P MorganChase	3.9	1.9	5.9	2.4	4.7	3.9	3.9	11.5	6.7	3.3	4.9	5.1	1.75	16.7	-647.8
National Assn. of Home Builders	3.9	1.9	5.9	2.4	4.0	3.7	3.5	10.0	10.0	3.0	4.5	5.3	1.90	17.3	-605.3
Morgan Stanley	3.9	1.9	5.8	2.7	4.4	5.1 H	3.6	12.5	11.5	3.2	4.8	5.2	1.98 H	16.9	-629.9
Mesirow Financial	3.9	1.8	5.8	2.2	3.6	4.4	3.7	11.9	20.0	2.8	4.5	5.3	1.84	16.6	-634.0
National Assn. of Realtors	3.9	1.7 L	5.6	2.5	4.3	3.9	3.7	8.9	9.9	3.0	4.5	5.1	1.92	17.5 H	-598.0
Goldman Sachs	3.8	2.3	6.2	2.6	3.8	3.5	3.5	10.7	9.0	3.1	4.8	5.1	1.88	17.2	-603.1
Banc of America Corp.*	3.8	2.2	6.0	2.4	3.8	3.6	3.7	9.0	9.0	3.1	4.5	5.3	1.85	17.1	-617.0
Moody's Investors Service	3.8	2.1	6.0	2.5	4.1	3.5	3.7	8.2	10.4	3.2	4.6	5.1	1.89	17.1	-603.0
Stanford Washington Research Group*	3.8	2.0	5.9	2.4	4.0	3.6	3.6	11.5	11.0	3.1	4.6	5.3	1.87	17.2	-617.0
Wayne Hummer Investments LLC*	3.8	2.0	5.9	2.5	4.4	3.7	3.6	9.3	9.3	3.0	4.7	5.2	1.80	17.4	-603.0
Fannie Mae	3.8	2.0	5.8	2.3	4.3	3.6	3.7	10.2	12.3	3.1	4.5	5.2	1.85	na	-601.5
U.S. Trust Co	3.8	1.7 L	5.6	2.4	5.1	3.6	3.5	8.6	8.9	3.4	4.5	5.1	1.94	16.8	-629.8
Wachovia	3.8	2.0	5.9	2.4	5.0	3.6	3.5	6.0	9.1	3.2	4.6	5.2	1.83	na	-620.0
Turning Points (Micrometrics)	3.7	2.2	6.1	2.8	4.5	4.0	3.3	10.5	10.4	3.3	4.5	5.2	1.84	16.9	-621.0
Credit Suisse First Boston	3.7	2.2	5.9	2.5	3.5	3.1	3.4	12.1	7.5	3.2	4.6	5.2	1.97	17.1	-640.8
Standard & Poors Corp.*	3.7	1.8	5.6	2.6	4.0	na	3.4	9.7	na	na	4.5	5.2	na	na	-633.5
Merrill Lynch Economics	3.7	1.8	5.6	2.0	3.6	3.3	3.5	6.1 L	32.7 H	3.0	4.6	5.1	1.84	16.7	-629.9
SOM Economics, Inc.	3.7	1.8	5.3	2.2	3.6	3.6	3.7	9.2	na	3.3	4.4	5.3	1.91	16.4	-624.8
Wells Capital Management	3.6	2.1	5.8	2.8	3.9	3.0	3.2	8.5	8.5	3.1	4.5	5.1	1.95	17.5 H	-611.0
LaSalle National Bank	3.6	2.0	5.7	2.1	4.3	4.7	3.2	9.1	9.5	3.2	4.8	5.2	1.70 L	17.4	-584.8
Comerica Bank*	3.6	2.0	5.6	2.6	4.1	3.6	3.5	8.0	10.5	3.2	4.6	5.3	1.85	17.0	-611.0
Prudential Equity Group, LLC	3.6	1.9	5.6	2.4	4.4	3.0	3.3	8.6	9.1	3.2	4.6	5.2	1.83	na	-620.0
UBS Warburg	3.6	1.7 L	5.4	2.1	4.7	3.5	3.3	10.4	5.8	3.6 H	4.8	5.3	1.83	na	-614.0
FedEx Corporation	3.5	2.5 H	6.0	3.0	3.7	4.0	3.5	9.0	6.3	3.1	5.1	5.3	1.90	16.7	-595.0
J.W. Coons Advisors	3.5	2.2	5.8	2.8	4.3	3.3	3.3	12.3	5.9	2.9	4.5	5.4	1.85	17.5	-643.0
Econoclast	3.5	2.1	5.6	2.2	4.0	3.0	3.1 L	8.0	9.0	2.9	4.4	5.3	1.74	16.9	-615.0
Perna Associates	3.5	2.0	5.6	2.7	3.7	3.3	3.3	10.6	5.4	3.1	4.9	5.1	1.91	16.7	-651.0
DuPont**	3.5	2.0	5.6	2.5	3.5	3.2	3.2	9.9	9.8	3.1	4.4	5.2	1.85	17.0	-616.0
Kellner Economic Advisers	3.5	2.0	5.5	2.5	4.2	3.1	3.2	8.0	9.5	3.0	4.5	5.3	1.79	17.0	-600.0
General Motors Corporation	3.5	1.9	5.6	2.4	3.9	3.3	3.2	9.9	9.8	3.1	4.6	5.4	1.85	na	-594.2
Motorola	3.5	1.8	5.4	2.0 L	3.4	2.8	3.4	9.7	na	3.1	4.7	5.2	1.85	17.2	-620.1
Global Insight	3.5	1.8	5.4	2.0 L	3.4	2.8	3.4	9.7	6.2	3.0	4.6	5.2	1.86	16.9	-620.0
ClearView Economics	3.5	1.8	5.3	2.8	4.4	2.7	3.4	9.7	6.8	3.1	4.5	4.9 L	1.89	17.1	-622.0
DaimlerChrysler AG	3.5	1.8	5.3	2.2	3.7	3.3	3.6	9.2	3.6 L	2.8	4.4	5.2	1.87	na	-607.8
BMO Nesbitt Burns	3.4	2.3	5.9	2.3	3.4	4.4	3.3	9.4	7.6	3.3	4.6	5.2	1.82	16.9	-616.0
Eggert Economic Enterprises, Inc.	3.4	2.2	5.6	2.4	4.3	3.4	3.1 L	8.6	9.5	2.9	4.8	5.3	1.75	17.5 H	-602.2
Northern Trust Company	3.4	2.0	5.5	2.6	3.2	na	3.2	10.5	na	3.2	4.5	5.4	1.85	16.3 L	-643.0
Inforum - Univ. of Maryland	3.4	2.0	5.5	2.6	4.2	2.5	3.1 L	9.2	3.7	3.0	4.7	5.3	1.90	17.0	-574.0
Naroff Economic Advisors	3.3	2.5 H	5.9	2.6	3.8	2.8	3.1 L	7.6	8.0	3.3	5.2 H	5.1	1.81	17.1	-595.0
Ford Motor Company*	3.3	2.0	5.4	2.4	3.4	3.0	3.3	7.9	na	3.2	4.6	5.3	1.81	na	-600.9
Swiss Re	3.3	1.9	5.4	2.6	4.4	3.3	3.3	10.0	7.3	3.3	4.5	5.0	1.93	17.0	-633.0
Daiwa Institute of Research America	3.2 L	2.4	5.6	2.7	4.7	3.6	3.7	9.6	11.5	2.4 L	4.2 L	5.6 H	1.94	16.9	-677.0 L
Georgia State University*	3.2 L	1.9	5.2 L	2.3	3.6	2.5	3.3	9.5	8.6	3.0	4.7	5.3	1.79	17.5 H	-630.1
UCLA Business Forecasting Proj.*	3.2 L	1.9	5.2 L	2.4	2.8 L	2.9	3.1 L	8.7	27.7	2.8	4.6	5.4	1.79	16.5	-613.2
2005 Consensus: March Avg.	3.7	2.0	5.8	2.5	4.0	3.4	3.4	9.9	10.4	3.1	4.6	5.2	1.86	17.0	-615.9
Top 10 Avg.	4.0	2.3	6.2	2.9	4.7	4.3	3.8	12.1	18.8	3.4	4.9	5.4	1.94	17.4	-586.3
Bottom 10 Avg.	3.3	1.8	5.3	2.1	3.3	2.6	3.1	8.0	5.6	2.8	4.4	5.0	1.77	16.6	-646.4
February Avg.	3.6	2.0	5.6	2.5	4.1	3.3	3.5	8.8	10.1	3.0	4.7	5.3	1.83	17.1	-608.8
Historical Data: 2001	0.8	2.4	3.2	2.8	-3.6	1.9	2.5	-4.2	-6.2	3.4	5.0	4.7	1.60	17.5	-399.1
2002	1.9	1.7	3.5	1.6	-0.3	3.1	3.1	-8.9	14.0	1.6	4.6	5.8	1.71	17.1	-472.1
2003	3.0	1.8	4.9	2.3	0.0	2.3	3.3	3.3	16.8	1.0	4.0	6.0	1.85	17.0	-518.5
2004	4.4	2.2	6.6	2.7	4.1	3.5	3.8	10.6	na	1.4	4.3	5.5	1.95	17.3	-584.3
Number Of Forecasts Changed From A Month Ago:															
Down	5	13	13	20	21	14	23	2	13	6	28	28	1	15	28
Same	12	24	10	19	18	14	13	10	16	28	17	24	16	22	7
Up	37	17	31	15	15	24	16	41	18	19	9	2	34	8	18
March Median	3.7	2.0	5.8	2.5	4.0	3.4	3.4	9.7	9.0	3.1	4.6	5.2	1.85	17.1	-616.0
March Diffusion Index	80 %	54 %	67 %	45 %	44 %	60 %	43 %	87 %	55 %	62 %	32 %	26 %	82 %	42 %	41 %

*Former winner of annual Lawrence R. Klein Award for Blue Chip Forecast Accuracy **Denotes two-time winner.

Figure 12.3

2006 Real GDP Consensus Forecast Remains At 3.4%

March 2005 Forecast For 2006 SOURCE:	Percent Change 2006 From 2005 (Year-Over-Year)									Average For 2005			Total Units-2006		2006-
	1 Real GDP (Chained) (2000 $)	2 GDP Price Index	3 Nominal GDP (Cur. $)	4 Consumer Price Index	5 Indust. Prod. (Total)	6 Dis. Pers. Income (2000 $)	7 Personal Cons. Exp (2000 $)	8 Non-Res. Fix. Inv. (2000 $)	9 Corp Profits (Cur. $)	10 Treas. Bills 3-mo.	11 Treas. Notes 10-Year	12 Unempl. Rate (Civ.)	13 Housing Starts (Mil.)	14 Auto/Truck Sales (Mil.)	15 Net Exports (2000 $)
Morgan Stanley	4.1 H	2.0	6.2	2.6	5.9 H	4.9	3.3	11.1	6.3	4.3	5.4	5.0	1.81	17.2	-594.3
Action Economics	4.0	2.6	6.7	2.7	4.0	4.0	3.7 H	8.6	8.1	4.6	5.2	4.9	1.93	17.6	-612.0
Mesirow Financial	4.0	1.4	5.5	1.9	3.6	3.6	3.4	12.2 H	14.8 H	3.8	5.4	5.1	1.53 L	16.4 L	-659.0
Banc of America Corp *	3.8	2.3	6.1	2.2	3.6	3.4	3.2	7.0	10.0	4.0	4.9	5.0	1.85	17.4	-595.0
Deutsche Bank Securities	3.8	2.2	6.0	2.2	2.7	3.8	2.9	6.5	na	5.0 H	5.8	4.9	na	na	-576.5
U S Chamber of Commerce	3.8	1.9	5.8	2.1	5.1	4.1	3.5	4.8	na	4.6	6.0	5.0	1.76	na	-632.0
Macroeconomic Advisers, LLC**	3.8	1.7	5.6	2.0	5.2	4.1	3.4	8.8	4.8	4.1	5.3	5.0	1.76	17.3	-569.4
National Assn. of Realtors	3.8	1.7	5.5	2.4	5.0	4.3	3.3	6.8	4.7	3.9	5.2	4.9	1.81	17.4	-548.0
Nomura Securities	3.8	1.6	5.5	2.2	3.1	4.0	3.4	9.8	7.0	3.5	5.1	5.0	1.75	17.4	-564.0
Fannie Mae	3.7	1.8	5.6	2.0	5.2	3.8	3.4	8.8	5.4	4.1	4.8	5.1	1.82	na	-582.4
Georgia State University*	3.7	1.6	5.4	1.6	4.9	4.0	3.4	7.2	3.9	3.7	5.4	5.2	1.67	18.1 H	-586.4
Credit Suisse First Boston	3.7	1.6	5.3	2.5	4.0	na	3.0	6.0	na	na	na	na	na	na	-629.4
Bear, Stearns & Co., Inc.	3.6	2.9 H	6.6 H	2.9	4.1	3.9	3.7 H	7.6	7.2	4.9	5.6	4.8	1.75	17.5	-672.9
Conference Board*	3.6	2.2	5.9	4.0 H	4.9	3.2	3.3	9.9	2.9	4.6	4.9	4.6	1.67	17.9	-579.9
Comerica Bank*	3.6	2.2	5.8	2.6	3.9	3.7	3.6	7.0	8.5	4.4	5.4	5.1	1.70	17.0	-605.0
National Assn of Home Builders	3.6	1.9	5.5	2.2	3.9	3.5	3.3	7.7	6.0	4.0	5.3	5.1	1.82	17.4	-582.0
National City Corporation	3.6	1.6	5.3	2.4	3.5	3.5	3.4	9.0	2.2	3.8	5.4	5.0	1.76	17.5	-604.9
Moody's Investors Service	3.5	2.3	5.8	2.7	4.2	3.0	1.2	6.8	8.0	4.5	5.4	4.7	1.70	16.9	-599.0
Eaton Corporation	3.5	1.4	5.0	2.2	4.7	3.3	2.8	9.3	8.8	3.9	4.6	5.2	1.76	17.5	-539.8
Wells Capital Management	3.4	2.4	5.8	2.9	4.0	3.0	2.8	10.2	5.6	3.7	4.8	5.1	1.72	16.7	-545.0
J P MorganChase	3.4	2.2	5.6	2.5	4.2	3.9	3.3	8.8	6.1	4.5	5.9	4.9	1.61	16.5	-645.0
Wayne Hummer Investments LLC*	3.4	2.1	5.6	2.5	4.2	3.4	3.2	8.6	6.1	3.6	5.3	5.0	1.69	16.9	-579.0
ClearView Economics	3.4	1.8	5.2	2.8	4.2	3.4	2.9	6.8	6.1	4.1	4.9	4.4 L	1.71	16.9	-621.0
Perna Associates	3.3	2.6	6.0	3.1	3.9	3.3	3.2	7.5	7.9	3.7	5.7	5.0	1.73	16.8	-669.0
Wachovia	3.3	2.6	6.0	2.8	4.8	3.0	2.7	8.7	5.1	4.6	5.6	5.1	1.77	17.1	-617.0
J.W. Coons Advisors	3.3	2.0	5.4	2.2	3.2	3.5	3.3	6.5	7.4	3.8	4.9	5.5	1.75	17.3	-674.0
Stanford Washington Research Group*	3.3	1.9	5.3	2.4	4.7	3.7	3.1	8.2	2.3	4.0	5.2	5.1	1.69	17.1	-571.0
Inforum - Univ. of Maryland	3.3	1.9	5.3	2.4	3.9	3.2	3.0	5.8	8.1	3.7	5.3	5.2	1.84	17.2	-550.0
LaSalle National Bank	3.3	1.8	5.2	1.6	2.8	5.2 H	2.9	6.9	7.5	3.8	5.0	5.3	1.70	17.6	-518.9 H
Standard & Poors Corp.*	3.3	1.8	5.1	1.7	3.6	3.4	2.9	2.9 L	0.3	3.7	5.3	5.1	1.70	16.8	-571.8
General Motors Corporation	3.3	1.8	5.1	2.6	5.0	3.7	3.1	7.4	2.4	4.1	5.3	5.5	1.60	na	-537.7
DaimlerChrysler AG	3.3	1.6	4.9	2.1	3.3	3.0	3.0	5.5	5.9	3.1	4.7	5.2	1.79	na	-577.8
Merrill Lynch	3.3	1.3 L	4.6	1.7	3.6	3.8	3.0	3.7	na	na	na	5.3	1.76	16.4 L	-563.8
FedEx Corporation	3.2	2.6	5.8	3.1	3.6	3.0	3.2	6.9	8.3	3.8	5.8	5.1	1.85	16.5	-588.0
Eggert Economic Enterprises, Inc.	3.2	2.3	5.5	2.5	4.1	3.5	3.0	7.8	8.0	3.3	5.4	5.2	1.68	17.3	-585.0
Turning Points (Micrometrics)	3.2	2.2	5.4	2.3	4.0	2.7	3.0	9.0	11.7	4.0	5.4	5.1	1.96 H	17.5	-668.7
Swiss Re	3.2	1.6	4.9	2.2	4.2	3.0	2.6	9.3	5.5	4.1	5.3	4.7	1.89	17.0	-642.0
Classicalprinciples.com	3.2	1.5	4.7	1.7	1.6 L	2.8	na	na	4.8	4.4	5.4	5.1	na	17.3	na
Goldman Sachs & Co.	3.1	2.6	5.8	2.5	4.2	3.7	2.6	7.7	3.4	3.9	5.4	5.0	1.67	na	-545.4
BMO Nesbitt Burns	3.1	2.1	5.3	2.4	3.1	3.3	2.5	7.3	5.0	4.4	4.8	5.0	1.68	16.7	-585.0
UBS Warburg	3.1	2.0	5.2	2.3	4.7	3.4	2.2 L	9.4	3.0	4.2	5.0	5.2	1.80	na	-614.0
Global Insight	3.1	1.7	4.9	1.6 L	2.8	3.2	2.9	7.0	2.3	3.4	5.1	5.2	1.71	17.1	-568.2
Motorola	3.1	1.7	4.9	1.6 L	2.8	3.2	2.9	7.0	na	3.5	5.2	5.1	1.72	17.4	-568.2
Naroff Economic Advisors	3.0	2.4	5.4	2.5	3.0	3.4	3.3	6.5	6.6	4.6	6.1 H	4.6	1.76	17.5	-540.0
Ford Motor Company*	3.0	2.2	5.1	1.9	4.2	2.9	3.0	7.9	na	3.9	5.5	5.3	1.66	na	-567.8
DuPont**	3.0	2.0	5.0	2.5	3.5	3.0	2.9	6.6	7.0	3.9	5.0	5.2	1.75	17.3	-625.0
Econoclast	3.0	2.0	5.0	2.3	3.5	3.2	2.8	6.5	5.8	3.2	4.6	5.1	1.65	16.8	-590.0
Kellner Economic Advisers	3.0	2.0	5.0	2.2	3.8	3.0	2.9	6.9	6.9	3.8	4.8	5.2	1.71	16.6	-560.0
SOM Economics, Inc.	3.0	1.9	5.0	2.5	3.7	2.7	2.9	4.5	3.7	3.9	4.8	5.0	1.90	16.6	-588.0
Daiwa Institute of Research America	2.8	2.0	4.8	1.8	2.6	2.2 L	3.5	5.8	5.4	1.6 L	3.7 L	5.8 H	1.84	16.8	-746.0 L
UCLA Business Forecasting Proj.*	2.5 L	1.7	4.3 L	1.8	1.9	3.1	2.5	4.4	-0.5 L	3.2	5.2	5.8 H	1.64	16.7	-553.9
2006 Consensus: March Avg.	**3.4**	**2.0**	**5.4**	**2.3**	**3.9**	**3.5**	**3.1**	**7.5**	**5.9**	**3.9**	**5.2**	**5.1**	**1.75**	**17.1**	**-594.2**
Top 10 Avg	3.8	2.5	6.0	3.0	5.1	4.2	3.5	9.9	9.4	4.6	5.7	5.4	1.86	17.6	-543.9
Bottom 10 Avg	3.0	1.5	4.8	1.7	2.6	2.8	2.6	5.0	2.2	3.2	4.7	4.8	1.64	16.6	-663.8
February Avg.	3.4	2.0	5.4	2.3	4.0	3.5	3.1	7.3	6.0	3.9	5.3	5.2	1.73	17.2	-584.4
Number Of Forecasts Changed From A Month Ago:															
Down	15	11	14	11	18	15	15	17	15	7	15	24	6	13	22
Same	25	30	23	33	22	25	23	17	20	27	24	23	27	22	10
Up	11	10	14	7	11	10	12	16	10	15	10	3	15	7	18
March Median	3.3	2.0	5.4	2.4	4.0	3.4	3.1	7.3	6.1	3.9	5.3	5.1	1.75	17.2	-585.0
March Diffusion Index	46 %	49 %	50 %	46 %	43 %	45 %	47 %	49 %	44 %	58 %	45 %	29 %	59 %	43 %	46 %

*Former winner of annual Lawrence R. Klein Award for Blue Chip Forecast Accuracy **Denotes two-time winner.

BASIC DATA SOURCES: [1]Gross Domestic Product (GDP), chained 2000$, National Income and Product Accounts (NIPA), Bureau of Economic Analysis (BEA); [2]GDP Chained Price Index, NIPA, BEA; [3]GDP, current dollars, NIPA, BEA; [4]Consumer Price Index-All Urban Consumers, Bureau of Labor Statistics (BLS); [5]Total Industrial Production, Federal Reserve Board (FRB); [6]Disposable Personal Income, 2000$, NIPA, BEA; [7]Personal Consumption Expenditures, 2000$, NIPA, BEA; [8]Non-residential Fixed Investment, 2000$, NIPA, BEA; [9]Corporate Profits Before Taxes, current dollars, with inventory valuation and capital consumption adjustments, NIPA, BEA; [10]Treasury Bills, 3-month, secondary market, bank discount basis, FRB; [11]10-Year Treasury note yield, FRB; [12]Unemployment Rate, civilian work force, BLS; [13]Housing Starts, Bureau of Census; [14]Total U.S. Auto and Truck sales (includes imports and all weight classes of trucks), BEA; [15]Net Exports of Goods and Services, 2000$, NIPA, BEA.

economists working for investment houses, banks, and businesses. For latest Blue

Chip Consensus survey results, go to www.aspenpublishers.com/bluechip.asp.

The National Association of Business Economists (NABE) conducts a similar type of survey on the future economic condition of the nation. There is a thriving industry of private consulting firms like DRI/McGraw-Hill, Inc. and Evans Economics, which provides economic forecasts based on their own econometric models.

Sources of General Economic Information: Aggregate Economic Data

Economic data are necessary for analyzing the past and forecasting future directions of the economy. The present economic environment and the one expected in the future will bear heavily on the types of investments selected when developing or managing an investment portfolio. Information on economic growth, inflation, employment, personal income, interest rate, money supply, and the like are important economic data that will influence investor decisions. This information is available in many publications from the government, banks, and periodicals. Below is a brief description of some of the major sources of economic data.

Economic Report of the President

It is a summary report concerning the state of the economy that the president sends to the Congress. The report includes over 200 pages covering such issues as monetary policy, inflation, tax policy, the international economy, and review and outlook. In addition, it contains over 100 pages of tables showing historical data for the gross domestic product (GDP), price indexes, savings, employment, production and business activity, corporate profits, agriculture, international statistics, and the like.

Federal Reserve Bulletin

The *Federal Reserve Bulletin* is published monthly by the Board of Governors of the Federal

Reserve System, Washington, D.C. It contains the following:

◆ Monetary data such as money supply figures, interest rates, bank reserves,

◆ Various statistics on commercial banks,

◆ Fiscal variables such as U.S. budget receipts and outlays and federal debt figures, and

◆ Data on international exchange rates and U.S. dealings with foreigners and overseas banks.

Below is a partial listing of the table of contents. Each heading may be divided into more detailed sections that provide information for the previous month, the current year on a monthly basis, and several years of historical annual data.

◆ Domestic Financial Statistics
◆ Federal Reserve Banks
◆ Monetary and Credit Aggregates
◆ Commercial Banks
◆ Financial Markets
◆ Federal Finance
◆ Securities Markets and Corporate Finance
◆ Real Estate
◆ Consumer Installment Credit
◆ Domestic Non Financial Statistics
◆ International Statistics
◆ Securities Holdings and Transactions
◆ Interest and Exchange Rates

The articles from the Federal Reserve Bulletin are available free from the Federal Reserve Board's Internet site (www.federalreserve.gov/pubs/bulletin/default.htm).

Quarterly Chart Book and Annual Chart Book

These two books are also published by the Federal Reserve Board depicting the data in the Federal Reserve Bulletin in graphic form.

The Report on Current Economic Conditions ("The Beige Book")

The Report, informally known as the Beige Book, is released about every six weeks by the Federal Reserve Board. It provides the most recent assessment of the nation's economy, with a regional emphasis. It is used to help the Fed decide on its monetary policy such as changes in interest rates. It can be accessed free from the Federal Reserve Board's Internet site (www.federalreserve.gov/pubs/bulletin/default.htm), as well as the Web site of the individual Federal Reserve Banks.

Monthly Newsletters and Reviews Published by Federal Reserve Banks

Each of the 12 Federal Reserve banks in the Federal Reserve System publishes its own monthly letter or review which includes economic data about its region and sometimes commentary on national issues or monetary policy. These can be accessed through the Internet sites of the individual Federal Reserve Bank . Their addresses and Internet sites are given at the end of the Chapter and in the Appendix.

U.S. Financial Data, Monetary Trends and National Economic Trends

The Federal Reserve Bank of St. Louis, publishes some of the most-comprehensive economic statistics on a weekly and monthly basis. They include: *U.S. Financial Data, Monetary Trends*, and *National Economic Trends*.

U.S. Financial Data is published weekly and includes data on the monetary base, bank reserves, money supply, a breakdown of time deposits and demand deposits, borrowing from the Federal Reserve Banks, and business loans from the large commercial banks. The publication also includes yields and interest rates on a weekly basis on selected short-term and long-term securities.

Monetary Trends, published monthly, includes charts and tables of monthly data. It covers a longer time period than U.S. Financial Data. The tables provide compound annual rates of change, while the graphs include the raw data with trend changes over time. Additional data are available on the federal government debt and its composition by type of holder and on the receipts and expenditures of the government.

National Economic Trends presents monthly economic data on employment, unemployment rates, consumer and producer prices, industrial production, personal income, retail sales, productivity, compensation and labor costs, the GDP implicit price deflator, and GD and its components, disposable personal income, corporate profits, and inventories. This information is presented in graphic form and in tables showing the compounded annual rate of change on a monthly basis.

Economic Indicators

It is a monthly publication of the Council of Economic Advisors. It contains data on income, spending, employment, prices, money and credit, and other factors on both a monthly and an annual basis.

Survey of Current Business, Weekly Business Statistics, and Business Conditions Digest

The Bureau of Economic Analysis of the U.S. Department of Commerce publishes two major economic source books: *Survey of Current Business, Weekly Business Statistics*, and *Business Conditions Digest*.

The *Survey of Current Business* is published monthly and contains monthly and quarterly raw data. It can be accessed free from the Bureau of Economic Analysis' Internet site (www.bea.doc.gov). It presents a monthly update and evaluation of the business situation, analyzing such data as GD, business inventories, personal consumption, fixed investment, exports, labor market statistics, financial data, and much more. For example, if personal consumption expenditures are broken down into subcategories, one would find expenditures on durable goods such as motor vehicles and parts and furniture and equipment; non-durables such as food, energy, clothing, and shoes; and services. *Note:* The Survey can be extremely helpful for industry analysis as it breaks down data into basic industries. For example, data on inventory, new plant and equipment, production, and more can be found on such specific industries as coal, tobacco, chemicals, leather products, furniture, and paper. Even within industries such as lumber, production statistics can be found on hardwoods and softwoods right down to Douglas fir trees, southern pine, and western pine.

Weekly Business Statistics is a weekly update to the Survey. It updates the major series found in the *Survey of Current Business* and includes 27 weekly series and charts of selected series.

To provide a more comprehensive view of what is available in the *Survey of Current Business* and *Weekly Business Statistics*, presented below is a list of the major series updates:

◆ GDP
◆ National Income
◆ Personal Income
◆ Industrial Production
◆ Manufactures' Shipments, Inventories, and Orders
◆ Consumer Price Index
◆ Producer Price Index
◆ Construction Put in Place
◆ Housing Starts and Permits
◆ Retail Trade
◆ Labor Force, Employment, and Earnings
◆ Banking
◆ Consumer Installment Credit
◆ Stock Prices
◆ Value of Exports and Imports
◆ Motor Vehicles

The *Business Conditions Digest*, published monthly, provides the information that differs from the other publications previously discussed in that its primary emphasis is on cyclical indicators of economic activity. The National Bureau of Economic Research (NBER) analyzes and selects the time series data based on each series' ability to be identified as a leading, coincident, or lagging indicator over several decades of aggregate economic activity. Over the years, the NBER has identified the approximate dates when aggregate economic activity reached its cyclical high or low point. Each time series is related to the business cycle. Leading indicators move prior to the business cycle, coincident indicators move with the cycle, and lagging indicators follow directional changes in the business cycle.

Monthly Business Starts

Dun & Bradstreet published "Monthly Business Starts," which report by industry and location the number of businesses on which Dun & Bradstreet opened files in a given month.

Other Sources of Economic Data

In addition to what we covered so far, much other data is available in other publications. They are summarized below.

◆ Many universities have bureaus of business research that provide statistical data on a statewide or regional basis.

◆ Major banks, such as Bank of America, Citicorp, Morgan Guaranty, and Manufacturer's Hanover, publish monthly or weekly letters or economic reviews, including raw data and analysis.

◆ Several other government sources are available, such as Economic Indicators and the *Annual Economic Report of the President* prepared by the Council of Economic Advisors.

◆ Moody's, Value Line's, and Standard & Poor's investment services all publish economic data along with much other market-related information.

◆ Economy.com, Inc. is an independent provider of economic, financial, country, and industry research designed to meet the diverse planning and information needs of businesses, governments, and professional investors worldwide.

Some useful web sites

The following Internet sites offer critical information about economic analysis:

Web Address	Primary Focus
www.economy.com	Economic data and user-friendly analysis
stats.bls.gov	Macroeconomic Data
minneapolisfed.org/research/qr/	Minneapolis Federal Reserve Bank
www.bea.doc.gov	Macroeconomic Economic Data
www.bls.gov	Most Economic Statistics And Data
www.federalreserve.gov/pubs/bulletin/default.htm	Federal Reserve Board -- Data & Statistics
www.bos.frb.org	Boston Federal Reserve Bank
www.census.gov/econ/www	Census Data
www.conference-board.org/	Macroeconomic Data
www.clevelandfed.org/index.cfm	Cleveland Federal Reserve Bank
www.dallasfed.org	Dallas Federal Reserve Bank
www.fedstats.gov	Government Economic Data And Statistics
www.frbatlanta.org	Atlanta Federal Reserve Bank
www.chicagofed.org/	Chicago Federal Reserve Bank
www.frbsf.org	San Francisco Federal Reserve Bank
www.kc.frb.org	Kansas City Federal Reserve Bank
www.moodys.com	Economic Commentary
www.ny.frb.org	New York Federal Reserve Bank
www.phil.frb.org	Philadelphia Federal Reserve Bank
www.rich.frb.org	Richmond Federal Reserve Bank
www.stls.frb.org	St. Louis Federal Reserve Bank
www.whitehouse.gov/fsbr/esbr.html	Economic Statistics Briefing Room

Chapter 13
Financial and Earning Forecasting

Financial forecasting, an essential element of planning, is the basis for *budgeting* activities. It is also needed when estimating future financing requirements. The company may look either internally or externally for financing. Internal financing refers to cash flow generated by the company's normal operating activities. External financing refers to capital provided by parties external to the company.

You need to analyze how to estimate *external* financing requirements. Basically, forecasts of future sales and related expenses provide the firm with the information to project future external financing needs. The chapter discusses (1) the *percent-of-sales method* to determine the amount of external financing needed, (2) the CPA's involvement in prospective financial statements, and (3) earnings forecast.

The Percent-of-Sales Method for Financial Forecasting

Percentage of sales is the most widely used method for projecting the company's financing needs. This method involves estimating the various expenses, assets, and liabilities for a future period as a percent of the sales forecast and then using these percentages, together with the projected sales, to construct pro forma balance sheets. *Note:* Pro forma financial statements are part of the budgeting process. Normally, the last pro forma statement prepared is the balance sheet. All other elements of the budget process must be completed before it can be developed.

Basically, forecasts of future sales and their related expenses provide the firm with the information needed to project its future needs for financing. The basic steps in projecting financing needs are:

1. Project the firm's sales. The sales forecast is the initial most important step. Most other forecasts (budgets) follow the sales forecast.

2.   Project additional variables such as expenses.

3.   Estimate the level of investment in current and fixed assets required to support the projected sales.

4.   Calculate the firm's financing needs.

The following example illustrates how to develop a pro forma balance sheet and determine the amount of external financing needed.

Example 13.1

Assume that sales for 20x0 = $20, projected sales for 20x1 = $24, net income = 5% of sales, and the dividend payout ratio = 40%. Figure 13.1 illustrates the method, step by step. All dollar amounts are in millions.

The steps for the computations are outlined as follows:

Step 1.

Express those balance sheet items that vary directly with sales as a percentage of sales. Any item such as long-term debt that does not vary directly with sales is designated "n.a.," or "not applicable."

Step 2.

Multiply these percentages by the 20x1 projected sales = $24 to obtain the projected amounts as shown in the last column.

Figure 13.1 Pro Forma Balance Sheet (in Millions of Dollars)

	Present (20x0)	% of Sales (20x0 Sales=$20)	Projected (20x1 Sales=$24)
ASSETS			
Current assets	2	10	2.4
Fixed assets	4	20	4.8
Total assets	6		7.2
LIABILITIES AND STOCKHOLDERS' EQUITY			
Current liabilities	2	10	2.4
Long-term debt	2.5	n.a.	2.5
Total liabilities	4.5		4.9
Common stock	0.1	n.a.	0.1
Paid-in-Capital	0.2	n.a.	0.2
Retained earnings	1.2		1.92 (a)
Total equity	1.5		2.22
Total liabilities and stockholders' equity	6		7.12
			0.08 (b) Total financing needed
			7.2

(a) 20x1 retained earnings = 20x0 retained earnings + projected net income -cash dividends paid

=$1.2+5%($24)-40%[5%($24)]

=$1.2+$1.2-$0.48=$2.4-$0.48=$1.92

(b) External financing needed=projected total assets - (projected total liabilities + projected equity)

=$7.2-($4.9+$2.22)=$7.2-$7.12=$0.08

Step 3.

Simply insert figures for long-term debt, common stock and paid-in-capital from the 20x0 balance sheet.

Step 4.

Compute 20x1 retained earnings as shown in (a).

Step 5.

Sum the asset accounts, obtaining a total projected assets of $7.2, and also add the projected liabilities and equity to obtain $7.12, the total financing provided. Since liabilities and equity must total $7.2, but only $7.12 is projected, we have a shortfall of $0.08 "external financing needed."

Although the forecast of additional funds required can be made by setting up pro forma balance sheets as described above, it is often easier to use the following formula:

External funds needed (EFN)	=	Required increase in assets	-	Spontaneous increase in liabilities	-	Increase in retained earnings
EFN	=	(A/S) ΔS	-	(L/S) ΔS	-	(PM)(PS)(1-d)

where A/S = Assets that increase spontaneously with sales as a percentage of sales.

L/S = Liabilities that increase spontaneously with sales as a percentage of sales.

ΔS = Change in sales.

PM = Profit margin on sales.

PS = Projected sales

d = Dividend payout ratio.

Example 13.2

In Example 13.1, A/S = $6/$20 = 30%

L/S = $2/$20 = 10%

ΔS = ($24 - $20) = $4

PM = 5% on sales

PS = $24

d = 40%

Plugging these figures into the formula yields:

EFN = 0.3($4) - 0.1($4) - (0.05)($24)(1 - 0.4)

= $1.2 - $0.4 - $0.72 = $0.08

Thus, the amount of external financing needed is $800,000, which can be raised by issuing notes payable, bonds, stocks, or any combination of these financing sources.

The major advantage of the percent-of-sales method of financial forecasting is that it is simple and inexpensive to use. Two important assumptions behind the use of the method are:

1.   The firm is operating at full capacity. This means that the company has no sufficient productive capacity to absorb a projected increase in sales and thus requires additional investment in assets. Therefore, the method must be used with extreme caution if excess capacity exists in certain asset accounts.

2.   The asset-to-sales ratios must be constant when applying the percentage-of-sales forecasting method. If the current levels of assets are considered to be optimal for the current sales level, that is, if assets are efficiently used, the asset-to-sales ratios are constant.

To obtain a more precise projection of the firm's future financing needs, however, the preparation of a cash budget may be required.

The Certified Public Accountant's Involvement and Responsibility with Prospective Financial Statements

Prospective financial statements encompass financial forecasts and financial projections. Pro forma financial statements and partial presentations are specifically excluded from this category.

Financial forecasts are prospective financial statements that present, to the best of the responsible party's knowledge and belief, an entity's expected financial position, results of operations, and cash flows. They are based on assumptions about conditions actually expected to exist and the course of action expected to be taken.

Financial projections are prospective financial statements that present, to the best of the responsible party's knowledge and belief, an entity's expected financial position, results of operations, and cash flows. They are based on assumptions about conditions expected to exist and the course of action expected to be taken, given one or more hypothetical (i.e., "what-if") assumptions.

Responsible parties are those who are responsible for the underling assumptions. While the responsible party is usually management, it may be a third party. EXAMPLE: If a client is negotiating with a bank for a large loan, the bank may stipulate the assumptions to be used. Accordingly, in this case, the bank would represent the responsible party.

The CPA's Reporting Responsibilities Regarding Prospective Financial Statements

Statement on Standards for Attestation Engagements #10 specifically precludes an accountant from compiling, examining, or applying agreed-upon procedures to prospective financial statements that fail to include a summary of significant assumptions. The practice standards in the Statement are not applicable:

To engagements involving prospective financial statements that are restricted to internal use

To those used solely in litigation support services (e.g., in circumstances where the practitioner is serving as an expert witness)

The Use of Prospective Financial Statements

The intended use of an entity's prospective financial statements governs the type of prospective financial statements to be presented.

◆ When all entity's prospective financial statements are for general use, only a financial forecast is to be presented. "General use" means that the statements will be used by persons not negotiating directly with the responsible party. **Example**: in a public offering of a tax shelter interest.

◆ When an entity's prospective financial statements are for limited use, either a financial forecast or a financial projection may be presented. "Limited use" refers to situations where the statements are to be used by the responsible party alone or by the responsible party and those parties negotiating directly with the responsible party. **Example**: If a client is negotiating directly with a bank, either a forecast or a projection is appropriate.

Compilation of Prospective Statements

Compilation procedures applicable to prospective financial statements are not designed to provide any form of assurance on the presentation of the statements or the underlying assumptions.

They are essentially the same as those applicable to historical financial statements. Additional procedures:

◆ Inquire of the responsible party as to the underlying assumptions developed.

◆ Compile or obtain a list of the underlying assumptions and consider the possibility of obvious omissions or inconsistencies.

◆ Verify the mathematical accuracy of the assumptions.

◆ Read the prospective financial statements in order to identify departures from AICPA presentation guidelines.

◆ Obtain a client representation letter in order to confirm that the responsible party acknowledges its responsibility for the prospective statements (including the underlying assumptions).

Caution: An accountant is precluded from compiling forecasts and projections that do not present the summary of significant assumptions. Furthermore, the practitioner should not compile a projection that foils to identify the underlying hypothetical assumptions or describe the limitations on the utility of the projection.

The accountant's report on compiled prospective financial statements should include:

◆ An identification of the prospective financial statements presented

◆ A statement as to the level of service provided and the fact that the prospective financial statements were compiled in accordance with attestation standards established by the AICPA

◆ A statement describing the limited scope of a compilation and the fact that no opinion or any other form of assurance is being expressed

◆ A warning that the prospective results may not materialize

◆ A statement that the accountant is under no responsibility to update his or her report for conditions occurring after the compilation report is issued

◆ The date of the report, which should coincide with the completion of the compilation procedures

◆ The accountant's signature

◆ In the case of a projection, a separate middle paragraph describing the limitations on the utility of the statements

◆ A separate paragraph when the statements present the expected results in the form of a range of values

◆ If the accountant is not independent, a statement as to this fact (No disclosure should be made as to the reasons why the accountant feels that he or she is not independent.)

◆ A separate explanatory paragraph when the prospective statements contain a departure from AICPA presentation guidelines or omit disclosures unrelated to the significant assumptions

Under the minimum presentation guidelines, prospective financial statements may take the form of complete basic statements or be limited to certain minimum items (when the items would be presented for the period's historical statements). A presentation is partial if it omits one or more of the following: (1) sales or gross revenues, (2) gross profit or cost of sales, (3) unusual or infrequently occurring items, (4) provision for income taxes, (5) discontinued operations or extraordinary items, (6) income from continuing operations, (7) net income, (8) primary and fully diluted earnings per share, (9) significant cash flows.

Figure 13.2 is a standard report on the compiled forecasts. Figure 13.3 presents a standard report on compiled projections.

Figure 13.2: Standard Report on Compiled Forecasts

I (We) have compiled the accompanying forecasted balance sheet, statement of income, retained earnings, and cash flows of Future Corporation as of (at) December 31, 20XX and for the year then ending, in accordance with attestation standards established by the American Institute of Certified Public Accountants.

A compilation is limited to presenting in the form of a forecast information that is the representation of management (or other responsible party) and does not include evaluation of the support for the assumptions underlying the forecast. I (We) have not examined the forecast and, accordingly, do not express an opinion or any other form of assurance on the accompanying statements or assumptions. Furthermore, there will usually be differences between the forecasted and actual results, because events and circumstances frequently do not occur as expected, and those differences may be material. I (We) have no responsibility to update this report for events and circumstances occurring after the date of this report.

Figure 13.3: Standard Report on Compiled Projections

I(we) have compiled the accompanying projected balance sheet, statements of income, retained earnings, and cash flows of Future Corporation as of December 31, 20XX, and for the year then ending, in accordance with attestation standards established by the American Institute of Certified Public Accountants.

The accompanying projection, and this report, were prepared for [state special purpose, for example, "the Takeover Corporation for the purpose of negotiating a buyout of the Company,"] and should not be used for any other purpose.

A compilation is limited to presenting in the form of a projection information that is the representation of management (or other responsible party) and does not include evaluation of the support for the assumptions underlying the projection. I (We) have not examined the projection and, accordingly, do not express an opinion or any other form of assurance on the accompanying statements or assumptions. Furthermore, even if [describe hypothetical assumption, for example, "the buyout is consummated"] there will usually be differences between the projected and actual results, because events and circumstances frequently do not occur as expected, and those differences may be material. I (We) have no responsibility to update this report for events and circumstances occurring after the date of this report.

Earnings Forecast

For many years financial analysts have predicted earnings per share and stock price performance. Considerable emphasis has been placed on such forecasts in order to provide guidance to investors. Recently, management forecast disclosures in financial statements have placed greater emphasis on the development of forecasting methodology in this area. The accuracy of these earnings forecasts has been given much attention recently primarily due to the SEC's position on financial forecasts.

Security Analysts vs. Time-Series Models

Forecasts of earnings per share for business firms are published by both management and security analysts. Unfortunately, however, the accuracy of EPS forecasts by security analysts have been shown to be little if any better than that produced by some "naive" models such as extrapolating the past trend of earnings. Indeed, it increasingly appears that the change in EPS may be a random variable.

Projections of EPS are frequently made by independent security analysts. Examples of forecast sources include (1) Value Line Investment Survey, (2) Lynch, Jones and Ryan's Institutional Brokers Estimate System (IBES), (3) Standard & Poor's The Earnings Forecaster, and (4) Zacks Investment Research (www.zacks.com or www. zackadvisor.com.

Figure 13.4 presents an excerpt from the monthly report from Zacks Investment Research's Icarus Service which contains various earnings forecasts by individual security analysts.

Figure 13.5 summarizes the pros and cons of both approaches.

Figure 13.4: Extract from Monthly Summary Report of the IBES Service

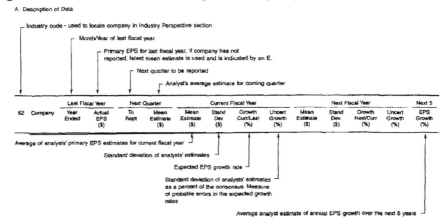

acks Investment Research, Inc. *The Icarus Service* (Chicago, Illinois).

Figure 13.5: Pros and Cons of Security Analyst and Univariate Time-Series Model Approaches to Forecasting

SECURITY ANALYST APPROACH TO FORECASTING

Pros
1. Ability to incorporate information from many sources.
2. Ability to adjust to structural change immediately.
3. Ability to update continually as new information becomes available.

Cons
1. High initial setup cost and high ongoing cost to monitor numerous variables, make company visits, and so on.
2. Heavy dependence on the skills of a single individual.
3. Analyst may have an incentive not to provide an unbiased forecast (e.g., due to pressure to conform to consensus forecasts).
4. Analyst may be manipulated by company officials (at least in the short run).

UNIVARIATE TIME SERIES MODEL APPROACH TO FORECASTING

Pros
1. Ability to detect and exploit systematic patterns in the past series.
2. Relatively low degree of subjectivity in the forecasting (especially given the availability of computer algorithms to identify and estimate models).
3. Low cost and ease of updating.
4. Ability to compute confidence intervals around the forecasts.

Cons
1. Limited number of observations available for newly formed firms, firms with structural change, and so on.
2. Financial statement data may not satisfy distributional assumptions of time series model used.
3. Inability to update forecasts between successive interim or annual earnings releases.
4. Difficulty of communicating approach to clients (especially the statistical methodology used in identifying and estimating univariate models).

Table 13.1 shows sources of earnings forecasting data preferred by financial analysts.

Table 13.1: What Are Your Present Sources of Earnings Forecasting Data?

Rank	1	2	3	4	5
Company contacts	56	28	24	8	9
Own research	55	15	5	1	
Industry statistics	19	14	14	7	
Other analysis	12	17	2	8	11
Historical financial data	8	12	8	5	4
Economic forecasts	7	7	10	3	
Competition	1	7	2	6	1
Computer simulation					2
Field trips		1			
Government agencies			2		
Industry & trade sources	1	7	17	3	5
Public relations of a promotional nature					1
Retired directors					1
Rumor					2
Wall Street sources	1	4	9	3	4
Rank					

1 = most preferred

5 = least preferred

Source: Carper, Brent W., Barton Jr., Frank M., Wunder Haroldene F. "The Future of Forecasting." *Management Accounting*. August, 2005. pp. 27-31.

Pro Forma EPS Confusion

Many companies are reporting pro forma EPS numbers along with U.S. GAAP-based EPS numbers in the financial information provided to investors. Pro forma earnings typically exceed GAAP earnings because the pro forma numbers exclude such items as restructuring charges, impairments of assets, R&D expenditures, and stock compensation expense. Some examples are given below

Company	GAAP EPS	Pro Forma EPS
Broadcom	(6.36)	(0.13)
Corning	(0.24)	0.09
General Motors	(0.41)	0.85
Honeywell	(0.38)	0.44
International Paper	(0.57)	0.14
Qualcomm	(0.06)	0.20

Source: Company Web site press releases.

The SEC has expressed concern that pro forma earnings may be misleading. For example, Trump Hotels & Casino Resorts (DJT) was cited for abuses related to its 1999 third-quarter pro forma EPS release. The SEC noted that the firm misrepresented its operating results by excluding a material, one-time $81.4 million charge in its pro forma EPS statement and including an undisclosed nonrecurring gain of $17.2 million. The gain enabled DJT to post a profit in the quarter. The SEC emphasized that DJT's pro forma EPS statement deviated from conservative U.S. GAAP reporting. Therefore, it was "fraudulent" because it created a "false and misleading impression" that DJT had actually (1) recorded a profit in the third quarter of 1999 and (2) exceeded consensus earnings expectations by enhancing its operating fundamentals.

The Sarbanes-Oxley Act of 2002 requires the SEC to develop regulations on pro forma reporting. As a consequence, the SEC now requires companies that provide pro forma financial information to make sure that the information is not misleading. In addition, a reconciliation between pro forma and CAAP information is required.

Sources: SEC Accounting and Enforcement Release No. 1499 (January 16, 2002); "SEC Proposes Rules to implement Sarbanes-Oxley Act Reforms," SEC Press Release 2002-155 (October 30, 2002).

Conclusion

Financial forecasting, an essential element of planning, is a vital function of financial managers. It is needed where the future financing needs are being estimated. Basically, forecasts of future sales and their related expenses provide the firm with the information needed to project its financing requirements.   Furthermore, financial forecasting involves earnings forecasts which provide useful information concerning the expectations of a firm's future total market return. This is of interest to security analysts and investors. Also presented was a CPA's involvement with prospective financial statements.

Chapter 14
Cash Flow Forecasting

Preparation of a cash budget requires incorporation of sales projections and credit terms, collection percentages, estimated purchases and payment terms, and other cash receipts and disbursements. In other words, preparation of the cash budget requires consideration of both inflows and outflows. A cash budget may be prepared monthly or even weekly to facilitate cash planning and control. The purpose is to anticipate cash needs while minimizing the amount of idle cash. The cash receipts section of the budget includes all sources of cash. One such source is the proceeds of loans.

A forecast of cash collections and potential writeoffs of accounts receivable is essential in *cash budgeting* and in judging the appropriateness of current credit and discount policies. The critical step in making such a forecast is estimating the cash collection and bad debt percentages to be applied to sales or accounts receivable balances. This chapter discusses two methods of estimating *cash collection rates* (or *payment proportions*) and illustrates how these rates are used for cash budgeting purposes.

The first approach involves account analysis. The second approach offers a more pragmatic method of estimating collection and bad debt percentages by relating credit sales and collection data. This method employs *regression analysis*. By using these approaches, a financial planner should be able to:

◆ Estimate future cash collections from accounts receivable

◆ Establish an allowance for doubtful accounts

◆ Provide a valuable insight into better methods of managing accounts receivable

Account Analysis

The most straightforward way to estimate collection percentages is to compute the percentages of collections realized from past months. Once the experience has been analyzed, the results can be adjusted for trends and applied to the credit sales portrayed in the sales forecast. An example illustrates the technique.

Total Month	Accounts Receivable	Aging by $ 0-30	30-60	60-90	Over 90
J	$50,000	$35,000	$ 8,000	$2,000	$ 5,000
F	52,000	40,000	3,200	1,000	7,800
M	58,000	45,000	2,000	600	10,400
A	71,000	48,600	6,000	2,200	14,200

Total Month	Accounts Receivable	Aging by % 0-30	30-60	60-90	Over 90
J	100%	70%	16%	4%	10%
F	100%	77%	6%	2%	15%
M	100%	78%	3%	1%	18%
A	100%	68%	8%	3%	20%

Example 14.1

Assume that an analysis of collection experience for August sales revealed the following collection data:

Description		% of Total Credit Sales
Collected in	August	2.3
	September	80.2
	October	9.9
	November	5.1
	December	.5
Cash discounts		1.0
Bad debt losses.		1.0
	Total	100.0

If next year's sales in August could be expected to fall into the same pattern, then application of the percentages to estimated August credit sales would determine the probable monthly distribution of collections. The same analysis applied to each month of the year would result in a reasonably reliable basis for collection forecasting. The worksheet (August column) for cash collections might look as follows:

Description

Month of Sale	% Total	Sales Net	August Collection
April	.5	$168,000	$ 840
May	4.2	192,000	8,064
June	8.9	311,100	2,768
July	82.1	325,600	267,318
August	2.3	340,000	7,820
Total Collections...			286,810
Cash Discounts (July)	1.0	325,600	(3,250)
Losses	1.0	(3,400)	
Total..			$ 280160

Lagged Regression Approach

A more scientific approach to estimating cash collection percentages (or payment proportions) is to utilize *multiple regression*. We know that there is typically a time lag between the point of a credit sale and realization of cash. More specifically, the lagged effect of credit sales and cash inflows is distributed over a number of periods, as follows:

$$C_t = b_1 S_{t-1} + b_2 S_{t-2} + ...b_i S_{t-i}$$

where C_t = cash collection in month t

S_t = credit sales made in period t

$b_1, b_2,...b_i$ = collection percentages (the same as P'_i,) and

i = number of periods lagged

By using the regression method discussed previously, we will be able to estimate these collection rates. We can utilize Excel or special packages such as *SAS, SPSS,* or *MINITAB.*

It should be noted that the cash collection percentages, $(b_1, b_2,...,b_i)$ may not add up to 100 percent because of the possibility of bad debts. Once we estimate these percentages by using the regression method, we should be able to compute the bad debt percentage with no difficulty.

Table 14.1 shows the regression results using actual monthly data on credit sales and cash inflows for a real company. Equation I can be written as follows:

$$C_t = 60.6\%(S_{t-1}) + 19.3\%(S_{t-2}) + 8.8\%(S_{t-3})$$

This result indicates that the receivables generated by the credit sales are collected at the following rates: first month after sale, 60.6 percent; second month after sale, 19.3 percent; and third month after sale, 8.8 percent. The bad debt percentage is computed as 6.3 percent (100-93.7%).

It is important to note, however, that these collection and bad debt percentages are probabilistic variables; that is, variables whose values cannot be known with precision. However, the standard error of the regression coefficient and the 5-value permit us to assess the probability that the true percentage is between specified limits. The confidence interval takes the following form:

$$b \pm t\, S_b$$

where S_b = standard error of the coefficient.

Table 14.1: Regression Results for Cash Collection (C_t)

Independent Variables		Equation I	Equation II
	S_{t-1}	0.606[a]	0.596[a]
		(0.062)[b]	(0.097)
	S_{t-2}	0.193[a]	0.142
		(0.085)	(0.120)
	S_{t-3}	0.088	0.043
		(0.157)	(0.191)
	St-4		0.136
			(0.800)
R^2		0.754	0.753
Durbin-Watson		2.52[c]	2.48[c]
Standard Error of the estimate(S_e)		11.63	16.05
Number of monthly observations		21	20
Bad debt percentages		0.063	0.083

a   Statistically significant at the 5% significance level.

b   This figure in the parentheses is the standard error of the e estimate for the coefficient (S_b).

c   No autocorrelation present at the 5% significance level.

Example 14.2

To illustrate, assuming $t = 2$ as rule of thumb at the 95 percent confidence level, the true collection percentage from the prior month's sales will be

$$60.6\% \pm 2(6.2\%) = 60.6\% \pm 12.4\%$$

Turning to the estimation of cash collections and allowance for doubtful accounts, the following values are used for illustrative purposes:

$S_{t-1} = \$77.6$, $S_{t-2} = \$58.5$, $S_{t-3} = \$76.4$, and forecast average monthly net credit sales $= \$75.2$

Then, (a) the forecast cash collection for period t would be

$$C_t = 60.6\%(77.6) + 19.3\%(58.5) + 8.8\%(76.4) = \$65.04$$

If the financial manager wants to be 95 percent confident about this forecast value, then the interval would be set as follows:

$$C_t \pm t\,S_e$$

where $S_e = $ standard error of the estimate.

To illustrate, using $t = 2$ as a rule of thumb at the 95 percent confidence level, the true value for cash collections in period t will be

$$\$65.04 \pm 2(11.63) = \$65.04 \pm 23.26$$

(b) the estimated allowance for uncollectible accounts for period t will be

$$6.3\% (\$75.2) = \$4.74$$

By using the limits discussed so far, financial planners can develop flexible (or probabilistic) cash budgets, where the lower and upper limits can be interpreted as pessimistic and optimistic outcomes, respectively. They can also simulate a cash budget in an attempt to determine both the expected change in cash collections for each period and the variation in this value.

In preparing a conventional cash inflow budget, the financial manager considers the various sources of cash, including cash on account, sale of assets, loan proceeds, and so on. Cash collections from customers are emphasized, since that is the greatest problem in this type of budget.

Example 14.3

	September	October	November	December
	Actual	Actual	Estimated	Estimated
Cash sales	$ 7,000	$ 6,000	$ 8,000	$ 6,000
Credit sales	50,000	48,000	62,000	80,000
Total sales	57,000	54,000	70,000	86,000

Past experience indicates net collection normally occurs in the following pattern:

◆ No collections are made in the month of sale.

◆ Eighty percent of the sales of any month are collected in the following month.

◆ Nineteen percent of sales are collected in the second following month.

◆ One percent of sales are uncollectible.

We can project total cash receipts for November and December as follows:

		November	December
Cash receipts:			
Cash sales		$ 8,000	$ 6,000
Cash collections:			
September sales:	$50,000 (19%)	9,500	
October sales:	$48,000 (80%)	38,400	
	$48,000(19%)		9,120
November sales:	$62,000(80%)		49,600
	Total cash receipts	$55,900	$64,720

Is Cash Flow Software Available?

Computer software allows for day-to-day cash management, determining cash balances, planning and analyzing cash flows, finding cash shortages, investing cash surpluses, accounting for cash transactions, automating accounts receivable and payable, and dial-up banking. Computerization improves availability, accuracy, timeliness, and monitoring of cash information at minimal cost. Daily cash information aids in planning how to use cash balances. It enables the integration of different kinds of related cash information such as collections on customer accounts and cash balances, and the effect of cash payments on cash balances.

Spreadsheet program software such as *Microsoft's Excel, Lotus 1-2-3,* and *Quattro Pro* can assist you in developing cash budgets and answering a variety of "what-if" questions. For example, you can see the effect on cash flow from different scenarios (e.g., the purchase and sale of different product lines).

There are computer software packages specially designed for cash management. Three popular ones are briefly described below.

1. Quicken (quicken.intuit.com/?src=www.quicken.com)

This program is a fast, easy to use, inexpensive accounting program that can help a small business manage its cash flow. Bills can be recorded as postdated transactions when they arrive; the program's *Billminder* feature automatically reminds the payer when bills are due. Then, checks can be printed for due bills with a few mouse and/or keystrokes. Similarly, he/she can record invoices and track aged receivables. Together, these features help maximize cash on hand.

2. Up Your Cash Flow XT (www.cashplan.com/)

Up Your Cash Flow XT creates financial forecasts for small to mid-size businesses with many features. This program automatically prepared spreadsheets for profit/loss forecasts, cash flow budgets, projected balance sheet, payroll analysis, term loan amortization schedule, sales/cost of sales by product, ratio analysis, and graphs. Accountants and consultants can use this software to provide management advice, secure financing, assist troubled businesses and offer other valuable services. CFOs, Controllers and financial managers use Up Your Cash Flow XT to make fast company budgets, manage cash flow and reach desired levels of profitability. Over 30 reports show the impact of Sales, Expenses, Cost of Sales, Financing, Payroll, Inventory and more. You can run "what-if" scenarios to see how changes in business activity affect the bottom line and compare plan to actual data to measure how close you've come to your goals and be able to predict any cash shortfalls before they happen.

3. Cashflow Plan – Cashflow Forecast Software (www.planware. org/cashshareware.htm)

Cashflow Plan is a range of powerful, easy-to-use software packages for preparing comprehensive monthly cashflow projections for 12 months ahead. You can use it for cashflow planning, budgets, business planning, fund raising etc. for young & established businesses of all sizes and types. It incorporates a roll-forward facility to help you to speedily update the projections every month. More powerful versions also include a tool for consolidating projections. Cashflow Plan will help plan your business's cash requirements, improve control over cashflows and conserve cash resources. It will be especially useful if you need to forecast cashflows in the context of:

◆ Tight cash/profit margins

◆ Limited financial resources

◆ Planning for growth or radical change

◆ Compiling cash budgets

◆ Preparing business improvement plans

Cashflow Plan is pre-formatted to handle the very wide range of the variables and functions normally encountered when preparing cashflow and financial projections. Based on your assumptions, it compiles detailed, fully-integrated financial projections for the coming year on a monthly basis, and for the initial three months on a weekly basis. It automatically produces 20+ pro-forma financial and management reports together with numerous graphs for key variables.

Conclusion

Two methods of estimating the expected collectible and uncollectible patterns were presented. The regression approach is relatively inexpensive to use in the sense that it does not require a lot of data. All it requires is data on cash collections, and credit sales. Furthermore, credit sales values are all predetermined; we use previous months' credit sales to forecast cash collections, that is, there is no need to forecast credit sales. The model also allows you to make all kinds of statistical inferences about the cash collection percentages and forecast values. Extensions of these models can be made toward setting credit and discount policies. By computing long-term collections and bad debts for each policy, an optimal policy can be chosen that maximizes expected long-run profits per period.

The most direct way of preparing a cash budget requires incorporation of sales projections and credit terms, collection percentages, estimated purchases and payment terms, and other cash receipts and disbursements. In other words, preparation of the cash budget requires consideration of both inflows and outflows.

Chapter 15

Analysis of Cost Behavior and Cost Prediction

Not all costs behave in the same way. There are certain costs that vary in proportion to changes in volume or activity, such as labor hours and machine hours. There are other costs that do not change even though volume changes. An understanding of cost behavior is helpful to budgeters, cost analysts, and managerial accountants as follows:

1. Cost prediction
2. Break-even and contribution margin analysis
3. Appraisal of divisional performance
4. Flexible budgeting
5. Short-term choice decisions
6. Transfer pricing decisions

A Look at Costs by Behavior

Depending on how a cost will react or respond to changes in the level of activity, costs may be viewed as variable, fixed, or mixed (semi-variable). This classification is made within a specified range of activity, called the *relevant range*. The relevant range is the volume zone within which the behavior of variable costs, fixed costs, and selling prices can be predicted with reasonable accuracy.

Variable Costs

Variable costs vary in total with changes in volume or level of activity. Examples of variable costs include the costs of direct materials, direct labor, and sales commissions. The following factory overhead items fall in the variable cost category:

Variable Factory Overhead

Supplies	Receiving Costs
Fuel and Power	Overtime Premium
Spoilage and Defective Work	

Fixed Costs

Fixed costs do not change in total regardless of the volume or level of activity. Examples include advertising expense, salaries, and depreciation. The following factory overhead items fall in the fixed cost category:

Fixed Factory Overhead

Property Taxes	Rent on Factory Building
Depreciation	Indirect Labor
Insurance	Patent Amortization

Mixed (Semi-Variable) Costs

Mixed costs contain both a fixed element and a variable one. Salespersons' compensation including salary and commission is an example. The following factory overhead items may be considered mixed costs:

Mixed Factory Overhead

Supervision	Maintenance and Repairs
Inspection	Workmen's Compensation Insurance
Service Department Costs	Employer's Payroll Taxes
Utilities Rental of Delivery Truck	
Fringe Benefits	Quality Costs
Cleanup Costs	

Note that factory overhead, taken as a whole, would be a perfect example of mixed costs. Figure 15.1 displays how each of these three types of costs varies with changes in volume.

Figure 15.1: Cost Behavior Patterns

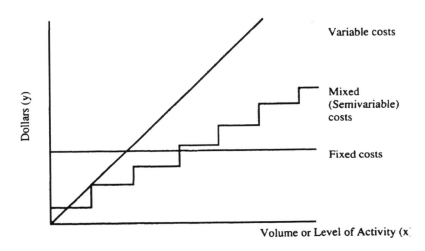

Analysis of Mixed (Semi-Variable) Costs

For forecasting, planning, control, and decision making purposes, mixed costs need to be separated into their variable and fixed components. Since the mixed costs contain both fixed and variable elements, the analysis takes the following mathematical form, which is called a cost-volume formula (or cost function):

$$Y = a + bX$$

where $Y =$ the mixed cost to be broken up.

$X =$ cost driver (any given measure of activity such as direct labor hours, machine hours, or production volume).

$a =$ the fixed cost component.

$b =$ the variable rate per unit of X.

Separating the mixed cost into its fixed and variable components is the same thing as estimating the parameter values a and b in the cost function. There are several methods available to be used for this purpose including the high-low method and regression analysis. They are discussed below.

The High-Low Method

The high-low method, as the name indicates, uses two extreme data points to determine the values of a (the fixed cost portion) and b (the variable rate) in the equation $Y = a + bX$. The extreme data points are the highest representative X-Y pair and the lowest representative X-Y pair. The activity level X, rather than the mixed cost item y, governs their selection.

The high-low method is explained, step by step, as follows:

Step 1: Select the highest pair and the lowest pair

Step 2: Compute the variable rate, b, using the formula:

$$\text{Variable rate} = \frac{\text{Difference in cost Y}}{\text{Difference in activity X}}$$

Step 3: Compute the fixed cost portion as:
Fixed cost portion = Total mixed cost - Variable cost

Example 15.1

Flexible Manufacturing Company decided to relate total factory overhead costs to direct labor hours (DLH) to develop a cost function in the form of $Y = a + b X$. Twelve monthly observations are collected. They are given in Table 15.1.

Table 15.1: Data on Factory Overhead and Direct Labor Hours

Month	Factory Overhead (Y)	Direct Labor Hours (X)
1	2510	82
2	2479	84
3	2080	74
4	2750	113
5	2330	77
6	2690	91
7	2480	95
8	2610	117
9	2910	116
10	2730	103
11	2760	120
12	2109	76

The high-low points selected from the monthly observations are

	X	Y
High	116 hours	$2910 (September pair)
Low	74	2080 (March pair)
Difference	42 hours	$830

$$\text{Variable rate b} = \frac{\text{Difference in Y}}{\text{Difference in X}} = \frac{\$830}{42 \text{ hours}} = \$19.76 \text{ per DLH}$$

The fixed cost portion is computed as:

	High	Low
Factory overhead (Y)	$2910	$2080
Variable expense ($19.76 per DLH)	(2292.16)*	(1462.24)*
	617.84	617.84

*$19.76 x 116 hours = $2292.16; $19.76 x 74 hours = $1462.24

Therefore, the cost volume formula for factory overhead is

$617.74 fixed plus $19.76 per DLH.

The high-low method is simple and easy to use. It has the disadvantage, however, of using two extreme data points, which may not be representative of normal conditions. The method may yield unreliable estimates of a and b in our formula. Be sure to check the scatter diagram for this possibility.

Simple Regression

One popular method for estimating the cost function is regression analysis. As was discussed in detail previously, simple regression involves one independent variable, e.g., DLH or machine hours alone, whereas multiple regression involves two or more activity variables. Unlike the high-low method, in an effort to estimate the variable rate and the fixed cost portion, the regression method includes all the observed data and attempts to find a line of best fit.

Figure 15.2: Excel Regression Output

SUMMARY OUTPUT

Regression Statistics	
Multiple R	0.84489
R Square	0.71384
Adjusted R Square	0.68522
Standard Error	145.759
Observations	12

ANOVA

	df	SS	MS
Regression	1	529979.3889	529979.389
Residual	10	212455.6111	21245.5611
Total	11	742435	

	Coefficients	Standard Error	t Stat
Intercept	1335.84	244.0486934	5.47367233
DLH	12.5504	2.512829835	4.99453875

From the regression output (Figure 15.2), the cost function is

$$Y = 1335.84 + 12.55\ X \qquad \text{with } R^2 = 71.38\%$$

or <u>$1335.84 fixed, plus $12.55 per DLH</u>

Example 15.2

Assume 95 direct labor hours are to be expended next year. The projected factory overhead for next year would be computed as follows:

$$Y = 1335.84 + 12.55\ X = 1335.84 + 12.55\ (95) = 2528.09$$

If the cost forecaster wants to be 95 percent confident in his/her prediction, the confidence interval would be the estimated cost (Y') $\pm$ t S_e. Note: As a rule of thumb, we may use t = 2.

Example 15.3

From Example 15.2, $Y' = \$2528.09$ and from Figure 15.2 we see, $S_e = 145.76$, and t= 2.

Therefore, the range for the prediction, given direct labor hours of 95 would be

$$= \$2528.09 \pm 2(145.76)$$
$$= \$2528.09 \pm 291.52, \text{ which means}$$
$$= \$2819.61 - \$2236.57$$

Multiple Regression

Regression analysis provides the opportunity for cost analysts to consider more than one independent variable. In case a simple regression is not good enough to provide a satisfactory cost function (as indicated typically by a low R-squared), the cost analyst should use multiple regression.

Presented below is an example of multiple regression.

Example 15.4

We add the data on machine hours to Table 15.1, as shown in Table 15.2.

Table 15.2: Extended data for cost prediction

Month	Factory Overhead (Y)	Direct Labor Hours (X_1)	Machine Hours (X_2)
1	2510	82	88
2	2479	84	101
3	2080	74	88
4	2750	113	99
5	2330	77	93
6	2690	91	109
7	2480	95	77
8	2610	117	102
9	2920	116	122
10	2730	103	107
11	2760	120	101
12	2109	76	65

First, we present two simple regression results (one variable at a time):

Simple regression 1
$$Y = b_o + b_1 X_1$$

Simple regression 2
$$Y = b_o + b_2 X_2$$

Then, we present the following multiple regression result:

Multiple regression
$$Y = b_o + b_1 X_1 + b_2 X_2$$

Figure 15.3 shows simple and multiple regression results (Excel output) for cost prediction.

Figure 15.3: Excel Output

SUMMARY OUTPUT

Regression Statistics	
Multiple R	0.7989
R Square	0.63825
Adjusted R Square	0.60207
Standard Error	163.884
Observations	12

ANOVA

	df	SS	MS
Regression	1	473856.0063	473856.006
Residual	10	268578.9937	26857.8994
Total	11	742435	

	Coefficients	Standard Error	t Stat
Intercept	1220.08	316.9563584	3.84936576
MH	13.7127	3.264643407	4.20036638

SUMMARY OUTPUT

Regression Statistics	
Multiple R	0.91977
R Square	0.84598
Adjusted R Square	0.81176
Standard Error	112.717
Observations	12

ANOVA

	df	SS	MS
Regression	2	628088.7656	314044.383
Residual	9	114346.2344	12705.1372
Total	11	742435	

	Coefficients	Standard Error	t Stat
Intercept	975.155	229.0522564	4.25734521
DLH	8.47915	2.433626337	3.48416437
MH	7.8143	2.81206043	2.77885304

As can be seen, simple regression 1 (overhead cost versus DLH) yielded:

$$Y = 1335.84 + 12.55 \, X \text{ with } R^2 = 71.38\%$$

$$S_e = 145.76$$

Due to a low R^2, trying the second regression (overhead cost versus MH) yielded:

$$Y = 1220.08 + 13.71 \, X \text{ with } R^2 = 63.83\%$$

$$S_e = 163.88$$

It shows that MH did not fare any better. In fact, R^2 and S_e were worse.

When we add machine-hours (MH) to the simple regression model, we obtain

$$Y' = 975.16 + 8.48 \, X_1 + 7.81 \, X_2$$

$$R^2 = 84.59\%, \, S_e = 112.72$$

The explanatory power (R^2) of the regression has increased dramatically to 84.59%, and the standard error of the regression has decreased to 112.72.

Use of Dummy Variables

In many cost analyses, an independent variable may be discrete or categorical. For example, in estimating heating and fuel bills, the season will make a big difference. To control this effect, a dummy variable can be included in the regression model. This variable will have a value equal to 1 during the winter months and 0 during all the other months.

A dummy variable can also be used to account for jumps or shifts in fixed costs. This situation is well illustrated by the data given in Table 15.3.

Table 15.3: Nonstationary Factory Overhead Costs

Month	Factory Overhead (Y)	Direct Labor Hours (X₁)	Shift Dummy (X₂)
1	2234	105	1
2	2055	89	1
3	2245	99	1
4	2110	85	1
5	2377	118	1
6	2078	89	1
7	2044	101	0
8	2032	112	0
9	2134	107	0
10	2090	100	0
11	2078	109	0
12	2007	93	0

A simple regression of overhead vs. DLH gives (Figure 15.4):

$$Y' = 1614 + 5.06\,X_1 \qquad R^2 = 22.42\%, S_e = 100.33$$

$$(2.98)$$

Figure 15.4: Excel Output

SUMMARY OUTPUT

Regression Statistics	
Multiple R	0.47354
R Square	0.22424
Adjusted R Square	0.14666
Standard Error	100.326
Observations	12

ANOVA

	df	SS	MS
Regression	1	29094.33565	29094.3357
Residual	10	100652.331	10065.2331
Total	11	129746.6667	

	Coefficients	Standard Error	t Stat
Intercept	1614.84	300.6752558	5.37072665
DLH	5.05871	2.97541537	1.70016982

The explanatory power of the model is extremely low, and the coefficient of DLH is barely statistically significant (i.e., $t = 5.06/2.98 = 1.7 < 2$). The data suggests that there might be a decrease around the end of the sixth month. To test this hypothesis, we define a dummy variable, X_2 as a shift or jump, where

$$X_2 = \begin{cases} 1 \text{ if } t = 1,2,..,6 \\ 0 \text{ if } t = 7,8,...12 \end{cases}$$

Rerunning the regression with the shift variable leads to the following printout (Figure 15.5):

Figure 15.5: Excel Output

SUMMARY OUTPUT

Regression Statistics	
Multiple R	0.89567
R Square	0.80402
Adjusted R Square	0.76047
Standard Error	53.1539
Observations	12

ANOVA

	df	SS	MS
Regression	2	104318.6442	52159.3221
Residual	9	25428.02251	2825.33583
Total	11	129746.6667	

	Coefficients	Standard Error	t Stat
Intercept	1258.13	173.6557749	7.24495057
DLH	7.7753	1.662006058	4.67826055
Shift Dummy	166.948	32.35461912	5.15993301

$$Y' = 1258.13 + 7.78\,X_1 + 166.95\,X_2 \qquad R^2 = 80.40\%, \quad S_e = 53.15$$

$$(1.66) \qquad\qquad (32.35)$$

The explanatory power of the model is quite good, and both the DLH shift variables are highly significant (t-values are 4.68 and 5.16, respectively).

Cost Prediction

1. If we wished to predict costs for the first six months of the following year, the predicted equation is:

$$
\begin{aligned}
Y' &= 1258 + 7.78\,X_1 + 166.95\,X_2 \\
&= 1258 + 7.78\,X_1 + 166.95\,(1) \\
&= 1424.95 + 7.78\,X_1
\end{aligned}
$$

2. If we wished to predict costs for the second six months of the following year, the predicted model becomes:

$$
\begin{aligned}
Y' &= 1258 + 7.78\,X_1 + 166.95\,X_2 \\
&= 1258 + 7.78\,X_1 + 166.95\,(0) \\
&= 1258 + 7.78\,X_1
\end{aligned}
$$

Conclusion

Cost analysts and financial managers analyze cost behavior for break-even and cost-volume-profit analysis, for appraisal of managerial performance, for flexible budgeting, and to make short-term choice decisions. We have looked at three types of cost behavior--variable, fixed, and mixed. We illustrated two popular methods of separating mixed costs in their variable and fixed components: the high-low method and regression analysis. Emphasis was placed on the use of simple and multiple regression. To account for jumps or shifts in fixed costs or seasonal change, a dummy variable can be incorporated into the model.

Chapter 16

Bankruptcy Prediction

There has recently been an increasing number of bankruptcies. Will the company of the stock you own be among them? Who will go bankrupt? Will your major customers or supplier go bankrupt - or even your employer? What warning signs exist and what can be done to avoid corporate failure?

Bankruptcy for a particular company is the final declaration of the inability to sustain current operation given the current debt obligations. The majority of firms require loans and therefore increase their liabilities during their operations in order to expand, improve or even just survive. The "degree" to which a firm has current debt in excess of assets is the most common factor in bankruptcy.

If you can predict with reasonable accuracy ahead of time, like a year or two, that the company you are interested in is developing financial distress, you could better protect yourself. For example, loan institutions face a major difficulty in calculating the "degree of debt relative to assets" or the likelihood of bankruptcy, yet this is precisely what these institutions must accomplish prior to issuing a financial loan to a firm.

Need of Prediction

Various groups of business people can reap significant rewards and benefits from a *predictive* model for their own purposes. For example,

1. *Merger analysis.* To help identify potential problems with a merger candidate.

2. *Turnaround Management.* To develop emergency action plans and turnaround strategies to quickly correct a deteriorating situation.

3. *Insurance Underwriting.* To evaluate the potential credit risk of the proposed insured including risk sharing and self-insured retentions.

4. *Corporate Governance.* For Board of Directors and Audit Committee analysis of going concern capability, consideration of corporate risk, and analysis of merger and acquisition scenarios.

5. *Investment analysis.* The model can help an investor selecting stocks of potentially troubled companies. For venture capitalists, investment bankers, and business valuation experts as they evaluate potential investment decisions.

6. *Auditing analysis.* For external CPA auditors to evaluate whether a firm is a going concern and to consider opinion qualification and financial statement disclosures

7. *Legal analysis.* Those investing or giving credit to your company may sue for losses incurred. The model can help in your company's defense.

8. *Loan credit analysis.* Bankers and lenders can use it to determine if they should extend a loan. If bankers can identify companies in danger of failure sufficiently far in advance, then corrective action can be taken. The banker can: (a) decline to accept the company as a customer, (b) encourage the company to identify its problems and take steps to rectify those problems, (c) encourage the principals of the company to inject more capital into the business, and (d) encourage the company to seek other financing. Other creditors such as vendors have used it to determine whether to extend credit.

Analysts have tried and will continue to try to build early warning systems to detect the likelihood of bankruptcy. Investment bankers, financial analysts, security analysts, auditors, and others have used financial ratios as an indication of the financial strength of a company, however, financial ratio analysis is limited because the methodology is basically *univariate*. Each ratio is examined in isolation and it is up to the financial analyst to use professional judgment to determine whether a set of financial ratios are developing into a meaningful analysis.

In order to overcome the shortcomings of financial ratio analysis, it is necessary to combine mutually exclusive ratios into groups to develop a meaningful predictive model. *Regression analysis* and *multiple discriminant analysis (MDA)* are two statistical techniques that have been used to predict the financial strength of a company.

Three Different Models

This chapter evaluates and illustrates three predictive bankruptcy models, with the aid of a spreadsheet program. They are the well-known Z-Score Model, the Degree of Relative Liquidity model, and the Lambda Index.

The *Z-Score* model evaluates a combination of several financial ratios to predict the likelihood of future bankruptcy. The model, developed by Edward Altman, uses multiple discriminant analysis to give a relative prediction of whether a firm will go bankrupt within five years. The *Degree of Relative Liquidity* model, on the other hand, evaluates a firm's ability to meet its short-term obligations. This model also uses discriminant analysis by combining several ratios to derive a percentage figure that indicates the firm's ability to meet short-term obligations. Third, the *Lambda Index* model evaluates a firm's ability to generate or obtain cash on a short-term basis to meet current obligations and therefore predict solvency.

These models are outlined and described in detail below. Spreadsheet models have been developed to calculate the prediction of bankruptcy using data extracted from *Moody's* and *Standard & Poor's*. Two companies--Navistar International (formerly International Harvester), the one that continues to struggle in the heavy and medium truck industry, and Best Products, Inc, the one that has declared bankruptcy as of January 1991--have been selected for our study. Financial data has been collected for the period 1979 through 1990 for Best and for the period 1981 through 2001 for Navistar.

Z-Score Analysis

Using a blend of the traditional financial ratios and multiple discriminant analysis, Altman[1] developed a bankruptcy prediction model that produces a Z score as follows:

$$Z = 1.2*X_1 + 1.4*X_2 + 3.3*X_3 + 0.6*X_4 + 0.999*X_5$$

where X_1 = Working capital/Total assets

X_2 = Retained earnings/Total assets

X_3 = Earnings before interest and taxes (EBIT)/Total assets

X_4 = Market value of equity/Book value of debt (or Net worth for *private firms*)

X_5 = Sales/Total assets

Altman also established the following guideline for classifying firms:

Z score	Probability of Short-Term Illiquidity
1.8 or less	Very high
1.81 - 2.99	Not sure
3.0 or higher	Unlikely

The Z score is known to be about 90 percent accurate in forecasting business failure one year in the future and about 80 percent accurate in forecasting it two years in

1   Edward I. Altman, *Corporate Financial Distress* (New York: John Wiley & Sons, 1983)

the future. It has been found that with the many important changes in reporting standards since the late 1960s, the Z-Score model is somewhat out of date in the 1980s. A second-generation model known as *Zeta Analysis* adjusts for these changes, primarily the capitalization of financial leases. The resulting Zeta discriminant model is extremely accurate for up to 5 years before failure. Since this analysis is a proprietary one, the exact weights for the model's seven variables cannot be specified here. The new study resulted in the following variables explaining corporate failure.

X_1 = Return on Assets. Earnings before interest and taxes to total assets.

X_2 = Stability of earnings. Measure by the "normalized measure of the standard error of estimate around a ten-year trend in X_1."

X_3 = Debt service. Earnings before interest and taxes to total interest payments.

X_4 = Cumulative profitability. Retained earnings to total assets.

X_5 = Liquidity. Current assets to current liabilities.

X_6 = Capitalization. Equity to total capital.

X_7 = Size measured by the firm's total assets.

Application

The graph shows that Navistar International performed at the edge of the ignorance zone ("unsure area"), for the year 1981. Since 1982, though, the company started signaling a sign of failure. However, by selling stock and assets, the firm managed to survive. Since 1985, the company showed an improvement in its Z scores, although the firm continually scored on the danger zone. Note that the 1991-2006. Z-score are in the high probability range of <1.81, except the year 1999.

Best Products, Inc. has had a Z-score in the 2.44 to 2.98 range from 1984 to 1988. The strong decline in 1989 may have correctly indicated that pending bankruptcy of Best that they file for in January 1991. (See Table 16.2 and Figure 16.2)

Table 16.1: Z score –navistar international

Year	Current Assets (CA)	Total Assets (TA)	Current Liability (CL)	Total Liability (TL)	Retained Earnings (RE)	Working Capital (WC)	Sales	EBIT	Market Value or Net worth (MKT-NW)	WC/TA (X1)	RE/TA (X2)	EBIT/TA (X3)	MKT-NW/TL (X4)	SALES/TA (X5)	Z Score	Top Gray	Bottom Gray
1981	2672	5346	1808	3864	600	864	7018	-16	376	0.1616	0.1122	-0.0030	0.0973	1.3128	1.71	2.99	1.81
1982	1656	3699	1135	3665	-1078	521	4322	-1274	151	0.1408	-0.2914	-0.3444	0.0412	1.1684	-0.18	2.99	1.81
1983	1388	3362	1367	3119	-1487	21	3600	-231	835	0.0062	-0.4423	-0.0687	0.2677	1.0708	0.39	2.99	1.81
1984	1412	3249	1257	2947	-1537	155	4861	120	575	0.0477	-0.4731	0.0369	0.1951	1.4962	1.13	2.99	1.81
1985	1101	2406	988	2364	-1894	113	3508	247	570	0.0470	-0.7872	0.1027	0.2411	1.4580	0.89	2.99	1.81
1986	698	1925	797	1809	-1889	-99	3357	163	441	-0.0514	-0.9813	0.0847	0.2438	1.7439	0.73	2.99	1.81
1987	785	1902	836	1259	-1743	-51	3530	219	1011	-0.0268	-0.9164	0.1151	0.8030	1.8559	1.40	2.99	1.81
1988	1280	4037	1126	1580	150	154	4082	451	1016	0.0381	0.0372	0.1117	0.6430	1.0111	1.86	2.99	1.81
1989	986	3609	761	1257	175	225	4241	303	1269	0.0623	0.0485	0.0840	1.0095	1.1751	2.20	2.99	1.81
1990	2663	3795	1579	2980	81	1084	3854	111	563	0.2856	0.0213	0.0292	0.1889	1.0155	1.60	2.99	1.81
1991	2286	3443	1145	2866	332	1141	3259	232	667	0.3314	0.0964	0.0674	0.2326	0.9466	1.84	2.99	1.81
1992	2472	3627	1152	3289	93	1320	3875	-145	572	0.3639	0.0256	-0.0400	0.1738	1.0684	1.51	2.99	1.81
1993	2672	5060	1338	4285	-1588	1334	4696	-441	1765	0.2636	-0.3138	-0.0872	0.4119	0.9281	0.76	2.99	1.81
1994	2870	5056	1810	4239	-1538	1060	5337	233	1469	0.2097	-0.3042	0.0461	0.3466	1.0556	1.24	2.99	1.81
1995	3310	5566	1111	4696	-1478	2199	6342	349	966	0.3951	-0.2655	0.0627	0.2057	1.1394	1.57	2.99	1.81
1996	2999	5326	820	4410	-1431	2179	5754	188	738	0.4091	-0.2687	0.0353	0.1673	1.0804	1.41	2.99	1.81
1997	3203	5516	2416	4496	-1301	787	6371	316	1374	0.1427	-0.2359	0.0573	0.3055	1.1550	1.37	2.99	1.81
1998	3715	6178	3395	5409	-1160	320	7885	515	1995	0.0518	-0.1878	0.0834	0.3688	1.2763	1.57	2.99	1.81
1999	3203	5516	2416	4496	-1301	787	8642	726	2494	0.1427	-0.2359	0.1316	0.5547	1.5667	2.17	2.99	1.81
2000	2374	6851	2315	5409	-143	59	8451	370	2257	0.0086	-0.0209	0.0540	0.4173	1.2335	1.64	2.99	1.81
2001	2778	7164	2273	6037	-170	505	6739	162	2139	0.0705	-0.0237	0.0226	0.3543	0.9407	1.28	2.99	1.81
2002	2607	6957	2407	6706	-721	200	7021	-85	1867	0.0287	-0.1036	-0.0122	0.2784	1.0092	1.02	2.99	1.81
2003	2419	6929	2272	6637	-883	147	7585	91	2965	0.0212	-0.1274	0.0131	0.4467	1.0947	1.25	2.99	1.81
2004	3167	7592	3250	7061	-604	-83	9724	438	2872	-0.0109	-0.0796	0.0577	0.4067	1.2808	1.59	2.99	1.81
2005	4852	10786	4688	12485	-2699	164	12124	453	1991	0.0152	-0.2502	0.0420	0.1595	1.1240	1.03	2.99	1.81
2006	6368	12830	5048	13944	-2399	1320	14200	826	2245	0.1029	-0.1870	0.0644	0.1610	1.1068	1.28	2.99	1.81

Note: (1) To calculate " Z " score for private firms, enter Net Worth in the MKT-NW column. (For public-held companies, enter Markey Value of Equity).

(2) EBIT = Earnings before Interest and Taxes

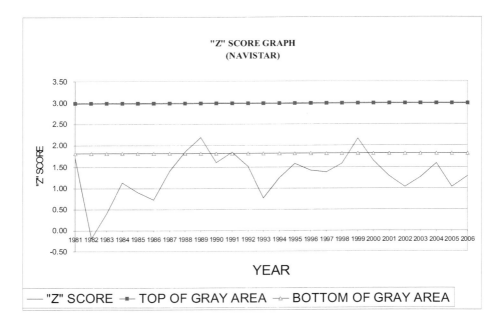

Table16.2: Best Product's Z score

			Balance Sheet					Income St		Stk Data	Calculations					Z	Misc Graph Values		
Year	Cur Asts	Total Asts	Current Liab	Total Liab	Retained Erngs	Net Worth	Wrkng Cap'l	SALES	EBIT	Market Val	WC/TA	RE/TA	EBIT/TA	MKT/TL	SALES/TA	Score	TOP GREY	BOTTOM GREY	Year
Graph	CA	TA	CL	TL	RE	NW	WC	SALES	EBIT	MKT						A	B	C	X
1984	745228	1202136	466590	787135	186486	415003	278628	2081328	106952	319048	0.2301	0.1551	0.0890	0.4053	1.7314	2.76	2.99	1.81	1984
1985	723684	1178424	443752	759278	193568	419146	279932	2252656	66705	407604	0.2375	0.1643	0.0586	0.5368	1.9116	2.93	2.99	1.81	1985
1986	840686	1331975	529690	916679	189306	415396	310996	2234768	47271	253041	0.2335	0.1421	0.0355	0.2761	1.6778	2.44	2.99	1.81	1986
1987	816853	1265637	400403	878479	160455	387158	416450	2142118	25372	202988	0.3290	0.1268	0.0200	0.2311	1.6925	2.47	2.99	1.81	1987
1988	811314	1299860	426065	836956	190960	402904	385249	2066589	93226	672300	0.3107	0.1540	0.0752	0.8033	0.6668	2.98	2.99	1.81	1988
1989	877937	1735595	738837	1646302	39293	89293	139100	809457	96440	672300	0.0801	0.0226	0.0556	0.4084	0.4664	1.02	2.99	1.81	1989
1990	583773	1438208	412732	1386974	−14516	71234	171041	2094570	73512	672300	0.1189	−0.0101	0.0511	0.4918	1.4564	2.05	2.99	1.81	1990

Figure 16.2:Best Product's Z Score

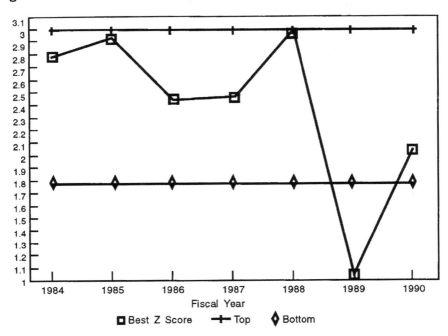

The Degree of Relative Liquidity (DRL)
===

The DRL, developed by Skomp and Edwards[2], has been proposed as an alternative method for measuring the liquidity of a small firm and can have significant applications for larger companies. It has been compared to the two common liquidity ratios, the *current* and *acid-test* (or *quick*) *ratios*, which are often used to evaluate the liquidity of a firm. However, under certain circumstances, these two ratios sometimes provide incomplete and often misleading indications of a firm's ability to meet its short-term obligations and may be opposite to the trend at hand. A logical approach to evaluating several liquidity measures simultaneously is to consider how appropriately each measure responds to changes relative to direction and degree of sensitivity. Examples where the current or acid-test ratio may give misleading indications are:

> *Current* – An obsolete or slow-moving inventory and uncollectible accounts receivable may distort this ratio.

> *Acid-test* – Uncollectible receivables and the exclusion of inventories can provide an incomplete picture.

The DRL represents the percentage of a firm's cash expenditure requirements which could be secured from beginning working capital and from cash generated

---

2   Stephen E. Skomp and Donald E. Edwards, "Measuring Small Business Liquidity: An Alternative to Current and Quick Ratios," *Journal of Small Business Management* (April 1978): Vol. 16,22

through the normal operating process. Emphasis is placed upon the availability of cash sources relative to cash needs, omitting sources and uses of cash such as:

◆ Capital expenditures and sale of fixed assets

◆ Sale and extinguishment of capital stock

◆ Receipt and repayment of long-term borrowings

◆ Investments and liquidations in marketable securities & bonds

The DRL is calculated by dividing the total cash potential by the expected cash expenditures.

In equation form,

$$DRL = \frac{TCP}{E} \text{ or } \frac{WC + (OT \times SVI)}{NSV - [(NI + NON) + WCC]}$$

where TCP = Total cash potential

E = Cash expenditures for normal operations

WC = Beginning working capital (Beginning current assets - Beginning current liabilities)

OT = Operating turnover, or

$$\frac{Sales}{Accounts\ Receivable + Inventory \times Sales/Cost\ of\ Sales}$$

SVI = Sales value of inventory (Inventory at cost x Sales/cost of sales)

NSV = Net sales values

NI = Net income

NON = Non-cash expenditures (such as depreciation and amortization)

WCC = Change in working capital

If the DRL ratio is greater than 1.00 (or 100%), the firm can meet its current obligations for the period and have *some* net working capital available at the end of the period. If the DRL is less than 1.00, the firm should seek outside working capital financing before the end of the period.

The DRL may be derived by dividing the total cash potential (TCP) by expected cash expenditures (E) in the operating period. The TCP is the sum of initial cash potential and the cash potential from normal operations. The initial cash potential is reflected in the beginning working capital (WC) assuming reported values can be realized in cash. The cash potential from operations can be determined by multiplying the operating turnover rate (OT) by the sales of value of existing finished goods inventory (SVI). The operating turnover rate (OT) reflects the number of times the sales value of finished goods inventory (at retail) and accounts receivables (net of uncollectibles) is converted into cash in an operating period. The sales value of finished goods inventory (SVI) is the adjustment of inventory at cost to retail value.

The expected cash expenditures (E) are derived by subtracting cash flow from operations from net sales (NSV). Cash flow from operations can be derived by accrual net income (NI) plus non-cash expenses (NON) plus the change in working capital (WCC).

Application

The DRL is calculated for the prior 19 years for Navistar International (see Table 16.3 and Figure 16.3). The results show a rather bleak liquidity position with all figures under the 1.00 zone except 1979. This indicates that Navistar has not been able to generate the working capital internally through operations, rather they have had to continually seek outside working capital sources since 1979. However, the DRL appears to bottom out in 1988 and show some sign of stability since then.

Best Products, Inc. has had a DRL which has remained above 1.000 since 1985, peaking at 1.194 in 1987. (See Table 16.4 and Figure 16.4). However, its DRL has been dropping since 1987 and took a significant plunge in 1990 down to 1.039. Although the DRL is above 1.000, the significant drop may have indicated a worsening situation for Best and predicted their bankruptcy in January 1991.

Table 16.3: Navistar's DRL

	Balance Sheet						Income Statement				Calculations						Graph Values		
Year	Acts Rec (AR)	Inv (INV)	Cur Asts (CA)	Cur Liab (CL)	End W.C. (E-WC)	Beg W.C. (B-WC)	N.S.V. (NSV)	Cost of Sales (COS)	Net Inc (NI)	Non-Cash Exp (NON)	Op TO (OT=)	Sales Val Inv (SVI=)	Oper Cash Pot (OCP=)	Chng Wrkg Cap (WCC=)	Total Cash Pot (TCP=)	Expen-ditures (E=)	Degree of Rel Liq (DRL=)	BASE	Year
1979	806	2343	3266	1873	1393	1210	8392	6904	370	127	2.3	2848	6541	183	7751	7712	1.005	1.000	1979
1980	769	2332	3427	2480	947	1393	6312	5700	-397	130	1.9	2582	4864	-446	6257	7025	0.891	1.000	1980
1981	555	1634	2672	1846	826	947	6298	5750	-351	144	2.7	1790	4807	-121	5754	6626	0.868	1.000	1981
1982	306	759	1768	1135	633	826	4292	4150	-1738	149	3.9	785	3088	-193	3914	6074	0.644	1.000	1982
1983	255	619	1388	1366	22	633	3601	3325	-485	131	3.9	670	2609	-611	3242	4566	0.710	1.000	1983
1984	226	693	1412	1257	155	22	3382	2934	-55	100	3.3	799	2636	133	2658	3204	0.830	1.000	1984
1985	133	334	1101	988	113	155	3508	3084	-364	41	6.8	380	2598	-42	2753	3873	0.711	1.000	1985
1986	111	293	680	797	-117	113	3357	3009	2	40	7.7	327	2506	-230	2619	3545	0.739	1.000	1986
1987	114	266	785	836	-51	-117	3530	3054	33	41	8.4	307	2575	66	2458	3390	0.725	1.000	1987
1988	1854	316	3410	1126	2284	-51	4080	3574	244	49	1.8	361	665	2335	614	1452	0.423	1.000	1988
1989	1629	336	2965	1731	1234	2284	4023	3637	87	60	2.0	372	747	-1050	3031	4926	0.615	1.000	1989
1990	1627	343	2663	1579	1084	1234	3854	3376	-11	66	1.9	392	748	-150	1982	3949	0.502	1.000	1990
1991	1316	332	2286	1145	1141	1084	3259	2885	-165	73	1.9	375	723	57	1807	3294	0.549	1.000	1991
1992	1479	365	2472	1152	1320	1141	3685	3248	-212	77	1.9	414	806	179	1947	3641	0.535	1.000	1992
1993	1550	411	2682	1338	1344	1320	4510	3925	-501	75	2.2	472	1053	24	2373	4912	0.483	1.000	1993
1994	1517	429	2870	1710	1160	1344	5153	4500	82	72	2.6	491	1261	-184	2605	5183	0.503	1.000	1994
1995	1854	416	3310	933	2377	1160	6125	5288	164	81	2.6	482	1263	1217	2423	4663	0.520	1.000	1995
1996	1655	463	2999	820	2179	2377	5508	4827	65	105	2.5	528	1333	-198	3710	5536	0.670	1.000	1996
1997	1755	483	3203	1100	2103	2179	6147	5292	150	120	2.7	561	1489	-76	3668	5953	0.616	1.000	1997

Figure 16.3: Navistar's DRL Graph

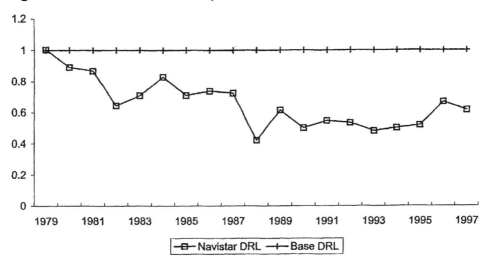

Table 16.4: Best product's DRL

Year	Balance Sheet						Income Statement				Calculations						Graph Values		Year
	Acts Rec (AR)	Inv (INV)	Cur Asts (CA)	Cur Liab (CL)	End W.C. (E-WC)	Beg W.C. (B-WC)	N.S.V. (NSV)	Cost of Sales (COS)	Net Inc (NI)	Non-Cash Exp (NON)	Op TO (OT=)	Sales Val Inv (SVI=)	Oper Cash Pot (OCP=)	Chng Wrkg Cap (WCC=)	Total Cash Pot (TCP=)	Expen-ditures (E=)	Degree of Rel Liq (DRL=)	BASE	
1979	806	2343	3266	1873	1393	1210	8392	6904	370	127	2.3	2848	6541	183	7751	7712	1.005	1.000	1979
1980	769	2332	3427	2480	947	1393	6312	5700	-397	130	1.9	2582	4864	-446	6257	7025	0.891	1.000	1980
1981	555	1634	2672	1846	826	947	6298	5750	-351	144	2.7	1790	4807	-121	5754	6626	0.868	1.000	1981
1982	306	759	1768	1135	633	826	4292	4150	-1738	149	3.9	785	3088	-193	3914	6074	0.644	1.000	1982
1983	255	619	1388	1366	22	633	3601	3325	-485	131	3.9	670	2609	-611	3242	4566	0.710	1.000	1983
1984	226	693	1412	1257	155	22	3382	2934	-55	100	3.3	799	2636	133	2658	3204	0.830	1.000	1984
1985	133	334	1101	988	113	155	3508	3084	-364	41	6.8	380	2598	-42	2753	3873	0.711	1.000	1985
1986	111	293	680	797	-117	113	3357	3009	2	40	7.7	327	2506	-230	2619	3545	0.739	1.000	1986
1987	114	266	785	836	-51	-117	3530	3054	33	41	8.4	307	2575	66	2458	3390	0.725	1.000	1987
1968	1854	316	3410	1126	2284	-51	4080	3574	244	49	1.8	361	665	2335	614	1452	0.423	1.000	1988
1989	1629	336	2965	1731	1234	2284	4023	3637	87	60	2.0	372	747	-1050	3031	4926	0.615	1.000	1989
1990	1627	343	2663	1579	1084	1234	3854	3376	-11	66	1.9	392	748	-150	1982	3949	0.502	1.000	1990
1991	1316	332	2286	1145	1141	1084	3259	2885	-165	73	1.9	375	723	57	1807	3294	0.549	1.000	1991
1992	1479	365	2472	1152	1320	1141	3685	3248	-212	77	1.9	414	806	179	1947	3641	0.535	1.000	1992
1993	1550	411	2682	1338	1344	1320	4510	3925	-501	75	2.2	472	1053	24	2373	4912	0.483	1.000	1993
1994	1517	429	2870	1710	1160	1344	5153	4500	82	72	2.6	491	1261	-184	2605	5183	0.503	1.000	1994
1995	1854	416	3310	933	2377	1160	6125	5288	164	81	2.6	482	1263	1217	2423	4663	0.520	1.000	1995
1996	1655	463	2999	820	2179	2377	5508	4827	65	105	2.5	528	1333	-198	3710	5536	0.670	1.000	1996
1997	1755	483	3203	1100	2103	2179	6147	5292	150	120	2.7	561	1489	-76	3668	5953	0.616	1.000	1997

Figure 16.4: Best product's DRL graph

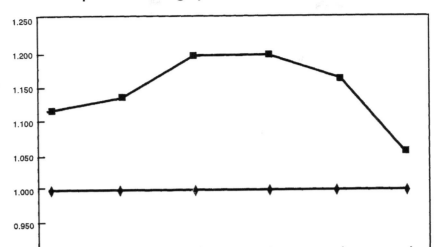

Based on just two companies, the DRL appears to have shown that the change in relative liquidity than the absolute measure is more relevant in predicting corporate bankruptcy.

Lambda Index

The Lambda Index, developed by Gary Emery and 1990 Nobel Laureate Merton Miller[3], is a ratio which focuses on two relevant components of liquidity - short-term cash balances and available credit to gauge the probability that a firm will become insolvent. The index measures the probability of a company going bankrupt and it includes the key aspect of uncertainty in cash-flow measurement by utilizing a sample standard deviation. In consequence, it can be used like a z value from the standard normal distribution table.

For a given period, Lambda is the sum of a company's initial liquid reserve and net flow of funds divided by the uncertainty associated with the flows:

$$\frac{\text{Initial Liquid Reserve} \quad + \quad \text{Total anticipated net cash during the analysis horizon}}{\text{Uncertainty about net cash flow during the analysis horizon}}$$

Net cash flow is the balance of cash receipts less cash outlays. Unused lines of credit, short-term investments, and cash balances make up the initial liquid reserve. The uncertainty is based on the standard deviation of net cash flow. In order to calculate and utilize the Lambda index, a cash forecast should be used.

A worksheet can be prepared to contain twelve line items in the following order from top to bottom: short-term line of credit, beginning liquid assets, adjustments, initial liquid reserve, total sources of funds, total uses of funds, ending liquid assets, ending liquid reserve, standard deviation, the Lambda index, and finally, additional cash required to maintain a Lambda of three.

A firm's short-term line of credit may not change during the course of the forecast (i.e. 1 year), which simplifies calculations. Liquid assets, by definition, include marketable securities and cash at the start of the forecast summary. By having an adjustments line item one can see the result of decreasing or increasing the cash level. The initial liquid reserve is the total short-term line of credit with any adjustments. The total sources and uses of funds are forecasts by company management, resulting in a positive or negative net cash flow. The Lambda value should rise if a firm's short-term line of credit doesn't change and it has a positive net cash flow. Ending liquid assets is the sum of three values: beginning liquid assets, adjustments, and net cash flow. Ending liquid reserve is the sum of two values: short-term line of credit and ending liquid assets. The standard deviation is drawn from the net cash flows from period to period. Next, the Lambda index is calculated by dividing the ending liquid reserve by the standard deviation.

And finally, the last line item is additional cash needed to hold a Lambda of three. A negative number here indicates a Lambda value of greater than three and hence, a safer firm financially. A high negative value here, assuming that management is confident of its forecasts, may point out that those funds could be better utilized somewhere else.

Once an index value has been determined using the equation, the pertinent odds can be found by referencing a standard normal distribution table (see Table A.1 in the Appendix). For example, a Lambda of 2.33 has a value of .9901 from the table, which says that there is a 99% chance that problems won't occur and a 1% chance that they will.

Generally, a firm with a Lambda value of 9 or higher is financially healthy. And firms with a Lambda of 15 or more are considered very safe. A Lambda value of 3 translates to one chance in a thousand that necessary cash outlays will exceed available cash on hand. A Lambda value of 3.9 puts the probability at one in twenty thousand. A low Lambda of 1.64 is equivalent to a one in twenty chance of required disbursements exceeding available cash on hand. A work sheet that keeps a running tally of Lambda shows how changes in the financial picture affect future cash balances.

There are a number of positive aspects to using the Lambda index. The Lambda index focuses on the key factors of liquidity, available unused credit and cash flows, which by contrast are ignored by standard cash forecasts. Further, by including the standard deviation of cash flows, Lambda penalizes irregular cash flows. The result of higher changes in cash flows would be a lower Lambda.

A drawback to Lambda, however, is the fact that it's significantly tied to revenue forecasts, which at times can be suspect depending on the time horizon and the industry involved. A strong Lambda doesn't carry much weight if a firm isn't confident about its forecast.

Application

Table 16.5 and Figure 16.5 shows that Navistar's Lambda index has remained very low since 1979, with a low point of 2.16 in 1982 to a high of 5.98 in 1989.

Table 16.5: Navixtar's Lambda Index

Year	1979	1980	1981	1982	1983	1984	1985	1986	1987	1988	1989	1990	1991	1992	1993	1994	1995	1996	1997
Short-term line of credit	100000	100000	100000	100000	100000	100000	100000	100000	100000	100000	100000	100000	100000	100000	100000	100000	100000	100000	100000
Beginning liquid assets	27256	25205	137103	393879	259452	391619	412970	323220	217745	383900	562400	674000	588000	604000	638000	734000	870000	798000	800000
Adjustments																			
Initial liquid reserve	127256	125205	237103	493879	359452	491619	512970	423220	317745	483900	662400	774000	688000	704000	738000	834000	970000	898000	900000
Total sources of funds	-2051	111898	256776	-134427	132167	21351	-89750	-105475	166155	178500	111600	-86000	16000	34000	96000	136000	-72000	2000	122000
Total uses of funds																			
Net cash flow	-2051	111898	256776	-134427	132167	21351	-89750	-105475	166155	178500	111600	-86000	16000	34000	96000	136000	-72000	2000	122000
Ending liquid assets, short-term debt, and adjustments (net)	5205	137103	393879	259452	391619	412970	323220	217745	383900	562400	674000	588000	604000	638000	734000	870000	798000	800000	922000
Ending liquid reserve	125205	237103	493879	359452	491619	512970	423220	317745	483900	662400	774000	688000	704000	738000	834000	970000	898000	900000	1022000
Standard deviation	NA	80574	129721	166384	147856	133909	135398	135804	135604	135181	129435	130297	125041	120167	116583	114801	115195	112221	110558
Calculated Lambda index	NA	2.94	3.81	2.16	3.32	3.83	3.13	2.34	3.57	4.90	5.98	5.28	5.63	6.14	7.15	8.45	7.80	8.02	9.24
Additional cash required (remaining) to maintain Lambda of 3.0	NA	4619	-104716	138701	-48050	-111243	-17027	89666	-77087	-256856	-385696	-297108	-328877	-377498	-484250	-625596	-552415	-563336	-690326
Very Safe	15.00	15.00	15.00	15.00	15.00	15.00	15.00	15.00	15.00	15.00	15.00	15.00	15.00	15.00	15.00	15.00	15.00	15.00	15.00
Healthy	9.00	9.00	9.00	9.00	9.00	9.00	9.00	9.00	9.00	9.00	9.00	9.00	9.00	9.00	9.00	9.00	9.00	9.00	9.00
Slight: 1 in 20000	3.90	3.90	3.90	3.90	3.90	3.90	3.90	3.90	3.90	3.90	3.90	3.90	3.90	3.90	3.90	3.90	3.90	3.90	3.90
Low: 1 in 20	1.64	1.64	1.64	1.64	1.64	1.64	1.64	1.64	1.64	1.64	1.64	1.64	1.64	1.64	1.64	1.64	1.64	1.64	1.64

Figure 16.5: Navixtar's Lambda Index Graph

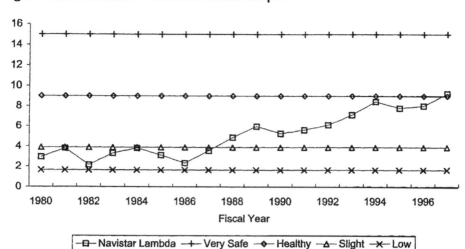

Its Lambda value had increased from 1986 through 1989, however it dropped again in 1990. Using a Lambda value of 9 as a bench mark for what is considered a healthy firm, Navistar has been in trouble for some time. Since 1989, however, the Lambda appears to improve constantly over time.

Best Product's Lambda index was far lower than that of Navistar, with a low of 2.39 in 1986 and a high of 4.52 in 1989. It Lambda index also dropped in 1990, reaching a level of .80. This is not surprising, since in January of 1991, Best filed for bankruptcy protection. (See Table 16.6 and Figure 16.6).

Table 16.6: Best Product's Lambda Index

YEAR	1985	1986	1987	1988	1989	1990
Short-term line of credit	100000	100000	100000	100000	100000	100000
Beginning liquid assets	62933	4915	115126	103197	110243	253278
Adjustments						
Initial liquid reserve	162933	104915	115126	203197	210243	353278
Total sources of funds	58018	10211	88071	7046	143035	−244843
Total uses of funds						
Net cash flow	−58018	10211	88071	7046	143035	−244843
Ending liquid assets, short-term debt, and adjustments (net)	4915	15126	106197	110243	253278	8435
Ending liquid reserve	104915	115126	203197	210243	353278	108435
Standard deviation	NA	48245	73097	59769	78245	135047
Calculated Lambda index	NA	2.39	2.78	3.52	4.52	0.80
Additional cash required (remaining) to maintain Lambda of 3.0	NA	29610	16095	−30936	−118542	296706
Very Safe		15.00	15.00	15.00	15.00	15.00
Healthy		9.00	9.00	9.00	9.00	9.00
Slight—1 in 20000		3.90	3.90	3.90	3.90	3.90
Low—1 in 20		1.64	1.64	1.64	1.64	1.64

Figure 16.6: Best Product's Lambda Index Graph

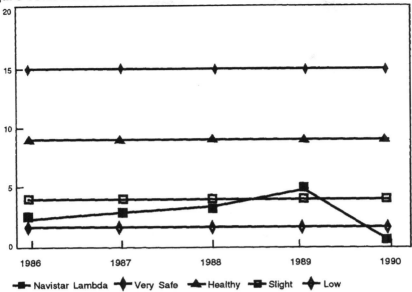

Table 16.7 summarizes guidelines for classifying firms under the three models.

Table 16.7: Classifying Guidelines Under the Three Models

	Model	*Guidelines*
(1) Z-Score Model	Z score	Probability of Short-Term Illiquidity
	1.8 or less	Very high
	1.81 - 2.99	Not sure
	3.0 or higher	Unlikely
(2) Degree of Relative Liquidity (DRL) Model	DRL score	Probability of Short-Term Illiquidity
	Less than 1.00	Very high
	Higher than 1.00	Unlikely
(3) Lambda Index	Lambda score	Probability of Short-Term Illiquidity
	1.64	
	3.9	1 in 20
	9.00 or higher	1 in 20,000
		Unlikely

203

A Word of Caution

The Z-Score may be used by a different people for varying uses. The Z-Score offers an excellent measure of the probability of a firm's insolvency, but like any tool, one must use it with care and skill. The Z-Score should be evaluated over a number of years and should not be the sole basis of evaluation.

The Z-Score may also be used to compare the stability of different firms. Care should also be exercised when the Z-Score is used for this purpose. The firms must be in the same market offering the same, if not very similar products. In addition, the measure must be taken across the same period of years. These similarities are requirements in order to eliminate external environmental factors which would be reflected in the score.

The DRL is a more comprehensive measure of liquidity than the current ratio or the acid-test ratio. However, like the current and the acid-test ratios, the DRL is a relative measure and should be used only in relation to either the firm's own historical DRL or to those of other businesses. Since the DRL does not incorporate the timing and variances in cash flows (assumed to be uniform and continuous), comparing the DRL of two dissimilar firms is hazardous. It is important to note that the DRL does correctly identify an improved or deteriorated liquidity position, however, it does not suggest explicit causes of change. On the other hand, the DRL does provide a basis from which to pursue an analysis and interpretation of those causes of change because the derivation of the DRL requires input for all the factors which are relevant to liquidity position.

As with DRL, the Lambda index is a method for gauging a firm's liquidity, but one should consider a firm's historical background and always use common sense in evaluating any calculated value. A weak point of this model is that in order to calculate the index, forecasted figures must be used, making the final Lambda value somewhat suspect in some cases.

Neural Bankruptcy Prediction

Neural networks appear to be a useful tool in bankruptcy prediction. They can use some of the tools already in place to improve prediction. If the ratios chosen for the Z model are used but the neural network is allowed to form its own functions, the predictive abilities of the Z formula can be much improved upon. This is of significant value to managers, creditors, and investors since misclassification, particularly of a firm that is going bankrupt, has huge monetary implications. The *Neural Bankruptcy Prediction Program* developed in 1995 by Dorsey, Edmister, and Johnson is a good example. This is a DOS-based software that is available and can be downloaded from the University of Mississippi Business School's Internet web page (http://school.it.bond.edu.au/INFM733/olemisdata/bankrupt.pdf)

The following example illustrates an application of this program. As an illustration, a set of financial data was obtained from America Online's "Financial Reports" database. The corporation's 1994 (one year prior to the insolvency) financial reports here. Then, the following 18 ratios required by the Neural Network Bankruptcy Prediction Program were calculated (see Table 16.8):

Table 16.8 : Data Set Ratio Definitions

Ratio	Definition
CASH/TA	Cash/Total assets
CASH/TS	Cash/Net sales
CF/TD	Cash flow operations income/Total liabilities
CA/CL	Total current assets/Total current liabilities
CA/TA	Total current assets/Total assets
CA/TS	Total current assets/Net sales
EBIT/TA	(Interest expense + Income before tax)/Total assets
LOG (INT+15)	LOG(Interest expense + Income before tax)/Total assets + 15)
LOG (TA)	LOG(Total assets)
MVE/TK	Shareholder's equity/(Total assets - Total current liabilities)
NI/TA	Net income/Total assets
QA/CL	(Total current assets - Inventories)/Total current liabilities
QA/TA	(Total current assets − Inventories)/Total assets
QA/TS	(Total current assets - Inventories)/Net sales
RE/TA	Retained earnings/Total assets
TD/TA	Total liabilities/Total assets
WK/TA	(Total assets/Net sales)/(Working capital/Total assets)
WK/TS	1/(Net sales/Working capital)

Table 16.9 shows the result of 1994 data analysis for a selected group of firms.

Table 16.9 : Bankruptcy Analysis for Selected Firms

Year	Company	Bankrupt (1-yes/0-no)	Value	Insolvency Predicted (1-yes/0-no)	Error
1994	Apparel Ventures Inc.	0	0.38085095	0	
1994	Apple Computer Inc.	0	0.00267937	0	
1994	Biscayne Apparel Inc.	0	0.43153563	1	
1994	Epitope Inc.	0	0.18238553	0	
1994	Montgomery Ward Holding Co.	0	0.06268501	0	30%
1994	Schwerman Trucking Co.	0	0.57828138	1	
1994	Signal Apparel Co.	0	0.37081639	0	
1994	Southern Pacific Transportation	0	-0.3514775	0	
1994	Time Warner Inc.	0	0.57828138	1	
1994	Warner Insurance Services	0	-0.1020344	0	
1994	Baldwin Builders	1	0.57828138	1	
1994	Bradlees Inc.	1	1.00828347	1	
1994	Burlington Motor Holdings	1	1.00828347	1	
1994	Clothestime Inc.	1	0.43153563	1	
1994	Dow Corning	1	0.65517535	1	0%
1994	Edison Brothers Stores	1	0.61124180	1	
1994	Freymiller Trucking Co.	1	1.00828347	1	
1994	Lamonts Apparel Inc.	1	1.28955072	1	
1994	Plaid Clothing Group Inc.	1	1.28955072	1	
1994	Smith Corona Co.	1	0.43153563	1	

Those companies with values over 0.4 (threshold value) are predicted as insolvent. Three of ten solvent companies (as of early 1998) received values over 0.4 indicating bankruptcy. Although those companies did not go bankrupt in 1995, they can be considered as "high risk" companies. The results of the insolvent companies' analysis was rather impressive; all of the insolvent corporations are recognized.

The foregoing analysis confirms that the Neural Network Bankruptcy Prediction Program is a reliable tool for screening financially distressed large companies. Despite the small sample size, 100% accuracy in predicting insolvency was remarkable. The program is a relatively simple and easy process for analyzing data and interpreting the results. It holds promise even to those who are not proficient in mathematics.

Conclusion

The three models discussed in this chapter appear to work well for both companies tested--Navistar International and Best products in the sense that they all point to early signs of financial distress. It is our contention, however, that the Z-score model is a more positive predictor for bankruptcy than the other two since it covers a wider range of financial ratios--especially, retained earnings divided by total assets. Note that *retained earnings* (of course backed by cash balance) is primarily the one that will save the company in financial trouble especially in economic hard times.

All developers of prediction models warn that the technique should be considered as just another tool of the analyst and that it is not intended to replace experienced and informed personal evaluation. Perhaps the best use of any of these models is as a "filter" to identify companies requiring further review or to establish a trend for a company over a number of years. If, for example, the trend for a company over a number of years is downward then that company has problems, that if caught in time, could be corrected to allow the company to survive.

Chapter 17

Forecasting Foreign Exchange Rates

This chapter addresses the problem of forecasting foreign exchange rates. Although currencies can be supported by various means for short periods, the primary determinant of exchange rates is the supply of and demand for the various currencies. The chapter explores the need for managers to forecast the exchange rates. It then establishes a framework of the international exchange markets and explores the relationship between exchange rates, interest rate, and inflation rate. The chapter focuses on the different types of forecasting techniques used to predict the foreign exchange rates and concludes by setting up a framework within which forecasts can be evaluated.

Why Forecast Exchange Rates?

Frequently multinational companies (MNCs) are subject to currency risk (exchange rate risk) and therefore are faced with a decision regarding forecasting foreign exchange rates. For example, when amounts to be paid or received are denominated in a foreign currency, exchange rate fluctuations may result in exchange gains or losses. For example, if a U.S. firm has a receivable fixed in terms of units of a foreign currency, a decline in the value of that currency relative to the U.S. dollar results in a foreign exchange loss.

Some companies choose to ignore forecasting, while others often rely on their banks for the answer. Very few companies dedicate resources to forecast foreign exchange rate.

Many companies argue that the forecasts of international exchange rates are often inaccurate and hence invalid. Therefore, there is no need to forecast. These companies, however, fail to understand that forecasting is not an exact science but rather an art form where quality of forecasts generally tend to improve as companies and mangers gain more experience in forecasting.

In today's global environment, companies trading across the national boundaries are often exposed to transaction risk, the risk that comes from fluctuation in the exchange rate between the time a contract is signed and when the payment is received. Historically, exchange rates have been fixed and there have been very few fluctuations within a short time period. However, most exchange rates today are floating and can easily vary as much as 5% within a week. Moreover, the recent crisis in the European monetary market illustrates the need for accurate exchange rate information. There are four primary reasons why it is imperative to forecast the foreign exchange rates.

Hedging Decision

Multinational companies (MNCs) are constantly faced with the decision of whether or not to hedge payables and receivables in foreign currency. An exchange rate forecast can help MNC's determine if it should to hedge its transactions. As an example, if forecasts determine that the Swiss franc is going to appreciate in value relative to the dollar, a company expecting payment from a Swiss partner in the future may not decide to hedge the transaction. However, if the forecasts showed that the Swiss franc is going to depreciate relative to the dollar, the U.S. partner should hedge the transaction.

Short Term Financing Decision for MNC

A large Corporation has several sources of capital market and several currencies in which it can borrow. Ideally, the currency it would borrow would exhibit low interest rate and depreciate in value over the financial period. For example, A U.S. firm could borrow in Japanese yens; during the loan period, the yens would depreciate in value; at the end of the period, the company would have to use fewer dollars to buy the same amount of yens and would benefit from the deal.

International Capital Budgeting Decision

Accurate cash flows are imperative in order to make a good capital budgeting decision. In case of international projects, it is not only necessary to establish accurate cash flows but it is also necessary to convert them into an MNC's home country currency. This necessitates the use of foreign exchange forecast to convert the cash flows and there after, evaluate the decision.

Subsidiary Earning Assessment for MNC

When an MNC reports its earning, international subsidiary earnings are often translated and consolidated in the MNC's home country currency. For example, when IBM makes a projection for its earning, it needs to project its earnings in Japanese, then it needs to translate these earnings from Japanese yens to dollars. A depreciation in marks would decrease a subsidiary's earnings and vice versa. Thus, it is necessary to generate an accurate forecast of marks to create a legitimate earnings assessment.

Some Basic Terms and Relationships

At this point, it is necessary to address some of the basic terminology used in foreign exchange as well as address the fundamental laws of international monetary economics. It is also necessary to establish a basic international monetary framework before forecasting.

Spot Rate

Spot rate can be defined as the rate that exists in today's market. Table 17.1 illustrates a typical listing of foreign exchange rates found in the Wall Street Journal. The British pound is quoted at 1.5685. This rate is the spot rate. It means you can go to the bank today and exchange $ 1.5685 for £1.00. In reality, for example, you need £10,000 for a paying off an import transaction on a given day, you would ask you bank to purchase £ 10,000. The bank would not hand you the money, but instead it would instruct its English subsidiary to pay £ 10,000 to your English supplier and it would debit you account by (10,000 x 1.5685) $ 15,685.

Forward Rate

Besides the spot rate, Table17.1 also quotes the forward rate. The 90 day forward rate for the pound is quoted as 1.5551. In forward market, you buy and sell currency for a future delivery date, usually, 1, 3, or 6 months in advance. If you know you need to buy or sell currency in the future, you can hedge against a loss by selling in the forward market. For example, let's say you are required to pay £10,000 in 3 months to your English supplier. You can purchase £10,000 today by paying $15,551 (10,000 x 1.5551). These pounds will be delivered in 90 days. In the meantime you have protected yourself. No matter what the exchange rate of pound or U.S. dollar is in 90 days, you are assured delivery at the quoted price.

Table 17.1: Sample Foreign Exchange Rates

Country	U.S.$ equiv.		Currency per U.S.$	
	Wed.	Tues.	Wed.	Tues.
Argentina (Peso)	1.01	1.01	.99	.99
Australia (Dollar)	.6952	.6932	1.4384	1.4426
Bahrain (Dinar)	2.6522	2.6522	.3771	.3771
Brazil (Cruzeiro)	.0000978	.0000987	10226.10	10128.01
Britain (Pound)	1.5685	1.6005	.6376	.6248
30-Day Forward	1.5637	1.5958	.6395	.6266
90-Day Forward	1.5551	1.5868	.6430	.6302
180-Day Forward	1.5440	1.5752	.6477	.6348
Canada (Dollar)	.7862	.7859	1.2720	1.2725
30-Day Forward	.7830	.7827	1.2772	1.2776
90-Day Forward	.7783	.7782	1.2848	1.2850
180-Day Forward	.7718	.7722	1.2957	1.2950
Chile (Peso)	.032704	.002704	369.87	369.87
China (Renminbi)	.181028	.181028	5.5240	5.5240
Colombia (Peso)	.001636	.001636	611.15	611.15
Czechoslovakia (Koruna)				
Commercial Rate	.0358938	.0357270	27.8600	27.9900
Denmark (Krone)	.1641	.1659	6.0935	6.0291
Ecuador (Sucre)				
Floating Rate	.000551	.000551	1814.03	1814.03

As can be seen in the example, the cost of purchasing pounds in the forward market ($15,551) is less than the price in the spot market ($15,685). This implies that the pound is selling at a forward discount relative to the dollar, so you can buy more pounds in the forward market. It could also mean that the U.S. dollar is selling at a forward premium.

Interest Rate Parity Theory

The interest rate parity theory says that interest rate differential must equal the difference between the spot and the forward rate. The validity of this theory can be easily tested by a simple example. Lets assume that interest rate in US is 10%. An identical investment in Switzerland yields 5%. Furthermore, the exchange rate in .7097 dollar per franc. Now an investor can invest $100,000 in the US and earn interest of $105,000 (100,000 x. 10/2)in six months. The same investor can today purchase 140,905 francs (100,000/.7097) and invest in a Swiss bank to earn 144,428 francs. Now when the investor decides to transfer his currency to the U.S., what will be the exchange rate? If the investor has sold francs in the 180 day forward market, the exchange rate should be 0.7270 and investor earnings would transfer to $ 105,000. If the exchange rate were lower, i.e. 0.7100, the amount would be $102,543 and no one would be interested to invest in Switzerland. All Swiss investors would want to invest in U.S., so they would buy dollars and drive down the exchange rate until the exchange rate was 0.7270 and excess profits disappeared.

Fisher Price Effect

Fisher Price effect states that difference in interest rates must equal expected difference in inflation rates. Interest rate is made up several different components:

$$\text{Interest Rate} = K_r + K + K_{drp}$$

where K_i = the inflation premium, K_{drp} = the default risk premium and K_r = the real interest rate. Fisher argued that the real interest rate remains the same for all countries. Thus the differences in exchange rate are a direct result of differences in inflation rate. (It is assumed that the investments are identical and therefore default risk would be the same). If the real interest rates were different, it provides an excellent opportunity for currency arbitrage and eventually, the market would make the exchange rates such that the real interest rate was identical.

Purchasing Power Parity

The law of purchasing power parity states that the expected difference in inflation rate equals the difference between the forward and the spot rate. This can be easily proven. According to the interest rate parity theory, the difference in interest rate equals the difference between the forward and spot rate. According to the Fisher price effect, the difference between interest rates also equals the difference between inflation rates. Therefore, the difference between the inflation rates should equal the difference between the forward and spot rate.

The three previously described theories form the corner stone of international finance. These theories are very important in that they are used in developing some fundamental forecasting models. These three models have been kept relatively simple although real life is not this simple. Frequently these models are modified to account for real world and market imperfections.

Forecasting Techniques

The international financial markets are very complex. Therefore, a variety of forecasting techniques are used to forecast the foreign exchange rate. A certain method of forecasting may be more suited to one particular exchange rate or scenario. There are four major ways of forecasting foreign exchange rates: Fundamental forecasting, market based forecasting, technical forecasting, and a mixture of the three.

Fundamental Forecasting

Fundamental forecasting is based on fundamental relationships between economic variables and exchange rates. Given current values of these variables along with their historical impact on a currency's value, corporations can develop exchange rate projections. In previous sections, we established a basic relationship between exchange rates, inflation rates, and interest rates. This relationship can be used to develop a simple a linear forecasting model for the pound (£/$).

$$UK = a + b\,(INF) + c\,(INT)$$

where UK = the quarterly percentage change in the pound, INF = quarterly percentage change in inflation differential (US inflation rate - British inflation rate), and INT = quarterly percentage change in interest rate differential (US interest rate - British interest rate). *Note*: This model is relatively simple with only two explanatory variables. In many cases, several other variables are added but the essential methodology remains the same.

The following example illustrates how exchange rate forecasting can be accomplished using the fundamental approach.

Example 17.1

Table 17.2 shows the basic input data (for an illustrative purpose only) for the ten quarters. Table 17.3 shows a summary of the regression output, based on the use of *Excel*.

Table 17.2: Quarterly Percentage Change (for 10 Quarters)

Period	£/$	Inflation Differential	Interest Differential
1	-0.0058	-0.5231	-0.0112
2	-0.0161	-0.1074	-0.0455
3	-0.0857	2.6998	-0.0794
4	0.0012	-0.4984	0.0991
5	-0.0535	0.5742	-0.0902
6	-0.0465	-0.2431	-0.2112
7	-0.0227	-0.1565	-0.8033
8	0.1695	0.0874	3.8889
9	0.0055	-1.4329	-0.2955
10	-0.0398	3.0346	-0.0161

Table 17.3: Regression Output for the Forecasting Model

SUMMARY OUTPUT

Regression Statistics	
Multiple R	0.9602
R Square	0.9219
Adjusted R Square	0.8996
Standard Error	0.0218
Observations	10.0000

ANOVA

	df	SS	MS	F	Significance F
Regression	2	0.03933	0.01966	41.32289	0.00013
Residual	7	0.00333	0.00048		
Total	9	0.04266			

	Coefficients	Standard Error	t Stat	P-value	Lower 95%	Upper 95%
Intercept	-0.01492	0.00725	-2.05762	0.07864	-0.03206	0.00223
INF Diff.	-0.01709	0.00510	-3.35276	0.01220	-0.02914	-0.00504
INT Diff.	0.04679	0.00557	8.39921	0.00007	0.03362	0.05997

Our forecasting model that can be used to predict the £/$ exchange rate for the next quarter is:

$$UK = -0.0149 - 0.0171 \, (INF) + 0.0468 \, (INT)$$

$$R^2 = 92.19\%$$

Assuming that INT = -0.9234 and INF = 0.1148 for the next quarter:

$$UK = -0.0149 - 0.0171 \, (-0.9234) + 0.0468 \, (0.1148) = 0.00623$$

$$£/\$ = (1 + 0.00623) \times (0.6376) = 0.6415$$

However, there are certain problems with this forecasting technique. First, this technique will not be very effective with fixed exchange rates. This technique also relies on forecast to forecast. That is, one needs to project the future interest rate and the future inflation rate in order to compute the differentials that are the used to compute the exchange rate. *Note:* These estimates are frequently published in trade publications and bank reports. Second, this technique often ignores other variables that influence the foreign exchange rate.

215

Market Based Forecasting

The process of developing forecasts from market indicators is known as *market-based forecasting*. This is perhaps the easiest forecasting model. While it is very simple, it is also very effective. The model relies on the spot rate and the forward rate to forecast the price. The model assumes that the spot rate reflects the foreign exchange rate in the near future. Let us suppose that the euro is expected to depreciate vs. the U.S. dollar. This would encourage speculators to sell euro and later purchase them back at the lower (future) price. This process if continued would drive down the prices of euro until the excess (arbitrage) profits were eliminated.

The model also suggests that the forward exchange rate equals the future spot price. Again, let us suppose that the 90 day forward rate is 1.20. The market forecasters believe that the exchange rate in 90 days is going to be 1.18. This provides an arbitrage opportunity. Markets will keep on selling the currency in the forward market until the opportunity for excess profit is eliminated.

This model, however, relies heavily on market and market efficiency. It assumes that capital markets and currency markets are highly efficient and that there is perfect information in the market place. Under these circumstances, this model can provide accurate forecasts. Indeed, many of the world currency markets such as the market for U.S. dollar, Euros, and Japanese Yen are highly efficient and this model is well suited for such markets. However, market imperfections or lack of perfect information reduces the effectiveness of this model. In some cases, this model cannot be used.

Technical Forecasting

Technical forecasting involves the use of historical exchange rates to predict future values. It is sometimes conducted in a judgmental manner, without statistical analysis. Often, however, statistical analysis is applied in technical forecasting to detect historical trends. There are also time series model that examine moving averages. Most technical models rely on the past to predict the future. They try to identify a historical pattern that seems to repeat and then try to forecast it. Most models try to break down the historical series. They try to identify and remove the random element. Then they try to forecast the overall trend with cyclical and seasonal variations.

A moving average is useful to remove minor random fluctuations. A trend analysis is useful to forecast a long term linear or exponential trend. Winter's seasonal smoothing and Census XII decomposition are useful to forecast long term cycles with additive seasonal variations. Many forecasting and statistical packages such as *Forecast Pro*, and *SAS* can handle these computations.

Mixed Forecasting

Mixed forecasting in not a unique technique but rather a combination of the three previously discussed methods. In some cases, mixed forecast is nothing but a weighted average of a variety of the forecasting techniques. The techniques can be weighted arbitrarily or by assigning a higher weight to the more reliable technique. Mixed forecasting may often lead to a better result than relying on one single forecast.

A Framework for Evaluating Forecasts

Forecasting foreign exchange is an ongoing process. Due to the dynamic nature of international markets, forecasts may not be accurate. However, the quality of forecast does improve with a forecaster's experience. Therefore, it is necessary to set up some kind of framework within which a forecast can be evaluated.

The simplest framework would be to measure the errors in forecasting, which was discussed in details in Chapter 4. Several measures such as MAD, MSE, and MPE can be calculated and tracked. If more than one forecasting technique is used, i.e., a mixed forecast is used, a company may be able to decide, which technique is superior. It may then adjust the weighting scale in a mixed forecast.

A good framework makes it easy for a company to predict errors in forecasting. For example, if a forecaster is consistently forecasting the foreign exchange rate for a foreign currency above its actual rate this would suggest that a forecaster needs to adjust the forecast for this bias. Furthermore, a tracking signal and the turning point error needs to be systematically monitored.

Conclusion

In reality, currency forecasting is neglected in many multinational firms. They often argue that forecasting is useless since it does not provide an accurate estimate. They do not even have a hedging strategy. Failure to accurately forecast currency can have a disastrous impact on earnings. Moreover, it is important to realize that forecasting is often undertaken so the corporation has a general idea about the overall trend of the future and that the companies are not caught off guard. While currency forecasts are not 100% accurate, they do provide some advance warning of future trends.

It is also important to realize that forecasting is not an exact science like mathematics, it is an art. The quality of forecasts tends to improve over time as the forecaster gains more experience. One can not ignore the value of judgment and intuition in forecasting, although evidence shows that forecasts using qualitative technique are not as accurate as those using quantitative technique.

Note: An experienced forecaster uses both qualitative as well as quantitative techniques to create a reasonable forecast.

Chapter 18
Interest Rate Forecasting

While there have been a number of efforts devoted to evaluating the accuracy of forecasts of sales and earnings per share, there have been little attention given to the reliability of interest forecasts. Noting that interest rates and earnings are closely linked more than ever before, interest rates need to be forecast accurately.

Furthermore, many corporate financial decisions such as the timing of a bond refunding are dependent on anticipated changes in interest rate. Especially for financial institutions, changes in the level of interest rates can be one of the most important variables determining the success of the enterprise sine both lending and investing decisions are heavily influenced by anticipated movements in interest rates. Clearly, the accuracy of interest rate forecasts is important from the perspective of the produced and the consumer of such forecast. Whether refinancing a mortgage or completing a multimillion-dollar acquisition, the future direction of interest rates is a key factor. It is important to develop a tracking and forecasting system that considers not only economic factors but also psychological and political forces.

Term Structure of Interest Rates

The term structure of interest rates, also known as a *yield curve*, shows the relationship between length of time to maturity and yields of debt instruments. Other factors such as default risk and tax treatment are held constant. An understanding of this relationship is important to corporate financial officers who must decide whether to borrow by issuing long-or short-term debt.

An understanding of yield-to-maturity for each currency is especially critical to a CFO. It is also important to investors who must decide whether to buy long- or short-term bonds. Fixed income security analysts should investigate the yield curve carefully in order to make judgments about the direction of interest rates. A yield curve is simply a graphical presentation of the term structure of interest rates. If short-term rates are higher than long-term rates, the curve will be downward sloping. If the reverse is true, the curve will be upward sloping. One facet of the term structure of interest rates (the relationship of yield and time to maturity) is that short-term interest rates have ordinarily been lower than long-term rates. One reason is that less risk is involved in the short run.

Interest Rate Fundamentals

Today's supply of and demand for credit determines today's short-term interest rate. Expectations about the future supply of and demand for credit determine the long-term interest rate. Therefore, it is safe to say that short- and long-term interest rates are impacted by similar factors.

Then what are the specific factors that determine interest rates? The business cycle is one factor. The cycle tends to dictate credit demands by the government and businesses. Economic growth is "credit and liquidity driven" in our economy. As the demand for funds strengthens during an expansion, there is an upward pressure on interest rates. The reverse will occur during a business contraction.

Although the demand side is stressed in this explanation of the cyclical effect on interest rates, the supply side of credit and liquidity should not be ignored. For example, foreign credit supplies are certainly an important factor these days. The larger the trade deficit, the larger will be the trade deficit of foreign capital into the U.S.—which, all things being equal, helps lower interest rates.

Any gap between the demand and supply will be accentuated by monetary policy. The Federal Reserve is supposed to "lean against the wind." TI-ms, the Fed's net addition to liquidity (growth of the monetary aggregates) will tend to raise interest rates near cyclical peaks and diminish them at cyclical troughs.

In addition, inflation impacts short- and long-term interest rates. One key factor is compensation for anticipated inflation, which would otherwise erode the purchasing power of principal and interest and hence ruin the supply of savings.

The stage is set for interest rate forecasting. Interest rates are the dependent variable within a multiple regression framework in which the state of the business cycle, monetary policy, and inflation anticipations are the right-hand explanatory variables.

The difficulties, however, are that the correct measurement of the explanatory factors are hard to find. For example, how do you represent the business cycle? It can be characterized by a multitude of business conditions and their statistical representations. The Fed's monetary policy is another example. Finding the right "proxies" would be a burdensome task.

Furthermore, the interest rate as the dependent variable is also hard to define since there are short-term rates, intermediate-term rates, and long-term rates. Table 18.1

presents a guide to selecting the dependent variable and conceivable independent variables. This table is by no means an exhaustive list and is only a suggested guide, based on a review of past efforts at forecasting interest rates.

Table 18.2 provides a list of variables that emerged from some selected prior empirical testing by interest rate experts.

Statistical Methodology and a Sample Model

Despite many difficulties, statistical forecasts of interest rates are commonly attempted by business economists and frequently structured along the lines of the sample equation shown in Table 18.3. Multiple regression analysis appears to be the dominant approach to building the model for interest rate forecasting.

In Table 18.2, we show the 20-year U.S. Treasury bond yield as a function of the unemployment rate, the growth in money supply, a weighted average of past inflation, and volatility in the three-month Treasury bill.

Checklist for Screening out Explanatory Factors

In order to pick the best regression equation for interest forecasting, you should pretty much follow the same criteria discussed in Chapter 5 (Multiple Regression). Some are repeated here.

Table 18.1: Commonly Used Variables in Interest Rate Forecasting

DEPENDENT VARIABLES

1. *Short-Term Rates*

    U.S. Treasury bill rates (notably three-month)

    Federal funds rate

    Prime rate

2. *Long-Term Rates*

    New AA utility bond yields

    20-year U.S. Treasury bond yields

    30-year U.S. Treasury bond yields

    10-year U.S. Treasury bond yields

    Commercial mortgage rates

    Residential mortgage rates

INDEPENDENT VARIABLES

1. *Real Economic Activity*
    Real GDP
    Change in real GDP
    Change in non-agricultural payroll employment
    Confidence index
    Leading economic indicators
2. *Capacity Utilization*
    Rate of growth in productivity
    Vendor performance
    New capacity utilization estimates
    Manufacturers capacity utilization
    Operating rates to preferred rates
    Utilization rate...Manufacturing
    Capacity utilization...Primary materials
    Capacity utilization...Advanced processing
    Buying policy
    Business equipment/consumer goods
    Help wanted/unemployment
    Number of initial jobless claims
    Change in unfilled orders
    Output/capacity
3. *Credit Demands by Government and Businesses*
    Income velocity (GDP/M-1)
    Federal budget deficit/GDP
    Change in mortgage debt
    Change in bank loans to business
    Change in installment debt
4. *Inflation Rate*
    Change in CPI (Consumer Price Index)
    Change in PPI (Producer Price Index)
5. *Monetary Aggregates*
    Change in money supply (M-I)
    Change in money supply (M-2)
    Real money base Money supply in constant dollars (M-I)

6. *Liquidity*

    Money supply (M-1)/GDP

    Money supply (M-2)/GDP

7. *Banking*

    Member bank borrowing

    Loans/deposits...Commercial banks

    Loans/investments...Commercial banks

8. *Households*

    Change in household net worth (flow of funds)

9. *Corporations*

    Internal cash flow/business capital spending

10. *Foreign Credit Supplies and Foreign Influences*

    Size of the current account (i.e., foreign trade) deficit/GDP Foreign interest rates

11. *Expectational-type Variables*

    Moving average of prior years of actual inflation

    Moving average of the change in the 3-month T-bill yield

    Polynomial distributed lag of the percentage change in the CPI

Table 18.2: Key Variables in Interest Rate Forecasting Found in the Literature

Dependent Variable	Independent (Explanatory) Variables
1. Roger Williams[1]	
Federal fund rate	Vendor performance
	Change in money supply M-1 or M-2
	Rate of change in the CPI
New AA utility bond yields	Vendor performance
	Rate of change in the CPI lagged one period
	Ration of bank loans to investments lagged one period

2. The Prudential[2]
    10-year Treasury bond yields

    Government deficits/GDP
    Foreign trade/GDP
    Rate of growth in productivity
    Moving average of the five prior years of
    Actual inflation
    Lagged change in GDP
    Foreign interest rates
    Variance and momentum indexes

3. Schott[3]
    20-year Treasury bond yields

    Log (unemployment rate)
    Percentage change in M-1
    Polynomial distributed lag of the percentage
    Change in the CPI
    Volatility = moving average of the change in
    the three-month T-bill

4. Horan[4]
    New AA utility bond yield

    Income volatility (GDP/M-1)
    Moving average of CPI change
    Commercial paper rate
    RHO (autoregressive error term)

[1]. Roger Williams, 'Forecasting Interest Rates and Inflation,' *Business Economics,*57-60. January 1979, pp. 57-60.

[2]. The Prudential, Understanding Long-Term Interest Rates,' *Economic Review.* July 1991, pp. 1-8.

[3]. Francis H. Schott, "Forecasting Interest Rates: Methods and Application,' *Journal of Business Forecast/~j,* Fall 1986, pp. 11-19.

[4]. Lawrence J. Horan, "Forecasting Long-Term Interest Rates – A New Method,' *Business Economics,* September 1978, pp. 5-8.

Table 18.3: Model and Values of Parameter Model

20-Year T-Bond Yield = b_o + b_1 × log (Unemployment Rate) + b_2 x % Change in M-1 + b_3 x Change in CPI, Annualized + b_4 x Volatility

VALUE OF PARAMETERS

	Independent Variable	*Coefficient*	*t-value**
1.	Constant	11.137	4.36
2.	Log (unemployment rate)	-3.297	-3.65
3.	Percentage change in M-1	-0.026	-2.16
4.	Polynomial distributed lag of the percentage change in the CPI annualized; lag of 4 quarters, 2nd degree polynomial	-0.24	-2.73
5.	Volatility; 4-year moving average of the absolute value of the change in the 3-month T-bill	1.726	2.05

n = 47

S_e = 0.4709

R_2 = 0.975

Durbin-Watson = 1.64**

* Statistically significant at the 5 percent significance level.

**No autocorrelation (serial correlation) at the 1 percent level.

Source: Schett, Francis H., "Forecasting Interest Rates: Methods and Application," *Journal of Business Forecasting,* Fall 1986, p. 18.

1. Many independent variables listed in Table 18.2 tend to be highly correlated with each other *(multicollinearity)*. This will help lead to the elimination of a number of overlapping series.

2. Variables cannot be retained unless the positive or negative signs of regression coefficients are consistent with theoretical expectations.

3. Traditional yardsticks such as R^2, t-test, F-test, and Durbin-Watson test must be used to select preliminary equations.

4. The predictive performance of the preliminary models needs to be tested based on *ex ante* and *ex post* forecasts.

    (a) It is usually measured by such metrics as MPE, RSME, MSE, MAD, and/ or Henry Theft U Coefficient, as was fully discussed in Chapter S.

(b)   Compare the forecasts with some "naive" (but much less costly) approach, such as assuming that rates in the future will be the same as today.

(c)   Compare quantitative approaches such as econometric forecasting with judgmental forecasts. Judgment can be the overriding factor in interest rate forecasting.

(d)   In addition to these evaluations, a separate evaluation of *turning point errors* needs to be made. A turning point error takes place when either you project an increase in interest levels when rates declined or when you anticipated its decline when rates increased. It often is argued that the ability of forecasters to anticipate reversals of interest rate trends is more important than the precise accuracy of the forecast. Substantial gains or losses may arise from a move from generally upward moving rates to downward rate trends (or vice versa), but gains or losses from incorrectly predicting the extent of a continued increase or decrease in rates may be much more limited.

A Word of Caution

No reasonable business planners should rely solely on statistical methods such as multiple regression. Other quantitative methods need to be attempted. It is important to realize that differences among forecasting methods and assumptions and in a choice of proxies regarding the explanatory variables can yield vastly different results from analyst to analyst. Judgments and expert opinions can help determine the future direction of interest rates. The right marriage between a quantitative evaluation and expert judgments is a must. Consensus forecasts such as those of the National Association of Business Economists (NABE), which receives wide coverage in the financial press, and econometric forecasts made by con-suiting firms such as The Wharton Econometric Associates, Chase Econometrics. and DRI/McGraw-Hill should be con-suited as well.

The cost of errors in interest rate forecasting can be as severe as that of exchange rate forecasting mistakes. Schott at Equitable Life suggests that businesses use specific strategies and policies to reduce their exposure to interest rate forecasting mistakes (e.g., asset/liability maturity matching and hedging with futures).

Conclusion

Interest rate forecasting is as treacherous as other economic forecasting, such as the prediction of corporate earnings and foreign exchange rates. The chapter briefly touched upon fundamentals: business cycles, the outlook for the demand and supply of credits, monetary policy, and the inflation rate. It also presented a sample model that reflects on the fundamental theory. The forecasting ability of the model also should be judged in terms of its ability to anticipate major changes in the direction (or turning point) of rates.

Chapter 19
Technological Forecasting

The effects of technological changes are felt in the following *ways:*

1. *New products or services.* The development of the internal combustion engine produced new products, from automobiles to lawn mowers to motorcycles, as innovators began to visualize better work methods and leisure applications for the engine.

2. *Alternate processing methods, raw materials, and service delivery.* The introduction of robotics to assembly line work has altered mass production technology in some sectors of the automobile industry, while the development of alloys and plastics has made cars lighter and more fuel-efficient.

3. *Changes in complementary products or services.* Blacksmiths have all but disappeared, but van customization has become a significant business in some areas of the country. Both related to the development and applications of the internal combustion engine.

All organizations feel the effects of **"progress,"** but the dramatic shifts in technology that render whole sectors of the economy almost obsolete are rare.

Technological forecasting is a discipline concerned with identifying new products that are based on innovative technologies that will produce growth markets. It attempts to predict changes in technology and the time frame in which new technologies are likely to be economically feasible. By its very nature, it is one of the most difficult kinds of forecasts to make because of the innumerable variables, unknowns and possible outcomes. However, being able to forecast technology with a reasonable degree of accuracy is becoming increasing important to the success of business managers in gaining a competitive edge or even remaining viable in the long run as evidenced by the tremendous pace of change occurring in today's dynamic times.

It is probably very safe to say that we have experienced greater technological change in the last 50 years than the total changes prior to that time from the beginning of recorded history. It is also just as certain that a similar comparison using the "last 50 years" at the end of this century, will show a very similar relationship. The implication is that technological growth will continue at an even accelerating rate.

In order to remain competitive and possibly even gain a competitive advantage in these times of change, management must engage in some level of technological forecasting. Nothing can be more damaging to a company than to allow competitors to get a jump on new products or techniques. Technological developments therefore, may not only be a requirement of competitiveness but also of self-preservation.

The planning of most areas affecting the operations of an enterprise will be predicated on some assumptions about future technology. Planning for capital investment in new machinery or equipment, planning of new facilities requirements, and the planning involved in the research and development activities of the enterprise are some examples.

Accuracy of Technological Forecasting

The need for technological forecasting is clear, but the ability to produce accurate forecasts is lacking. There are so many intangibles involved in the development of technological break-through that the forecaster is severely limited. It is doubtful that anyone could have predicted the many technical spinoffs from the space program. Nor, for that matter, can we surmise the full results of the unforeseen development of some method of immunization against cancer, or AIDS.

Once a breakthrough occurs, however, prediction of the growth of the development is more feasible. A historical analysis of the progress of the technology of any given development will most likely show an exponential improvement rate. The progress can be represented by a curve like that shown in Figure 19.1.

Figure 19.1: Exponential Curve Projecting Bit Density in Computer Memory

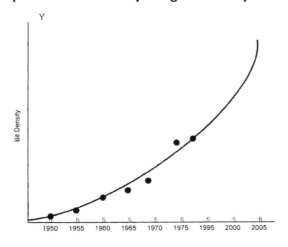

This curve, however, has certain underlying assumptions. Early progress is very small for a period of time. At some point very rapid progress begins, probably as a result of a specific breakthrough. This may be the result of a discovery making a useful item possible; e.g., splitting the atom made atomic energy feasible. This discovery could result from a production technology making economic production possible. Following the period of rapid growth, a leveling off is seen. This could represent a period of saturation, where only by another breakthrough could any further significant progress take place. It is conceivable that another curve of the same shape could start where this curve left off. For example, television could be represented by two sequential curves: the first showing progress for black and white; the second, for color television.

S-Curve as a Guide for Technological Forecasting

The S-type curve is one of the most common (but not the only) curves used in technological forecasting. It implies a slow beginning, a period of rapid growth, and finally a plateauing of the trend. The S-curve is indicative of many technological developments, such as incandescent and fluorescent lighting efficiency, the maximum speed of aircraft, and the efficiency of commercial electric power plants, as well as the sales of many new products including color TVs, CB radios, and small calculators.

The S-curve graphs the relationship between effort put into improving a product or process and the firm's results from making the investment. The S-curve reveals the life cycle of a particular product or process. It shows how one technology eventually outperforms another previously higher-performance technology when a discontinuity exists. It can be used as a guide because at the point of maturity (increased efforts and investment result in small productivity improvements) firms need to look for higher performing technologies which frequently involve radical changes. It is strategically important to organizations because they may be leapfrogged by other competitors who adopt a radical different technology and achieve a competitive advantage. The notion of S-curves suggests that organizations need to manage a portfolio of technologies in order to compete in the long term.

Methodology of Technological Forecasting

Despite what has been said above about the problems of accurate technological forecasting, the company should develop this kind of forecast. For short-term periods, acceptable forecasts should be possible by means of historical trends and statistical probability analysis. This does not mean that "history repeats itself," and, therefore, because a certain progress took place in the past that here will be a continued similar progress. It is possible to determine the pertinent elements of the environment and to be cognizance of their impact. Technological forecasting must recognize the strong influence of environmental factors. This type forecast is only a part of a total attempt to relate the enterprise to its environment. It is not possible to produce a technological forecast without this recognition. The relationship of technology to society appears to be of particular significance.

There are two general classes of technological forecasting techniques. The *exploratory approach* begins with today's knowledge, projects potential future progress, and then considers the effects of this future technological environment on the firm's decisions. In contrast, the *normative approach* attempts to assess future goals and objectives and then to identify the technological requirements for meeting these goals. The final step of normative models is to identify limits and barriers in the current state of technology that preclude the achievement of the identified objectives. It is these technological gaps that become prime candidates for research and development efforts by the firm.

The types of methods that have been devised to forecast technology are:

1.   Delphi method
2.   Simple trend extrapolation and lead-lag relationships
3.   Input-output models
4.   Production models
5.   Diffusion models

The Delphi Method

According to various surveys and expert opinions on technological forecasting, intuition appears to play a very important role in exploratory technological forecasting. For instance, suppose that a company wants to forecast the maximum speed of PCs in the year 2010. One way of obtaining such a forecast would simply be to ask an expert, or, a group of experts, to make an educated guess as best they can what they think the speed will be at that time. This approach is relatively straightforward and inexpensive, but it suffers from a number of difficulties. First, answers are likely to vary depending on the choice of expert. Second, even when based on the opinion of distinguished experts such forecasts can contain large errors. For example, some experts predicted in 1985 that there would be a near disaster of small nuclear war.

To deal with some of the inherent problems involved in simply asking a group of experts for a consensus guess, the *Delphi method* can be used to attempt to utilize expert opinion more effectively. For example, to forecast the maximum speed of PCs in the year 2010, users of the Delphi method would ask a number of experts to formulate separate and independent estimates. Then the median and interquartile range of the estimates would be communicated to each of the experts, and they would be asked to reconsider their previous answers and revise them if they wanted to. Then those people whose answers lie outside the interquartile range would be asked to state why they disagree to this extent from the other members of the group. Then their replies would be circulated among the group, and the members would be asked once again to make a forecast. This interactive process would continue until there was a reasonable convergence of the individual forecasts.

Advocates of the Delphi approach argue that it is superior to conventional approaches designed to achieve consensus through open discussion because direct contact between the panelists is eliminated. This eliminates the influence of such factors as the persuasive ability of individual panel members, the reluctance to abandon publicly stated opinions, and the bandwagon effects of majority opinions.

The disadvantages of this approach are as follows: (1) the experts may be unable to reach a consensus view, (2) the results may be widely divergent if different panels of experts are used, (3) it is difficult to take into account the unexpected, and (4) the technique has a considerable sensitivity to the ambiguity of the questions initially posed. It should be noted that, to a large extent, these limitations exist for other techniques as well. In spite of these disadvantages the Delphi approach has been successfully used to forecast the need for new products and processes and to determine the most attractive possibilities and the best time for introduction. For such new product or process forecasting in a firm, the panel may consist of knowledgeable individuals from both inside and outside the firm. It is usually preferable to have a wide range of expertise represented on the panel.

Simple Trend Extrapolation and Lead-Lag Relationships

Another technique that plays an important role in exploratory technological forecasting is *simple trend extrapolation*. For example, to forecast the maximum speed of PCs in 2015, one could obtain a time series of the maximum speed of such PC at various points in history, and project the historical trend into the future. In fact, Nesbitt used this approach to project the future trends in our society, such as a shift from an industrial to an information society and globalization of the economy.

The problem with these types of naive extrapolation techniques is that, unless the fundamental factors determining the technological parameter in question operate much as they have in the past, previous trends will not necessarily be a good guide to the future. For example, a host of factors, including the allocation of R & D resources, data processing needs, and the competitive pressure of the industry may see to it that maximum speed of PCs increases at quite a different rate than it has in the immediate past. Or take the case of productivity increase. There is considerable evidence that productivity increase has not occurred at a constant rate in the United States. The moral well known to economists, is that a naive projection of historical trends is a dangerous business, particularly when long-term forecasts are being made.

Besides trend extrapolation, the technological forecasters have adopted another old favorite of the economic forecasters – *lead-lag relationships*. For example, to forecast the maximum speed of PCs in 2015, the forecaster could plot the maximum speed of PCs against the maximum speed of mainframe. Finding that PC speeds have lagged mainframe speeds, he or she might be able to use this relationship to make the desired forecast. Again, the problem here is that the historical relationship may not prevail into the future.

There are plenty of examples of technological forecasting that utilized a combination of simple extrapolation and lead-lag relationships. For example, Marvin Minsky, a pioneer in the field of artificial intelligence see computerized robots and smarter machines as a growing trend. Jack Kilby predicts the development of integrated-circuit research will result in many new products and applications of technology. Jerome Feldman sees neutral networks, connectionist systems, and parallel-distributed processing systems becoming practical applications in the next decade. The huge growth of genetic engineering and biotechnology is already underway. By the year 2010, $1 trillion worth of biotech drugs, plants, chemicals, and other products is expected to be sold worldwide.

Input-Output Models

There has been some experimentation with the projection of input-output structures into the future. In order to make such projections, one must forecast both the input requirements of future techniques and the rate of diffusion of future techniques, since the input-output coefficients will be a weighted average of existing and future techniques, the weights depending on the rate of diffusion.

This approach requires the estimation of the input requirements for future techniques. One way that economists have tried to forecast input-output coefficients in a particular industry is to assume that new technologies have a weight proportional to investment in new capacity. By observing the changes in the industry's average input-output structure, and its expenditures on new plant and equipment, one can estimate what the input-output coefficients for the new "layer" of capital must have been. Then, to make short-term projections, one can assume that the coefficients for the new "layer" will remain constant, and increase the weight given to these coefficients (in proportion to expected investment). This method, however, is crude at best. All that its users claim is that it gives "ball park" estimates.

Another way of projecting input-output structures is through the use of expert opinion. This method, however, suffers from by the same sorts of difficulties mentioned in connection with the Delphi method. Moreover, there are other problems as well. For one thing, the industrial classification employed in the input-output model is broader than the product categories that the technologists making the forecasts are used to dealing with. For another thing, it is difficult to include qualitative changes, like new products, within the input-output framework. At present, the use of input-output analysis in connection with technological forecasting is still in its infancy. All that can be said is that it represents a promising area for future research.

Production Models

Some economists consider the use of production models containing R & D expenditures for technological forecasting. In recent years, many researchers have attempted to formulate econometric models of production in which research and development plays a role. These models are oversimplified and incomplete in many respects. Yet they provide reasonably persuasive evidence that R & D has a significant effect on the rate of productivity increase in the industries and time periods that have been studied. The models utilize regression and econometric techniques.

These models can be used for technological forecasting. In particular, they can be used to forecast the effects on productivity or output of a certain investment in research and development at various points in time. Moreover, they can be used to forecast future requirements for labor and other inputs. Of course, they cannot be used to forecast the precise nature of the technology that will result from an investment in R & D. But they can provide some idea of the input-output relationships that this technology will permit--and for many purposes these relationships are what really count. For example, if we can be reasonably sure that a given investment in R & D will result in a certain reduction in cost or in the use of certain crucial inputs, (for example, alternative energy sources such as hydropower, solar energy, alcohol fuels, photovoltaic cells, and geothermal energy) this may be all that is really relevant in making certain decisions. The precise nature of the new technology may not matter much.

It might be noted that some of our government agencies have become interested in these models in recent years. Specifically, these models suggest that the marginal rate of return from certain types of civilian R & D is very high, and that we may be underinvesting in such R & D. It is difficult, of course, to tell how much influence these models had on the recent decisions by the American government to experiment with various devices to encourage additional R & D in various civilian areas. But we can rest assured that they are one of the influences at work. However, lest anyone gets the impression that these models are sufficiently dependable to play a dominant role in influencing such decisions, let's add that they are extremely crude and subject to considerable error. Much more work still needs to be done.

Diffusion Models

In the past thirty years, a number of studies have been made of the diffusion of innovations. The results suggest that it is possible, on the basis of fairly simple econometric models, to explain fairly well the differences among industrial innovations in their rate of diffusion. A simple model--based on variables like the profitability of the innovation, the size of the investment required to adopt the innovation, and the organization of the industry of potential users—can be built to explain differences in the rate at which innovations spread. This model would explain the rates of diffusion of a dozen major innovations in the United States very well. Moreover, it may be also useful in explaining the rates of diffusion of other innovations--and in other countries.

Models of this sort can be used for technological forecasting. For many purposes, it is extremely important to know how rapidly a new technique will displace an old one. Obviously, this is of crucial importance to the firm marketing the new technique. But it may be of great importance to other groups as well. For example, government agencies are sometimes concerned with the extent to which labor will be displaced and the way in which particular areas will be affected. Also, labor unions and competing firms have a great interest in this question. For many purposes, the important consideration is not when an entirely new process or product will be invented in the future. Instead, it is how rapidly one can expect the new processes and products that have already been invented to diffuse. Certainly, in view of the long time lags in many sectors of the economy, this often is all that matters in the short run--and the intermediate run as well.

For forecasting growth markets, however, research arising out of the diffusion of innovations is not without limitations. The problem stems from the fact that market growth is not automatic or even likely. Forecasts based on such theories have a built-in tendency to be overly optimistic. They presuppose strong market growth and do not address adequately the possibility of failure. There is no law or inherent tendency for products to exhibit growth as some formulations would have people believe. In fact, nearly every study that has looked at the issue has concluded that most products never make it past stage one.

This is not to suggest however, that the work in these areas is flawed but to rather point out that since the theories rely so heavily on after-the-fact explanations, they are of little help in predicting which technologies will go on to spawn huge growth markets and which will repeat previous failures.

Diffusion models nevertheless, have found a variety of uses in technological forecasting. This model has been used by a number of firms in a variety of industries. For example, a leading electronics firm has been experimenting with the use of this model to forecast the market penetration of its new products. Of course, the fact that this model has been used does not mean that it is other than a simple first approximation. We are continually refining it and testing it on a wider and wider variety of technological and product areas. We are still far from having a satisfactory understanding of the diffusion process.

An Evaluation

The present state of the art in technological forecasting can be characterized as follows:

1. Most of the techniques commonly used for exploratory forecasting seem crude and hence inaccurate. Among other things, there have been no studies measuring the track record of various kinds of technological forecasting techniques. Such studies seem to be called for. It would be useful to have some idea of how well these techniques have performed under various circumstances, and of which sorts of techniques seem to do better under particular kinds of circumstances. Without such information, it is hard for anyone to make decisions concerning the types of exploratory forecasting activities that are worth carrying out.

2. Despite the crudeness of most existing techniques, no one can argue that technological forecasting is not a necessary part of the decision-making process in firms and government agencies. The potential gains seem to outweigh the costs. However, given the lack of reliable data regarding the likely gains from various kinds of technological forecasting, this is not an easy comparison to make.

3. There is a great need for studies leading toward a better understanding of the process of technological change. Until the fundamental processes are somewhat better understood, it seems unlikely that much improvement will occur in exploratory forecasting techniques. The area that is perhaps best understood at present is the diffusion process--and this is the area where forecasting currently seems most effective. More emphasis must be placed on the accumulation of the basic knowledge that is required if this field is to become more a science and less of an art.

4. If normative technological forecasting is to become of widespread use, it is important that better methods be developed to estimate development cost, time, the probability of success, and the value of the outcome if achieved. At present, such estimates tend to be so biased and error-ridden that it is difficult to place much dependence on the results. In view of the inaccuracy of these estimates, companies that use normative technological forecasting techniques must to carry out "what-if" analyses to see the effect of such errors on the results. Further, they must see how big the errors in these estimates have been in the recent past--since there seems to be some tendency to underestimate their size.

5. The work of the technological forecasters needs to be integrated properly with the decisions of the strategic planners. Frequently, the work of the technological forecasters is largely ignored in the decision-making process. If this work is worth doing at all, it should be related and coupled with long range planning and decision-making.

6. It is important to recognize that technological forecasting is just a thing of science and engineering. One cannot estimate the probability that a particular technology will come into being on the basis of technological considerations alone. Economic, social, political, and business anomalies considerations often play an equally important role. Furthermore, managers cannot decide how a firm's technological resources should be allocated and utilized on the basis of technological considerations alone.

Chapter 20

Forecasting in the 21st Century

Any discipline or managerial function can be expected to change over time, and forecasting is no exception. Alterations in the methodology and uses of forecasting can be expected to increase. These changes can be expected to take the form of more sophisticated forecasting techniques, wide availability of expert system-based forecasting software, and their increased employment by management. The critical element in any supply chain plan is the demand forecast.

More Sophisticated Techniques and User-Friendly Software

The passage of time should witness advances in the quality of forecasting technology. Among the forces contributing to the elevation of the art are new developments in the social sciences, mathematics, research techniques, and information technology. Progress to date has been considerable, as witnessed by analysts who use innovations in simulation, brand-share models, and survey techniques.

A survey of the literature suggests that sensitivity analysis (or what-if analysis) -- a refined feature of model building -- is being widely adopted by analysts. Sensitivity analysis involves manipulating a mathematical model and observing the effect on the dependent variable. If' the effect is small, analysts need not concern themselves with attempting to develop more precise estimates of the magnitude of that variable. If the effort is substantial, attempts to improve preciseness may be in order. Increasing use of sensitivity analysis is only one indicator of advances in methodology. Virtually every phase of the forecasting process can be expected to become more sophisticated in upcoming years.

Increased Use of Forecasting by Management

It is likely that managers of the future will use forecasting to a larger extent than is the case now. Part of the impetus for this development will evolve from increasing educational levels of executives. Larger numbers of managers have MBA degrees. These better-educated managers are likely to give more importance to forecasting as a planning and control tool than did their predecessors. The modern manager is more likely to have the training required to understand the methodology and even to construct forecast models.

The increased pace of change is a second force that contributes to increased employment of forecasting. More and more products are displaying shorter life cycles. Industry sales change abruptly, producing rapid and significant fluctuations in company sales. These changes make it necessary for managers to be in possession of methods which will signal what is expected to take place in the future. No longer are managers able to sit back and assume that their sales will more or less automatically grow at a pace of 5 percent annually. They must continually monitor sales levels and be prepared to respond to change.

In the future, cost pressures on management are expected to be a continuing reality. These take the form of increments in wages, power rates, interest rates, and costs of raw materials, supplies, parts, and equipment. These cost advances put pressure on management to produce effective plans and controls. Such plans and controls are dependent on the sales forecast.

Business valuations that are essential for such key strategic activities as mergers and acquisitions require more precise prediction of future earnings, cash flows, and sales.

Increases in the intensity of global competition can be expected to generate increments in forecasting use. Rivalry from both foreign and domestic firms is increasing, especially in industries such as packaged foods, automobiles, and computers. As competition steps up, managers are forced to use effective forecasting processes to compete with rivals who are enhancing their own forecasting abilities. Forecasting and its connection to supply chain management are greatly being stressed. If your forecasts and orders are the input to your Enterprise Resource Planning (ERP) system's material requirement planning (MRP), the output of your MRP should be the input to your suppliers' MRP.

Advancing inability to predict the future behavior of the consumer through simplistic methods that were effective in the past tends to induce further use and sophistication in sales forecasting. Increments in consumer education and discretionary income tend to render consumers less brand-loyal and more inclined to attempt new forms of behavior, including purchase and use of previously unknown products. Consumers are tending to become more fickle and more difficult to predict, despite considerable advances in the quality of consumer behavior research and theory.

The increasing sophistication of methods and modeling software should help produce more usage of forecasting. As methodology improves and becomes more accurate and precise, managers can be expected to rely on forecasting more than they did in the past. Better tools and computer software are likely to yield wider use. Data mining, data warehousing, and business intelligence are increasingly used for forecasting purposes. For example, inn *data mining*, the data in a data warehouse are processed to identify key factors and trends in historical patterns of business activity that can be used to help managers make decisions about strategic changes in business operations to gain competitive advantages in the marketplace.

Conclusion

Some generalizations help in placing the forecasting process in proper perspective. One is that forecasting is an ongoing process; another is that it is essential. Forecasting is *not* an activity that takes place at periodic intervals, such as once a year, and ceases entirely between these intervals.

Both short- and long-term forecasts are continually being made, evaluated, and revised. As new products are considered or are adopted, their sales potential is assessed. Changes in the environment and internal structure of the firm are likely to be continual. Factors such as price alterations by competitors, strikes by labor unions, and changes in the advertising strategy of the firm occur from time to time. Many of these phenomena are of sufficient significance to warrant alterations in existing sales forecasts. Forecasting is not a one-time and static activity. It is a continuing process that should merit constant attention.

Forecasting is also essential. It is difficult and in some cases impossible for the firm to develop and implement effective plans in the absence of well-conceived sales forecasts that provide managers with the means for planning, organizing, and controlling all of the resources at their disposal. In the absence of forecasts, these activities must be based on mere hunch and guesswork. The dynamic and uncertain nature of the business world dictates that sales forecasts be the springboard for virtually all major decisions made by management.

Glossary

ACCURACY: The criterion for evaluating the performance of alternative forecasting methods and models. It refers to the correctness of the forecast as measured against actual events. Accuracy can be measured using such statistics as mean squared error (MSE) and mean absolute percentage error (MAPE).

BANKRUPTCY PREDICTION: Prediction of the financial distress of corporations, municipalities, universities, and other institutions.

BUSINESS VALUATIONS: the process of determining the value of a business or an asset.

CASH BUDGET: A budget for cash planning and control presenting expected cash inflow and outflow for a designated time period. The cash budget helps management keep its cash balances in reasonable relationship to its needs. It aids in avoiding idle cash and possible cash and possible cash shortages.

CASH FLOW FORECASTING: Forecasts of cash flow including cash collections from customers, investment income, and cash disbursements.

CAUSAL FORECASTING MODEL: A forecasts model that relates the variable to be forecast to a number of other variables that can be observed.

CENSUS X-II DECOMPOSITION: A refinement of the classical decomposition method, developed by the U.S. Bureau of Census.

CLASSICAL DECOMPOSITION METHOD: The approach to forecasting that seeks to decompose the underlying pattern of a time series into cyclical, seasonal, trend, and random sub-patterns. These subpatterns are then analyze individually, extrapolated into the future, and recombined to obtain forecasts of the original series.

COEFFICIENT OF DETERMINATION: A statistical measure of how good the estimated regression equation is, designated as R^2 (read as R-squared). Simply put, it is a measure of "goodness of fit" in the regression. Therefore, the higher the R-squared, the more confidence we can have in our equation.

CONSTANT VARIANCE: *See **Homoscedasticity**.*

CORRELATION COEFFICIENT (R): A measure of the degree of correlation between two variables. The range of values it takes is between -1 and +1. A negative value of R indicates an inverse relationship; a zero value of R indicated that the two variables are independent of each other; the closer R is to + or -1, the stronger the relationship between the two variables.

CORRELATION: The degree of relationship between business and economic variables such as cost and volume. Correlation analysis evaluates cause / effect relationships. It looks consistently at how the value of one variable changes when the value of the other is changed. A prediction can be made based on the relationship uncovered. An example is the effect of advertising on sales. A degree of correlation is measured statistically by the coefficient of determination (R-squared).

COST OF PREDICTION ERRORS: The cost of a failure to predict a certain variable (such as sales, earnings, and cash flow) accurately.

COST PREDICTION: Forecast or prediction of costs for managerial decision-making purposes. The terms " cost estimation" and "cost prediction" are used interchangeably. To predict future costs, a cost function often is specified and estimated statistically. The cost function may be either linear or nonlinear. The estimated cost function must pass some statistical tests, such as having a high R^2 and a high t-value, to provide sound cost prediction.

DEGREE OF RELATIVE LIQUIDITY (DRL): The percentage of a firm's cash expenditures, which can be secured from (1) beginning fund and from (2) cash generated from its normal operation.

DEGREE OF FREEDOM (DF): Indicates the number of data items that are independent of one another. Given a sample of data and the computation of some statistic (e.g., the mean), the degrees of freedom are defined as (number of observations included in the formula) minus (number of parameters estimated using the data). For example, the mean statistic for N sample data points has n DF, but the variance formula has (n-1) DF because one parameter (the mean X) has to be estimated before the variance formula can be used.

DELPHI METHOD: A qualitative forecasting method that seeks to use the judgment of experts systematically in arriving at a forecast of what future events will be or when they may occur. It brings together a group of experts who have access to each other's opinions in an environment where no majority opinion is disclosed.

DEPENDENT VARIABLE: A variable whose value depends on the values of other variables and constants in some relationship. For example, in the relationship $Y = f(X)$, Y is the dependent variable influenced by various independent variables, such as earnings per share, debt / equity ratio, and beta (see also Independent Variable).

DESEASONALIZED DATA: Removal of the seasonal pattern in a data series. Deseasonalizing facilitates the comparison of month-to-month changes.

DUMMY VARIABLE: Often referred to as a binary variable whose value is either 0 of 1, a dummy variable frequently is used to quantify qualitative or categorical events. For example, a peace or war situation could be represented by a dummy variable.

DURBIN-WATSON STATISTIC: A summary measure of the amount of autocorrelation in the error terms of the regression. By comparing the computed value of the Durbin-Watson test with the appropriate values from the table of values of the D-W statistic (Appendix Table A.4), the significance can be determined (see also Autocorrelation).

EARNINGS FORECAST: Projection of earnings or earnings per share (EPS) frequently made by management and independent security analysts. Examples of forecast sources include (1) Lynch, Jones and Ryan's Institutional Brokers Estimate System (IBES), (2) Standard & Poor's The Earnings Forecaster, and (3) Zacks Investment Research's Icarus Service.

ECONOMETRIC FORECASTING: A forecasting method that uses a set of equations intended to be used simultaneously to capture the way in which endogenous and exogenous variables are interrelated. Using such a set of equations to forecast future values of key economic variables is known as econometric forecasting. The value of econometric forecasting is connected intimately to the value of the assumptions underlying the model equations.

ERROR TERM: Deviation of the actual value of an observation from the true regression line (*see also* **Residual**).

EX ANTE FORECAST: A forecast that uses only the data available at the time at which the actual forecast is prepared.

EX POST FORECAST: A forecast that uses some information beyond the period for which the actual forecast is made.

EXPONENTIAL SMOOTHING: A forecasting technique that uses a weighted moving average of past data as the basis for a forecast. The procedure gives heaviest weight to more recent information and smaller weights to observations in the more distant past. The method is effective when there is random demand and no seasonal fluctuations in the data. The method is popular technique for short-run forecasting by business forecasters.

EXPONENTIAL SMOOTHING ADJUSTED FOR TREND: Also called Holt's two-parameter method, it is an extension by Winter of Holt's two-parameter exponential smoothing by including an additional equation that is used to adjust the smoothed forecast to reflect seasonality.

EXPONENTIAL SMOOTHING, SEASONAL: Also called Winter's three-parameter method, it is an extension by Winter of Holt's two-parameter exponential smoothing by including an additional equation that is used to adjust the smoothed forecast to reflect seasonality.

F-TEST: In statistics the ratio of two mean squares (variances) often can be used to test the significance of some item of interest. For example, in regression, the ratio of (mean square due to the regression) to (mean square due to error) can be used to test the overall significance of the regression model. By looking up F-tables, the degree of significance of the computed F-value can be determined.

FINANCIAL PROJECTION: An essential element of planning that is the basis for budgeting activities and estimating future financing needs of a firm. Financial projections (forecasts) begin with forecasting sales and their related expenses.

FORECAST: 1. A projection or an estimate of future sales revenue, earnings, or costs (see also Sales Forecasting). 2. A projection of future financial position and operating results of an organization (see also Financial Projection).

GOODNESS OF FIT: A degree to which a model fits the observed data. In a regression analysis, the goodness of fit is measured by the coefficient of determination (R-squared).

GROSS DOMESTIC PRODUCT (GDP): A measure of the value of all goods and services produced by the economy within its boundaries. It is the nation's broadest gauge of economic health.

HOLT'S TWO-PARAMETER EXPONENTIAL SMOOTHING: *See Exponential Smoothing Adjusted for Trend*.

HOMOSCEDASTICITY: One of the assumptions required in a regression in order to make valid statistical inferences about population relationships, also known as constant variance. Homoscedasticity requires that the standard deviation and variance of the error terms is constant for all Xs, and that the error terms are drawn from the same population. This indicated that there is a uniform scatter or dispersion of data points about the regression line. If the assumption does not hold, the accuracy of the b coefficient is open to question.

INDEPENDENT VARIABLE: A variable that may take on any value in a relationship. For example, in a relationship $Y = f(X)$, X is the independent variable. For example, independent variables that influence sales are advertising and price (see also Dependent Variable).

INPUT-OUTPUT ANALYSIS: Models concerned with the flows of goods among industries in an economy or among branches of a large organization. This method of analysis is concerned with the interindustry or interdepartmental flows of goods or services in the economy, or a company and its markets. An input-output matrix table is the source of this method. The table is very useful in evaluating the effects of a change in demand in one industry on other industries (i.e., a change in oil prices and its resulting effect on demand for cars, then steel sales, then iron ore and limestone sales).

INTEREST RATE FORECASTING: Projection of short-term or long-term interest rates. The forecasting of the future direction of interest rates is required whether refunding a bond or completing an acquisition.

JUDGMENTAL (QUALITATIVE) FORECAST: A forecasting method that brings together, in an organized way, personal judgments about the process being analyzed.

LEAST-SQUARES METHOD: A statistical technique for fitting a straight line through a set of points in such a way that the sum of the squared distances from the data points to the line is minimized.

LIFE CYCLE: A movement of a firm or its product through stages of development, growth, expansion, maturity, saturation, and decline. Not all products go through such a life cycle. For example, paper clips, nails, knives, drinking glasses, and wooden pencils do not seem to exhibit such a life cycle. Most new products seem to, however. Some current examples include high-tech items such as computers, DVDs, and black-and-white TVs (see also Product Life Cycle).

LIFE-CYCLE ANALYSIS: Forecasts new product growth based on S-curves. Central to the analysis are the phases of product acceptance by the various groups such as innovators, early adapters, early majority, late majority, and laggards.

LINEAR REGRESSION: A regression that deals with a straight line relationship between variables. It is in the form of $Y = a + bX$ whereas nonlinear regression involves curvilinear relationships such as exponential and quadratic functions (see also Regression Analysis).

LOGISTIC CURVE: This curve has the typical S-shape often associated with the product life cycle. It frequently is used in connection with long-term curve-fitting as a technological method.

MARKOV ANALYSIS: A method of analyzing the current behavior of some variable to predict the future behavior of that portion of the accounts receivable that will eventually become uncollectible.

MEAN ABSOLUTE DEVIATION (MAD): The mean or average of the sum of all the forecast errors with regard to sign.

MEAN ABSOLUTE PERCENTAGE ERROR (MAPE): The mean or average of the sum of all the percentage errors for a given data set taken without regard to sign. (That is, their absolute values are summed and the average computed.) It is one measure of accuracy commonly used in quantitative methods of forecasting.

MEAN SQUARE ERROR (MSE): A measure of accuracy computed by squaring the individual error for each item in a data set and then finding the average or mean value of the sum of those squares. The mean squared error gives greater weight to large errors than to small errors because the errors are squared before being summed.

MOVING AVERAGE (MA): (1) For a time series an average that is updated as new information is received. With the moving average, the analyst employs the most recent observations to calculate an average, which is used as the forecast for next period. (2) In Box-Jenkins modeling the MA in ARIMA stands for "moving average" and means that the value of the time series at time t is influenced by a current error term and (possibly) weighted error terms in the past.

MULTICOLLINEARITY: The condition that exists when the independent variables are highly correlated with each other. In the presence of multicollinearity, the estimated regression coefficients may be unreliable. The presence of multicollinearity can be tested by investigating the correlation between the independent variables.

MULTIPLE DISCRIMINANT ANALYSIS (MDA): A statistical classificatory technique similar to regression analysis that can be used to evaluated financial ratios.

MULTIPLE REGRESSION ANALYSIS: A statistical procedure that attempts to assess the relationship between the dependent variable and two or more independent variables. For example, sales of Coca-Cola is a function of various factors such as its price, advertising, taste, and the prices of its major competitors. For forecasting purposes, a multiple regression equation falls into the category of a causal forecasting model (see also Regression Analysis).

NAIVE FORECAST: Forecasts obtained with a minimal amount of effort and data manipulation, and based solely on the most recent information available. One such naive method would be to use the most recent datum available as the future forecast.

OPTIMAL PARAMETER OR WEIGHT VALUE: Those values that give the best performance for a given model applied to a specific set of data. It is those optimal parameters that then are used in forecasting.

PRODUCT LIFE CYCLE: The concept that is particularly useful in forecasting and analyzing historical data of new products. It presumes that demand for a product follows an S-shaped curve growing slowly in the early stages, achieving rapid and sustained growth in the middle stages, and slowing again in the mature stage.

PROGRAM EVALUATION AND REVIEW TECHNIQUE (PERT): Useful management tool for planning, coordinating and controlling large complex projects.

PROJECTED (BUDGETED) BALANCE SHEET: A schedule for expected assets, liabilities, and stockholders' equity. It projects a company's financial position as of the end of the budgeting year. Reasons for preparing a budgeted balance sheet follow: (1) discloses unfavorable financial condition that management may want to avoid; (2) serves as a final check on the mathematical accuracy of all other budgets; and (3) highlights future resources and obligations.

PROJECTED (BUDGETED) INCOME STATEMENT: A summary of various component projections of revenues and expenses for the budget period. It indicates the expected net income for the period.

QUANTITATIVE FORECASTING: A technique that can be applied when information about the past is available - if that information can be quantified and if the pattern included in past information can be assumed to continue into the future.

R-SQUARED: See *Coefficient of Determination*.

R-BAR SQUARED $(\overline{R^2})$: R^2 adjusted for the degrees of freedom. (See R-Squared.)

REGRESSION ANALYSIS: A statistical procedure for estimating mathematically the average relationship between the dependent variable (sales, for example) and one or more independent variables (price and advertising, for example).

REGRESSION COEFFICIENTS: When a dependent measure Y is regressed against a set of independent measures X_1 through X_k the analyst wishes to estimate the values of the unknown coefficients by least-squares procedures. For example, in a linear regression equation $Y = a + bX$, a and b are regression coefficients. Specifically, a is called the y-intercept or constant, while b is called a slope. The properties of these regression coefficients can be used to understand the importance of each independent variable (as it relates to Y) and the interrelatedness among the independent variables (as they relate to Y).

REGRESSION EQUATION (MODEL): A forecasting model that relates the dependent variable (sales, for example) to one or more independent variables (advertising and income, for example).

RESIDUAL: A synonym for error. It is calculated by subtracting the forecast value from the actual value to give a " residual" or error value for each forecast period.

ROOT MEAN SQUARED ERROR (RMSE): The square root of the mean squared error (MSE).

S-CURVE: The most frequently used form to represent the product life cycle. Several different mathematical forms, such as the logistic curve, can be used to fit an S-curve to actual observed data.

SALES FORECASTING: A projection or prediction of future sales. It is the foundation for the quantification of the entire business plan and a master budget. Sales forecasts serve as a basis for planning. They are the basis for capacity planning, budgeting, production and inventory planning, manpower planning, and purchasing planning.

SERIAL CORRELATION: *See Autocorrelation*.

SEASONAL INDEX: A number that indicates the seasonality for a given time period. For example, a seasonal index for observed values in July would indicate the way in which that July value is affected by the seasonal pattern in the data. Seasonal indexes are used to obtain deseaonalized data.

SIMPLE REGRESSION: A regression analysis that involves one independent variable. For example, the demand for automobiles is a function of its price only (see also Multiple Regression; Regression Analysis).

SLOPE: The steepness and direction of the line. More specifically, the slope is the change in Y for every unit change in X.

STANDARD ERROR OF THE REGRESSION COEFFICIENT: A measure of the amount of sampling error in a regression coefficient.

STANDARD ERROR OF THE ESTIMATE: The standard deviation of the regression. The static can be used to gain some idea of the accuracy of our predictions.

t-STATISTIC: *See* ***t-value***.

SUPPLY CHAIN MANAGEMENT: Management of the integration of the functions, information, and materials that flow across multiple firms in a supply chain-- i.e., buying materials, transforming materials, and shipping to customers.

t-TABLE: A table that provides t-values for various degrees of freedom and sample sizes. The t-table is based on the student t-probability distribution (see also t-value).

t-TEST: In regression analysis, a test of the statistical significance of a regression coefficient. it involves basically two steps: (1) compute the t-value of the regression coefficient as follows: t-value = coefficient / standard error of the coefficient; (2) compare the value with the t-table value. High t-values enhance confidence in the value of the coefficient as a predictor. Low values (as a rule of thumb, under 2.0) are indications of low reliability of the coefficient as a predictor (see also t-Value).

t-VALUE: A measure of the statistical significance of an independent variable b in explaining the dependent variable Y. It is determined by dividing the estimated regression coefficient b by its standard error.

TEMPLATE: A worksheet or computer program that includes the relevant formulas for a particular application but not the data. It is a blank worksheet that we save and fill in the data as needed for a future forecasting and budgeting application.

THEIL U STATISTIC: A measure of the predictive ability of a model based on a comparison of the predicted change with the observed change. The smaller the value of U, the more accurate are the forecasts. If U is greater than or equal to 1, the predictive ability of the model is lower than a naive, no-change extrapolation.

TIME SERIES MODEL: A function that relates the value of a time series to previous values of that time series, its errors, or other related time series (see ARIMA).

TRACKING SIGNALS: One way of monitoring how well a forecast is predicting actual values. The running sum of forecast is predicting actual values. The running sum of forecast error is divided by the mean absolute deviation (MAD). When the signal goes beyond a set range, corrective action may be required.

TREND ANALYSIS: A special form of simple regression in which time is the independent variable (see also Trend Equation).

TREND EQUATION: A special case of simple regression, where the X variable is a time variable. This equation is used to determine the trend in the variable Y, which can be used for forecasting.

TREND LINE: A line fitted to sets of data points that describes the relationship between time and the dependent variable.

TURNING POINT ERROR: Also known as "error in the direction of prediction." It represents the failure to forecast reversals of trends. For example, it may be argued that the ability to anticipated reversals of interest rate trends is more important than the precise accuracy of the forecast.

WEIGHT: The relative importance given to an individual item included in forecasting, such as alpha in exponential smoothing. In the method of moving averages all of those past values included in the moving average are given equal weight.

WINTER'S THREE-PARAMETER METHOD: *See Exponential Smoothing, Seasonal*.

Z-SCORE: A score produced by Altman's bankruptcy prediction model, known to be about 90 percent accurate in forecasting business failure one year in the future and about 80 percent accurate in forecasting it two years in the future.

Appendix

Table A.1 – Standard Normal Distribution Table

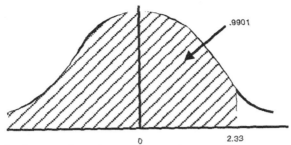

Areas under the normal curve

Z	0	1	2	3	4	5	6	7	8	9
.0	.5000	.5040	.5080	.5120	.5160	.5199	.5239	.5279	.5319	.5359
.1	.5398	.5438	.5478	.5517	.5557	.5596	.5636	.5675	.5714	.5753
.2	.5793	.5832	.5871	.5910	.5948	.5987	.6026	.6064	.6103	.6141
.3	.6179	.6217	.6255	.6293	.6331	.6368	.6406	.6443	.6480	.6517
.4	.6554	.6591	.6628	.6664	.6700	.6736	.6772	.6808	.6844	.6879
.5	.6915	.6950	.6985	.7019	.7054	.7088	.7123	.7157	.7190	.7224
.6	.7257	.7291	.7324	.7357	.7389	.7422	.7454	.7486	.7517	.7549
.7	.7580	.7611	.7642	.7673	.7703	.7734	.7764	.7794	.7823	.7852
.8	.7881	.7910	.7939	.7967	.7995	.8023	.8051	.8078	.8106	.8133
.9	.8159	.8186	.8212	.8238	.8264	.8289	.8315	.8340	.8365	.8389
1.0	.8413	.8438	.8461	.8485	.8508	.8531	.8554	.8577	.8599	.8621
1.1	.8643	.8665	.8686	.8708	.8729	.8749	.8770	.8790	.8810	.8830
1.2	.8849	.8869	.8888	.8907	.8925	.8944	.8962	.8980	.8997	.9015
1.3	.9032	.9049	.9066	.9082	.9099	.9115	.9131	.9147	.9162	.9177
1.4	.9192	.9207	.9222	.9236	.9251	.9265	.9278	.9292	.9306	.9319
1.5	.9332	.9345	.9357	.9370	.9382	.9394	.9406	.9418	.9430	.9441
1.6	.9452	.9463	.9474	.9484	.9495	.9505	.9515	.9525	.9535	.9545
1.7	.9554	.9564	.9573	.9582	.9591	.9599	.9608	.9616	.9625	.9633
1.8	.9641	.9648	.9656	.9664	.9671	.9678	.9686	.9693	.9700	.9706
1.9	.9713	.9719	.9726	.9732	.9738	.9744	.9750	.9756	.9762	.9767
2.0	.9772	.9778	.9783	.9788	.9793	.9798	.9803	.9808	.9812	.9817
2.1	.9821	.9826	.9830	.9834	.9838	.9842	.9846	.9850	.9854	.9857
2.2	.9861	.9864	.9868	.9871	.9874	.9878	.9881	.9884	.9887	.9890
2.3	.9893	.9896	.9898	.9901	.9904	.9906	.9909	.9911	.9913	.9916
2.4	.9918	.9920	.9922	.9925	.9927	.9929	.9931	.9932	.9934	.9936
2.5	.9938	.9940	.9941	.9943	.9945	.9946	.9948	.9949	.9951	.9952
2.6	.9953	.9955	.9956	.9957	.9959	.9960	.9961	.9962	.9963	.9964
2.7	.9965	.9966	.9967	.9968	.9969	.9970	.9971	.9972	.9973	.9974
2.8	.9974	.9975	.9976	.9977	.9977	.9978	.9979	.9979	.9980	.9981
2.9	.9981	.9982	.9982	.9983	.9984	.9984	.9985	.9985	.9986	.9986
3.	.9987	.9990	.9993	.9995	.9997	.9998	.9998	.9999	.9999	1.0000

Table A.2 – T-Distribution Table

Critical Values for the t Statistic

			Values of t			
d.f.	$t_{0.100}$	$t_{0.050}$	$t_{0.025}$	$t_{0.010}$	$t_{0.005}$	**d.f.**
1	3.078	6.314	12.706	31.821	63.657	1
2	1.886	2.920	4.303	6.965	9.925	2
3	1.638	2.353	3.182	4.541	5.841	3
4	1.533	2.132	2.776	3.747	4.604	4
5	1.476	2.015	2.571	3.365	4.032	5
6	1.440	1.943	2.447	3.143	3.707	6
7	1.415	1.895	2.365	2.998	3.499	7
8	1.397	1.860	2.306	2.896	3.355	8
9	1.383	1.833	2.262	2.821	3.250	9
10	1.372	1.812	2.228	2.764	3.169	10
11	1.363	1.796	2.201	2.718	3.106	11
12	1.356	1.782	2.179	2.681	3.055	12
13	1.350	1.771	2.160	2.650	3.012	13
14	1.345	1.761	2.145	2.624	2.977	14
15	1.341	1.753	2.131	2.602	2.947	15
16	1.337	1.746	2.120	2.583	2.921	16
17	1.333	1.740	2.110	2.567	2.898	17
18	1.330	1.734	2.101	2.552	2.878	18
19	1.328	1.729	2.093	2.539	2.861	19
20	1.325	1.725	2.086	2.528	2.845	20
21	1.323	1.721	2.080	2.518	2.831	21
22	1.321	1.717	2.074	2.508	2.819	22
23	1.319	1.714	2.069	2.500	2.807	23
24	1.318	1.711	2.064	2.492	2.797	24
25	1.316	1.708	2.060	2.485	2.787	25
26	1.315	1.706	2.056	2.479	2.779	26
27	1.314	1.703	2.052	2.473	2.771	27
28	1.313	1.701	2.048	2.467	2.763	28
29	1.311	1.699	2.045	2.462	2.756	29
Inf.	1.282	1.645	1.960	2.326	2.576	Inf.

Note:The t value describes the sampling distribution of a deviation from a population value divided by the standard error.

Degrees of freedom (d.f.) are in the first column. The probabilities indicated as subvalues of t in the heading refer to the sum of a one-tailed area under the curve that lies outside the point t. For example, in the distribution of the means of samples of size $n = 10$, $d.f. = n - 2 = 8$; then 0.0025 of the area under the curve falls in one tail outside the interval $t \pm 2.306$.

Table A.3 – F-Distribution Table

Values of F_P for specified probabilities P and degrees of freedom in the numerator n_1 and degrees of freedom in the denominator n_2

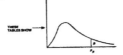

F_P is the value of the Snedecor F random variable such that the probability of obtaining a sample F value at least as large as F_P is P. In the first comprehensive table, the level of significance P is 0.05 *for all lightface entries* and 0.01 *for all boldface entries*. This table continues on four pages with the degrees of freedom in the numerator specified across the top and the degrees of freedom in the denominator specified along the side. The areas are shown in the illustration above. For example, given $n_1 = 4$ and $n_2 = 9$, the value of F is 3.63 when 5% of the total area is in the right tail of the distribution.

F Distribution

	n_1 = degrees of freedom for numerator = k						n_2 = degrees of freedom for denominator = n − k − 1					
	1	2	3	4	5	6	7	8	9	10	11	12
1	161	200	216	225	230	234	237	239	241	242	243	244
	4,052	**4,999**	**5,408**	**5,625**	**5,764**	**5,559**	**5,928**	**5,981**	**6,023**	**6,054**	**6,082**	**6,106**
2	18.51	19.00	19.16	19.25	19.30	19.33	19.36	19.37	19.38	19.39	19.40	19.41
	98.49	**99.01**	**99.17**	**99.25**	**99.30**	**99.33**	**99.34**	**99.36**	**99.38**	**99.40**	**99.41**	**99.42**
3	10.13	9.55	9.28	9.12	9.01	8.94	8.88	8.84	8.81	8.78	8.76	8.74
	34.12	**30.81**	**29.46**	**28.71**	**28.24**	**27.91**	**27.67**	**27.49**	**27.34**	**27.23**	**27.13**	**27.06**
4	7.71	6.94	6.59	6.39	6.26	6.16	6.09	6.04	6.00	5.96	5.93	5.91
	21.20	**18.00**	**16.69**	**15.98**	**15.52**	**15.21**	**14.98**	**14.80**	**14.66**	**14.54**	**14.45**	**14.37**
5	6.61	5.79	5.41	5.19	5.05	4.95	4.88	4.82	4.78	4.74	4.70	4.68
	16.26	**13.27**	**12.06**	**11.39**	**10.37**	**10.67**	**10.45**	**10.27**	**10.15**	**10.05**	**9.96**	**9.89**
6	5.99	5.14	4.76	4.53	4.39	4.28	4.21	4.15	4.10	4.06	4.03	4.00
	13.74	**10.92**	**9.78**	**9.15**	**8.76**	**8.47**	**8.26**	**8.10**	**7.98**	**7.87**	**7.79**	**7.72**
7	5.59	4.74	4.35	4.12	3.97	3.87	3.79	3.73	3.68	3.63	3.60	3.57
	12.25	**9.55**	**8.45**	**7.85**	**7.44**	**7.19**	**7.00**	**6.84**	**6.71**	**6.62**	**6.54**	**6.47**

Table A.4: Durbin-Watson Table

Values of the Durbin–Watson d for Specified Samples Sizes (T) and Explanatory Variables
Significance level = 0.01

Number of Residuals	K = 1		K = 2		K = 3		K = 4		K = 5	
T	d_L	d_U	d_L	d_U	d_L	d_U	d_L	d_U	d_L	d_U
15	1.08	1.36	0.95	1.54	0.82	1.75	0.69	1.97	0.56	2.21
16	1.10	1.37	0.98	1.54	0.86	1.73	0.74	1.93	0.62	2.15
17	1.13	1.38	1.02	1.54	0.90	1.71	0.78	1.90	0.67	2.10
18	1.16	1.39	1.05	1.53	0.93	1.69	0.82	1.87	0.71	2.06
19	1.18	1.40	1.08	1.53	0.97	1.68	0.86	1.85	0.75	2.02
20	1.20	1.41	1.10	1.54	1.00	1.68	0.90	1.83	0.79	1.99
21	1.22	1.42	1.13	1.54	1.03	1.67	0.93	1.81	0.83	1.96
22	1.24	1.43	1.15	1.54	1.05	1.66	0.96	1.80	0.86	1.94
23	1.26	1.44	1.17	1.54	1.08	1.66	0.99	1.79	0.90	1.92
24	1.27	1.45	1.19	1.55	1.10	1.66	1.01	1.78	0.93	1.90
25	1.29	1.45	1.21	1.55	1.12	1.66	1.04	1.77	0.95	1.89
26	1.30	1.46	1.22	1.55	1.14	1.65	1.06	1.76	0.98	1.88
27	1.32	1.47	1.24	1.56	1.16	1.65	1.08	1.76	1.01	1.86
28	1.33	1.48	1.26	1.56	1.18	1.65	1.10	1.75	1.03	1.85
29	1.34	1.48	1.27	1.56	1.20	1.65	1.12	1.74	1.05	1.84

Index